A FISH EAGLE CALLS

MEMORIES OF GROWING UP IN MALAWI 1975-1988

RUPERT WILKEY

Njoka Books

ARISTOTLE

"If you do not wont to be criticised,
SAY NOTHING and DO NOTHING and BE NOTHING.

∽

SIGMUND FREUD

"I cannot think of any need in childhood
as strong as the need for a father's protection."

∽

ERNEST HEMINGWAY

"I never knew of a morning in Africa
when I woke up that I was not happy."

Published by Njoka Books

Copyright© Rupert Wilkey
First Edition 2020
Second Edition 2020
Third Edition 2021 with photos

ISBN:9798685892850 (paperback)

~

This book is dedicated to my

Dad

I often wonder what I would have become and what I would have achieved, had I not been taken from you in Kenya all those years ago. Thank you for helping me find out who I really was.
I love you

ACKNOWLEDGMENTS

∼

Firstly, I'd like to thank the wonderful people of Malawi for allowing me to call Malawi home for thirteen amazing years. It was a privilege to grow up in the "Warm Heart of Africa".

I'd like to thank Richard Terrell for his friendship. I would be in a very different place had we not been friends. The snakes you introduced me to have brought me so much pleasure over the years. I'm also grateful to the Terrell family for their friendship after Richard's passing.

I would like to say thank you to the late "Snake Man" who provided me with many specimens some of which I had been unable to find.

For my time at Blantyre Zoo I'd like to thank Paul Taylor, Justin Albert, Laxon and Baison Lidi. *Zikomo kwambiri!*

To Samuel, my cook, you were a godsend. You took care of me while I was at FES, keeping the house in order and providing me with three good meals every day. Thank you for sleeping at the foot of my bed when I was sick with Malaria.

Thank you to Roger Ling for employing me at Farming &

Engineering Services in Namwera. They were great memories and ones that still make me chuckle to this day.

Let me thank Elias, Chilangwe and Kawale (Eros) at FES Namwera. You all made my days a work an absolute joy.

To Denis Phocus, my "uncle" - thanks for your friendship and happy memories in Namwera. We had some good times together.

To Jorge and his family, what can I say? The years with you moulded me forever. I appreciate what you did for me, without reward for yourself.

For their friendship and numerous suppers at their house I'd like to the Pantazis family. To Taki, thank you for coming into my office every day for a coffee and chat, I do miss our conversations immensely. To my "κουμπάρος" Thanasi, you were a good friend and I miss you. I hope one day we will meet up again when the world is a better place, where wrongs are righted and where truth prevails. You are a good man.

To Jordan Price in the US, thank you for rekindling my love of Malawi, and for being there to talk about the great books on Nyasaland and "old Africa".

I'd like to thank Kathy Sheppard for he "research" and my various questions about old Malawi.

My thanks have to go to Ian "Witty" Whitfield for his help with researching St Andrews and it's staff.

Thanks also to Mike Bamford for allowing me to tap into his vast knowledge of Malawi's historical subjects.

To Angus John Welford I want to say how much I appreciate you writing the foreword. I know it has made you return to those days in Kenya but your help in me understanding what happened has been a great comfort to me - Thank you.

Lastly I'd like to thank my father. If I had not found you, this book would have not been written.

INTRODUCTION

~

At the age of twenty, I read a book entitled *Locksley* by Nicholas Chase. It was a story about Robin Locksley, the man who was assumed to be the real Robin Hood. The author wrote the novel as if looking through the eyes of Locksley, who had fled to find peace in France. The opening line of the book was "As I sit here at my window and look out, I see the waves crashing upon the shore. My memories are like those incoming waves. I see one come in but just as I try to hold its image in my mind, it breaks and my mind rushes forward to meet the next oncoming wave".

Now, almost three decades later, I sit here at my farm looking out across the valley to the hills of the Sierra d'Esparreguera beyond, my memories flood towards me, yet, and just like they did for Locksley, I can't seem to hold onto one for very long before the next memory comes in. I can now relate to that book I read all those years ago.

My time in Malawi has given me so many memories and they consume my mind on a daily basis. All of us are getting older and I wanted to write these memories down before I cannot recall places, people or events anymore. Some people have asked "why write this story now?" Well It's been thirty-three years since I left Malawi and there are many reasons for me writing it now.

Firstly, I wanted to sit and write down my memories for my father. We were separated for almost thirty-eight years. He didn't see me growing up, he couldn't share things with me or lend fatherly advice. I wanted him to be able to read this book and have an insight into my life.

The second reason for writing this book was that I am not the most talkative person in the world and find it very hard to tell people things about me. Friends and family often feel shut out, complaining that they know nothing about me. I just don't find it easy to tell "stories" or talk about myself because I don't think anybody will be interested to hear. The writing of this book will enable me to talk about my life through the pages and if the reader does indeed get bored, then they can make no excuses to me; they may just simply close the book, put it down or throw it in the bin.

The third reason for this book was to try and explain how the experiences, the places and indeed the people I lived and grew up with have shaped my life and made me the very person I am today. I have tried to write this book in a chronological way but my memories don't flow from one date to another but are more of the places and the people from those places. Like a good play is about the individual actors, and the way they play their characters, it's their parts that make it a great play. For me it has been the scenes and the individual characters that have shaped my life, and that is what I have tried to convey in this book. Finally, I wanted to "set the records straight" on many events described in this book. Over the years I have heard so many versions of events I was actually present at, and I know there version they had heard was, how shall we say, far from the truth. A lot has been said about my time in Malawi by other people, much of it has been aired for their own benefit, and I have to say, to the detriment of my own character. Like I say, after thirty-three years I'm setting the records straight.

Having said that, when the first edition came out I did receive some criticism from people who were upset by the way members of their extended family had been portrayed in the book. I told them that I was hurt that they wanted events removed to paint a better picture of those people, who had in fact both passed away. Be all this as it may, I agreed to remove sections and chapters of the book where their family were mentioned. I have taken heart from the masses of emails from other people who where either still in Malawi or had been there at the time I was. The emails were all the same - total shock at events, with messages of "Oh my god, we had no idea it was like that...or that happened....or he did that......we are so sorry". Those emails have meant a great deal to me. I'm sad that I have been asked to seal the lid once again on an aspect of my life. I guess Namwera wins again!

Let me say at this point that my command of English is lacking at times and I have written this book as I speak. I've not even tried to be creative with the language and while there will be many who will tut and shake their head as they read, my English teachers through the years for a start; but the aim of the pages is to convey the story and for the reader to understand me as a person. My language is that part of me.

Looking back, my childhood was in many ways a lucky one. I grew up in Africa where fences, boundaries or rules were few. I feel blessed to have grown up there and had the chance to have experienced Africa. Not the "Real Africa", I think I was almost a hundred years too late for that. That Old Africa was enjoyed by people like Henry M. Stanley, F. C. Selous and in some respects C.J.P. Ionides. Someone once told me that the only thing that remains constant in Africa is the rate of change. They were and still are wise words. All us "African children" look back and miss our time in Africa but those moments we had are gone, the people we knew are gone, and the places we knew have changed beyond recognition. We miss the times we had then and re-visiting Africa is usually a very saddening and upsetting experience for us all, I know it is for me.

Having said that, Africa is always "home" to me and always will be. They say that "Africa is like a lion and its claws dig deep" and they are right. My "African" memories fill my mind every day. Sometimes when it rains and there is that smell of wet soil in the air, my mind will instantly flash back to Africa. Anyone who has lived there through a rainy season will understand exactly what I mean. I, like so many ex-"Africans", still shake out my shoes just to make sure there is nothing lurking inside like a scorpion, spider or snake. I still always slow down when coming over the crest of a hill expecting to see a broken-down lorry and I always check my bag of flour for weevils. Africa takes hold of you when you have lived in its countries, grown up with its people, its wildlife, its seasons and its troubles.

As the South African poet Bridget Dore said, "You may leave Africa but Africa never leaves you".

Rupert Wilkey
    Spain

FOREWORD

Rupert Wilkey, farmer, herpetologist, business consultant, CEO, businessman ... How else to describe him?

Let me see, now... For me Rupert's story is inextricably tied to, and interwoven with, the story of my best friend at school, but that will become clear as you read the following pages.

I knew Rupert before he became even a schoolboy. I knew him just about as well as a teenager can know a babe-in-arms who he has to look after from time to time. I watched him take his first steps and felt privileged to see that happen. I heard him learn to talk. I loved him and knew that when the time came, I wanted a son just like him. It was 1963, I was sixteen, nearly seventeen and at a boy's boarding school in Nairobi, Kenya; the Prince of Wales School. I had a year and a term to go before I finished school. In that country at the time, there were three terms in the school year.

When our old Art Master retired, Rupert's father came to my school to teach Art. He was Michael Wilkey from Sheffield, Yorkshire. He had Art qualifications from Leeds University. A few weeks after Mr Wilkey arrived at my school, his wife and their baby son arrived as well and the small family was given a house to live in which was at the end of the school drive. All members of the school staff were expected to live on campus and were given a house or flat within the school grounds. My own mother was a member of staff. She was the Matron, the school nurse in charge of the Sanatorium (San for short) which was the school's small, 16 bed hospital. She lived in a flat attached to the San. The Assistant Matron, also had a flat attached to the San. When I was at the school I lived in a boarding House,

Rhodes House, which was more than half a mile from the Wilkey's house at the end of the drive into the school grounds. Later the Wilkey's moved into a staff house right next to the San where my mother lived, thus they became next-door-neighbours. My best friend and I used to baby-sit for his parents. My mother and Rupert's mother became friends and his family and mine went on holidays together. I did not know then how my life and baby Rupert's would be affected by my friendship with his parents, nor how all our relationships would be irrevocably altered.

In 1961 I had been selected for the school shooting team. In 1962 I broke my left arm. I couldn't shoot a rifle with my arm in plaster that came nearly to my armpit. Therefore, I made myself useful to my team by working in the rifle-butts as often as I could persuade the shooting master to let me go out to the range with them. I learnt how to score each target and where to put the indicators and how to patch the holes one by one and place the scoring indicator when the target was lowered after a shot was fired. While I was in the butts, I took the chance to smoke illegally. Not that I was a habitual smoker even though I'd started at primary school but I'd smoke to impress my mates. It was the 'done thing' to smoke while you were in the rifle-range butts, although by this age (nearly sixteen) I was priding myself in not necessarily following what others were doing. In this case I allowed myself to be dragged along and began to like smoking, whereas before that I had only done it to show others my toughness and machismo. Not that I was aware of the term 'machismo' at that time.

During that same year I had made that friend who was to have a major influence on my life: his name was John Prickett.

Rupert's book will tell you some of what happened in those early days in Kenya but I hope to add some detail that he never knew because he was much too young at the time. His mother kept the story from him and in effect, denied him any knowledge of his real father. My friend John became Rupert's de facto father. Rupert Wilkey became Rupert Prickett without any legal basis to the name change. Rupert's mother, Peggy, called John "Jungle Jim" because of his tales about hunting in the forest. It soon became shortened to Jim. He was never known as Jim at school even though Peggy told Rupert that that was his nickname there. John often referred to me by my initials, AJW, and Peggy did likewise. Her little boy, Rupert, was "Grub" which I took to be an affectionate family name and then gradually he became "Totty" though I never quite figured out how this happened. Peggy liked to give people nicknames.

I last saw Rupert in December 1968, but a few years ago, through the modern miracle that is the internet, I managed to get in touch with Rupert again and we have since exchanged many emails and then messages via Facebook.

Looking at Rupert's story in this book and thinking back, I learned that there are some amazing parallels between his life and mine. Apart from the times we shared in Kenya at my school and elsewhere, I note that I also spent time within a Greek community... in a place called Tanga in Tanzania... for three months after I left school.

Also, in 1978, only two years after I married my wife, Gaye, whom I met at the school I was teaching at in Kenya, I learned to fly - in a Cessna 150. I never quite managed to get my full Private Pilot's Licence because I could not afford the costs of the last part – cross-country navigation – of the course. I had a restricted licence and that meant I could take the 150 Aerobat up and learn to do aerobatics! One time, I stalled the little plane upside-down and fell out of the sky that way... I don't remember being frightened and just calmly remembered what my instructor had told me: to centre all the controls, cut the power, push the control yoke forward a little and wait until the airspeed built up enough for the control surfaces to work again, then smoothly bring the plane back from the dive it would be in. It all happened just as he said it would and I regained control just as he predicted, even though my eyes and nose were full of the dust that up until then had been on the floor of the little plane! I had to be a minimum of 5,000 feet above the land to do aerobatics and that was just as well because I pulled out of the dive when the altimeter registered just a bit over 1,500 feet. Hmmm! Oh well, time to do some more practice.

Through the stories in the following pages, I am delighted to have found out a great deal that I never knew previously about how the boy I knew and came to love all those years ago, has survived through tough times, to be a success in this world. I have read this book, his autobiography, and laughed and cried with him. I wish him every success.

Angus John Welford
    Lal Lal
    Victoria
    Australia

A. J. Welford holding me as a baby

PROLOGUE

Most books tend to kick off the first page with something dramatic to catch the reader and hold them. So, I suppose I should start with the story of lion hunts or swimming in hippo infested rivers, maybe fishing for crocodiles or catching some of Africa's most deadly snakes; but I won't, I'll start at the beginning.

This is a book about me, the person I am, as much as what I have done; so, I'd like to start off by telling you about my early childhood. But the truth is I can't. Most kids can remember back to when they were four or five years old so I'm told; but I can't. I remember nothing of my early childhood.

The earliest memory I have is probably nine years old and that's maybe one moment, one incident that has stuck in my mind from that time.

I'd look at photos taken when I was a small child and although I could see it was me in the photo, it might as well have been anyone in the picture. My memories are not made up of remembering actual events but are built around photos and what people have told me. I see me in the photo holding a ball so I must have had a ball. I see a photo of me in a swimming pool and I'm told, "oh that picture of you was taken in Nairobi", therefore I must have been to Nairobi.

Slowly over the years I would piece together my early years, the most crucial bits not being able to fit into place until very recently; and its only now that I have come to realise that subconsciously, as I child, I blocked out the first nine or so years of my life from my memory. It's from this jigsaw of pieces gathered from relations and people who knew me as a young child that I write this prologue. As I say I have no memory of the events I am about to describe.

Let me start from the facts I do have. My birth certificate, which I didn't see till I was almost twenty-four years old, gives my date of birth and says I was born James Rupert Moore Wilkey at Nether Edge Hospital in Sheffield in Yorkshire. Sadly, the hospital has long since been demolished to make way for up-market apartment housing.

My parents, Michael and Peggy were living at Thornsett Road in Ecclesall at the time, which could not have been more removed from Africa if it had tried. However, something at that time must have sown a seed of "Africa" in my father's mind. Maybe it was a geography lesson at school or looking through an old atlas; or maybe it was the talk he'd been to as a young boy when a missionary man had stood in the local church hall and spoken about his travels in Africa. Whatever it was, he thought more and more about Africa.

With that my father set about applying for jobs in Africa, anywhere in Africa but his heart was set on Kenya. After a few weeks he was offered a teaching post at the Prince of Wales School in Freetown, Sierra Leone, which he wasn't too thrilled about but hey, it was still Africa right and he was just happy to get out of Sheffield and start a new life under the warm African sun. A few weeks after he had been offered the job, he received a telegram asking him to go to London to discuss the position and so he hot-footed it down to London. When he walked into the meeting my father was told that the post in Sierra Leone was no longer available but they would be able to offer him a post at the Prince of Wales School in Nairobi, Kenya. He was over the moon; finally, he was going to the one country he had dreamed of. It was ironic that both schools had the same name.

This must have been quite a brave move from the streets of Sheffield but in 1963 my father went out to Kenya ahead of my mother to set up home and await his new family. My mother and I would follow about ten days after that.

Kenya gained independence in December 1963 and I have certainly seen photographs of me as a baby in my mother's arms watching as Kenya's first president, Jomo Kenyatta drove past. Kenya changed fast in those early days as the country tried to stamp its own mark on developing the country.

My father appeared to embrace Kenya and was fully taken in by its beautiful landscapes and amazing wildlife. He had bought a series I Land Rover to tackle the rough Kenyan roads and later bought a .276 calibre Mannlicher Schoenaur rifle for £70 and with both he emerged himself in the "African Safari" life, hunting at weekends and during school holidays. His new post as Art Teacher was even going well. I had a Kikuyu nanny called Mongui who was very fond of me and I would spend most of the day with her and her children while my father was at work.

The Prince of Wales, or "Prince-o" as it was known, was a long established school in Nairobi. It had first been conceived in 1902 as The European Nairobi School and consisted of a few rooms near the Railway Station. In 1916 the school was moved to the hilly grounds of Protectorate Road (current grounds of Nairobi Primary School). In 1925 His Excellency Sir Edward Grigg (later Lord Altrincham), Governor of the Kenya Colony, supported Lord Delamere's idea of establishing a Senior Boy's School, to run as a Public School. Captain B.W.L. Nicholson from Royal Naval College in Dartmouth was appointed Head-master of the European Nairobi School while planning went under way for the New Boys School to be built at Kabete (the present Nairobi School grounds). Sir Herbert Baker was commissioned to plan a school similar to Winchester Public School in England and Captain Nicholson even designed the school uniform and discipline to be based on Naval system. The foundation stone of the new School was finally laid on 24th September 1929 by Sir Edward Grigg, in the area directly beneath the Clock Tower. Under the foundation stone was placed a copy of the then East African Standard and some coins of the colony. Generations of boys would walk over this stone daily.In 1931 the school finally opened for boarders and day boys; however the headmaster at the time felt the old name 'Kabete Boys Secondary School' was too clumsy and it was given the name Prince of Wales School; as a special case, the Prince of Wales feathers were to be inserted between the horns of a Royal Impala as the School badge, accompanied by the school motto "TO THE UTTERMOST"

In 1962 Mr. O.C. Wigmore was appointed as Headmaster and ran the school when my father arrived.

The wilkey's lived in a nice cottage in the grounds of the Prince of Wales School. As I've said the school was run on naval discipline and boys were encouraged to help teachers with babysitting, in exchange for a few shillings or a top-up meal and boys would usually bring their homework to pass the time. Since my father had a young family it wasn't long before two boys would become regulars at the Wilkey house; they were Angus John Welford (who I will call Angus) and John Prickett, two close friends from Rhodes House. From this point in the book I will always refer to John Prickett as Jim, which was his nick-name at Prince-o where according to my mother he was always called "Jungle Jim", although Angus disputes this and says that Jim was always known as "Bush Pig". I can understand why my mother may not have thought this a very pleasant name.

So Angus and Jim were at the house most evenings doing

their homework and some evenings were baby-sitters while my parents were out attending various parties around the community in Nairobi.

Life in the Wilkey house seemed all well and good in photos I have seen recently but behind the scenes and unbeknown to my father, my mother was far from happy. According to my father her unhappiness was never discussed and he was oblivious to tensions that were brewing.

I am not sure whether I was a good child, most of my character then is only described to me over the years by my mother and frankly it is now hard to separate fact from fiction. One story that was always related to me was how I disrupted the embassy garden party; however I now understand that this may have been a party at one of the staff houses at the school. Be it as it may, my mother had been busy chatting and kept hearing this "thud, thud, thud" noise, then realised I was missing. It didn't take her long to follow the sound of the thudding to find me. There I was, sat on the floor removing the contents of a very full nappy and throwing handfuls of it at the nice clean lounge wall. I was quite a handful then!

The months rolled by, my mother soon got friendly with Jim's parents when they came to collect their son for school holidays. Jims father Dick ran a forester station close to the border with Uganda and my parents and I were often invited up to Kakamega to stay with them.

Dick was a keen hunter and eventually my father and mother were invited on a hunting trip to Meru and Mt Kenya by Dick and Jim. I was left with Mongui and Dick's wife Gertrude Annie at the forest station in Kakamega.

By all accounts the trip went off badly, Jim "showed off a lot" and there were many disagreements. Eventually Jim and my mother went off alone to hunt zebra. By the end of the day they had not returned to camp and with light fading Dick and my father went off to look for them. After much searching they were found skinning a zebra they had shoot and both seem unconcerned about the worry they had caused. Eventually the four of them came back to camp and a huge argument about the whole incident and my father lost his cool and decided the safari was over and announced he was leaving the next morning. My mother wouldn't sleep in my fathers tent that night and the next morning when my father got ready to return to Kakamega, my mother refused to leave; so my father left without her.When my father got back to the forest station at Kakamega he found that I had developed an eye infection, so took me to the local clinic in Kakamega. When he got back to the house Dick, Jim and my mother had arrived. Dick was furious that my father had left them, although they had all the food, camping equipment and a vehicle. Dick then demanded that my father "leave his property!".So my father took my nanny but left me with my mother in Kakamega and headed back to work. A few days later, while my father was teaching, he received a message from Mongui's son, Njoroge, telling him that he "must come to the house immediately". My father was in the middle of teaching a class and it took a while for him to finish up the lesson and get over to the house. By the time he got there he was really not prepared for the sight that was to greet him.

The house was empty of all personal effects and when I say empty of all personal effects, I mean ALL. The only thing that was left was the government furniture that the house came with. Books, ornaments, plates, cutlery, bedding, photo albums; everything was gone.

My fathers first thought was that we had been robbed and he called for my nanny, Mongui, who came in floods of tears to explain that "a large green forestry lorry and a Consul station-wagon belonging to Bwana Dick had emptied the house of all belongings!"

This must have been devastating for my father and I guess he must have just sat there in that empty house with his head in his hands in total disbelief. I doubt whether he had any idea of the reality of the situation.

My father did what any man would have done, and decided to drive back up to Dick's house at Kakamega to find out what was going on. My father had every intention of at least collecting me and took Mongui along to hold me on the journey back in the Land Rover. Kakamega in 1965 was over a day's drive from Nairobi, some 250 miles. This was before the more direct road was built that you see today. When he arrived at the house he was met at the closed gate by Dick who was carrying a shot-gun and made it clear that my father was not welcome at the house. My father said that "both Dick pointed the barrels at my chest and told me to leave!"

There was little my father could do but drive the 250 miles back to Nairobi and an empty house. The journey was made even harder since Mongui cried all the way home, which just shows the bond between Mongui and me.

Over the coming weeks the story did come out, as these stories always do. I appears that my mother had been having an affair with Jim for quite a while behind my father's back. Jim had been visiting the house while my father wasn't there and heading to the bedroom with my mother. Obviously the house staff all knew what was going on but hadn't dare tell my father. Jim had told Angus and it appeared most of the students in the school knew. With Jim being an eighteen or nineteen year old school boy and my mother a married woman of twenty nine, it must have been the talk of Nairobi.

When I made contact with Angus some forty five years later he was able to give his version of events, and I was actually sickened by the way the affair had been conducted, especially between a teachers wife and student of the school.

My father remained at Prince-o till the end of the school year before returning to England a broken man. Before he left

Kenya he did make one more attempt to see me and drove up to Eldoret where Dick Prickett was now stationed together with my mother, Jim and I. Again my father was turned away. I guess it hits people differently but with my father he chose to let the bottle ease his sorrows, while he picked up the pieces of his life in Sheffield. Sheffield must have seemed a million miles away from his life in Kenya and me. At this point I want to say how different our lives may have been if he had actually gone to Sierra Leone instead of Kenya. It's a funny old world.

Me? So what was I doing? Well my mother enjoyed this second lease of life that she had found with Jim and the two of them spent days, sometimes weeks on hunting safari while I was left in the care of Dick and Gertrude Annie Prickett. Again I have no memories of this time but photos in the family collection show me at various forest stations where Dick was posted. It was also around this time that I acquired two names. The first was Grub, however this was then dropped as Hugo and Jane van Lawick-Goodall started calling their son Grub, much to my mother's annoyance. The second name was Totty, taken from the Swahili word Mtoto for child. This name stayed with me for many years.

Whether it was a term of endearment or just the fact that no one could remember my name, I don't know.

While all traces of my father were erased, including the total destruction of any photo that he appeared in; there was also a total absence of photos of Jim taking on the role of step-father. I presume because he must have still looked like the school boy he obviously was at the time. Over the years I never questioned this fact and it only registered with me when I was writing this book.

As for Jim I have to say I don't really think he knew what he was getting himself into in terms of the responsibility of an "instant family" at that young age. I suspect that initially he enjoyed the affair with my mother while he was at school but didn't know or appreciate the events that were about to unfold and by the time he did realise, he was too committed to step away.

Having grown up with Dick as my step-grandfather I also have to say that I guess he did what any father would do when a son "gets himself into trouble" and that is to protect his son; whether he agreed with what Jim was doing or not. Again knowing Dick, who was married to his childhood sweet-heart for all his life, the act that Jim had committed must have torn him apart inside. A few years before his death Dick did finally speak to me about the events that brought me into his life and he was truly upset by the way it had come about and how it was subsequently handled by both my mother and Jim. He said he and his wife, Gertrude Annie, had always treated me as their own. I will come back to this towards the end of the book.

Anyway come-what-may, the years slowly rolled on in Kenya for me, learning Swahili and running around the various forest stations where Dick worked.

Finally Dick must have had a few discussions with Jim regarding his future and asking how he was going to support his new family, so finally it was agreed that "we", Jim, my mother and I, would go to England where Jim would enrol in Art School in Manchester.

Again the memory of this time is nil but my father tells me that he did visit the house in Manchester one Christmas when I was three years old. Hy father had Christmas presents for me from him and his parents. My mother refused the presents and handed them back to my father, who had arrived in a little red MG sports car. He asked if he could take me for a spin around the block in it but again my mother said no and I was only allowed to sit in the front seat while she kept a step away should my father attempt to drive off with me. Apparently Jim was in the house at the time but did not show his face. During this Christmas Angus also came to visit, but again I can't remember this. Recently Angus shared his experience of that visit with me and how he struggled with Jim's relationship with my mother.

I struggle to understand why my real grandparents were punished by having their gifts returned. In fact I was punished too as I was denied those presents, mainly by spite I guess. Recently I spoke to my aunt Kath Wilkey who was married to my father's brother Peter. She told me that my mother and father regularly ate at my grandparents' house prior to going out to Kenya but this obviously was quickly forgotten by my mother.

Anyway the pretend ride in the MG ended and that would be the last time my father and I would see each other for thirty eight years!

Eventually Jim must have finished his Diploma in Art and we moved into "Woodcroft", Dick's house in Cumbria. It was here that Jim and my mother had their first child, Amy.

It's worth mentioning that growing up my mother always used to recount how she had suffered while in Manchester saying "there were times when I went without food just to put food on your plate." She said this with bitterness and I always assumed it was directed at my father's feet but today I realise that at that point she had already left my father and was living with Jim. Either way it is a strange thing to tell a child and made me feel that it was my fault.

Shortly after Amy was born the four of us moved back to Kenya, where Jim managed to find a job with Root & Leakey Safari's. RLS was a photographic safari business set up by Allan Root and Richard Leakey and Jim worked as a driver-guide for them. He would be away for weeks at a time in places as far away as Uganda and Tanzania.

During this time we lived in a house on the Hinger Estate in Thika. Hinger was the Commissioner of Police. Although I would have been six or seven years old I only have a few vague memories of living there. I do remember that the place was infested with snakes, to the point that they were almost coming up through the plug holes in the bathroom! My mother was not impressed and had all snakes killed on sight.

An ironic story is that despite the house being owned by the Commissioner of Police and being on his private estate we got broken into one day while we were at Lake Nivasha. The thieves took everything although I have to say once the robbery was reported Mr Hinger had his policemen round within the hour but none of our belongings were ever recovered. I remember our little sausage dog, Klaus came in for some criticism when we entered the house as he was nowhere to be seen and my parents assumed that he had done a runner at the first sign of danger. However a few minutes later Klaus timidly appeared from one of the bedrooms sporting a large bump on his head and had obviously got stuck into the fight before being beaten up by the thieves. Maybe the robbery made my mother and Jim realise what it is like to come back to a home and find everything gone, as my father did.

As I say I must have been six or seven at this time but there was never any mention of me going to school or even mixing with other European kids. The only contact I really had was with the local children or occasionally a few European kids at the Safari Park Hotel between Nairobi and Thika. I do have memories of interacting with other European children at the pool side of the hotel that would consist of removing the back legs off grasshoppers we had caught around the potted bougainvillea. In the late nineteen sixties The Safari Park Hotel was nothing like it is today although the rectangular pool I played around as a kid is still there at the side of the hotel.

No school and running around the garden all day avoiding snakes was my upbringing and for a young boy life was good. There was a small ditch between the house and the road, which for some reason usually flowed with water. I remember spending hours in this ditch building water-wheels out of old cans. I'd cut small flaps in the can and suspend them in the flow of water with the aid of a stick spindle. I'd sit for hours as the can spun round and round. Such were my days.

Another highlight of my small world was going into Nairobi on the rare occasions that Jim was home and we would all pile into the ten-seater Land Rover and head into "town". I'm not sure why but for some reason I was always left in the car. I'm not sure this was a punishment for my behaviour on the journey in or for other reasons. What I do remember was being given strict instructions not to open the roll back roof that the Land Rover had; but as soon as I was alone the roof would be opened and I would stand up on the back seats to take in the hustle and bustle of those Nairobi streets. Often we would park in front of what I think was a small travel agents but I can't be sure. The doorway was set back off the street and either side were two bay-style windows, one considerably larger than the other. In the small one was a very realistic model of an African waterhole, complete with plastic zebras and little pink flamingos. I would lean out of the Land Rover roof and gaze at the model for ages, memorised by the creation. The layout of the animals would never change but trip after trip I would never get tired of looking at this window.

Another vague memory I do have is of a supermarket somewhere in Nairobi that had a roof car park and again I would have the vehicle roof open once I was alone and would survey my "kingdom".

I can't really say whether I was a happy child or a sad one as I remember very little of this time.

If it was a happy time it was soon to be shattered one morning, when we received a letter informing us that we were in Kenya illegally due to Jim not having a work permit.

This must have been a devastating blow to Jim whose father had first come to Kenya in 1938 during the war; Jim himself had been in Kenya since 1957. Even though Jim was under contract with Root & Leakey Safaris and no one gives you a contract in Africa without you having a work permit, it was still a case of guilty until proven innocent. Jim hot-footed it to Nairobi to see what the mistake was but the meeting at the ministry had not gone well. Basically they had given us seven days to leave the country.

Since the Commissioner of Police was in affect our landlord it was decided that if anyone had an influence it was Bernard Hinger; so Jim headed to his house next. Hinger said he would look into it but a few days later came back and said that the problem was that Jim did not even have a file or any documentation so there was nothing he could do.

Calls were made to everyone we knew but nothing could be done. Dick was in England at the time so he was powerless to do anything.

The seven days drifted by, Jim's bank account was frozen, and we were given twenty four hours to pack what we could carry and get to the airport. The contents of the house were left as they were and that was that.

As a seven year old boy I was oblivious to the stress being caused and as I say I have no memory of that moment.

It was a quick and sad end to our time in Kenya.

For me I guess it was ok, I appear to have blocked out most of my memories of this time and everything prior to it. However if I sit now I can still smell the vinyl seats of the ten-seater Land Rover we had at the time. It's funny how certain things do stay with you.

We arrived in London with very little money in 1970. Mothers plan was to get a train to Cumbria where Dick had his empty house, however at the rail station they soon found out that they could only afford a family ticket a few stops up the line to a place called Harlow; so at Harlow station we got off the train. Again I have no memory of what happened and where we stayed that night but home ended up being number 21 Potter Street in Harlow.

We hadn't been back in England long when we received a letter from Jim's father, Dick, saying that the Immigration Department in Kenya had found his file and all paperwork was correct and that they were very, very sorry and had made a huge mistake. Jim's father pleaded for us all to return to Kenya but Jim refused.

Jim got various jobs but ended up getting a teaching job at Netwswell Secondary School, as did mother. I was sent to school for the first time ever at the age of seven going on eight and I hated every minuet of it. I was bullied and teased for five years. It was horrific.

I remember Dick and his wife coming to visit from Kenya, but as I saw them I didn't recall any memories of them, they were strangers to me, which I find very odd thinking about it now.

The years in Harlow dragged by when suddenly it was announced that mother was going to have another baby and soon after Isabel is born. A few weeks later I heard that Jim was applying for jobs overseas, Africa, Papua New Guinea, anywhere, just to get out of England. This seemed strange to me as he had been given the chance to go back to Kenya in 1970 and decided to stay in England.

Jim would always tell people that "it took us five years to get out" like he had done everything in his power to escape England. It had never seemed like that to me as a kid.

Eventually after much application writing by my mother, as she did everything when it came to that sort of thing, Jim finally got an interview in London. I remember Jim getting dressed up and heading down to London for his interview with the Overseas Development Agency, or ODA. He was going for a teaching job in Papua New Guinea or some remote place like that. When he got to the interview the job had somehow vanished but Jim asked if they had any other jobs going, "I'll go anywhere". he told them. They said they had a job in Africa, and was he interested? He said he was and left the interview with a job, now he just had to tell my mother!

"You've got a job where?" mother demanded when Jim came home and told us the news.

"Malawi" said Jim, trying to sound like he had just won the lottery.

"Where the bloody hells that?" she said, showing a lack of African geography.

"Somewhere in Africa they said" Jim stuttered, waiting for some approval.

"Oh really? Somewhere in Africa? Where in Africa?"

"I don't know" said Jim sheepishly. He always found himself in situations like this where he had not done his homework and was ill-prepared for the questions.

"You don't bloody know?!!!!!! Well I suggest we blessed find out!" Mother then went to the atlas and found Malawi.

Malawi was a small country sandwiched between Zambia, Tanzania and Mozambique, at least it wasn't near Chad or Ethiopia so Jim breathed a sigh of relief at this small respite. The next weekend we all went off by train to the Commonwealth Institute in West London to find out what we could about this country we were going to be spending 3 years in. Jim was visibly nervous as we walked round the Malawi cubicle and kept saying positive things like "Look love, it's got a lake...look love they call it the Warm Heart of Africa.... and look love, it has mountains with everlasting flowers. At the end of the day mother reserved judgment and agreed to go.

ODA had informed Jim that Malawi had some rules on dress code and that all men were required to have short hair so on Saturday I went with Jim to a barber's shop in Harlow to have a haircut.

It was the first time I had been to a barber in my life, mother had always cut my hair. I sat there rigid in the chair, frozen with fear. The barber turned to Jim, "what's he having?" he asked.

"Short back and sides" was Jim's reply.

It might have well been cut his ears off and slit his throat as far as I was concerned. I don't think I moved a muscle until the barber said "All done".

Back at 21 Potter Street there was plenty to do. The flat had to be cleared, cherished items packed and shipped to Malawi, other items sold, given away or binned. I was told I could take three toys only, and I remember taking my Red Devil Action Man, and a couple of toy cars. I never understood why so many of my things vanished, but the promise of a land where Coca-Cola was 5p and pineapple 1p soon had my tears dried.

We had to get Cholera and Yellow Fever injections so that was booked in. There was one last thing to endure and that was my first visit to the dentist - yes that's right, I was twelve years old and had never been for so much as a check-up. I can't say I was really worried as I did not know what to expect. The family kept saying it was just a check-up before going to Africa so off I went for the "check-up". As soon as the dentist saw the result of twelve years of neglect, he proceeded to remove one tooth and fill three others! I remember coming out of there shell-shocked. That would be the last time I would be taken to the dentist for another twelve years! Shocking really but there we are.

We continued the readiness for the move. Mother wanted to take her two Siamese cats so that had to be arranged. Finally, it was all done and we were ready.

Then we got a call from mothers' dad in Yorkshire to say that my grandmother Mattie was ill in hospital with a rare skin disease and was not expected to live long. This threw all the plans into question but my grandfather Tom Moore being the level headed man he was demanded that we go to Malawi as planned and were not to give up returning to Africa for the sake of Mattie who may pass away in a few days anyway. He said that

Mattie was in such a bad state that he did not want her to be seen like this and that mother should not come up to Derbyshire to visit her in hospital.

We then caught the plane as planned to Malawi on the 5th of May 1975. My grandmother died a few days later. I wasn't sad; I had not really known her. I think I can remember seeing her twice and, on both occasions, there was very little love from her, not the love you would expect from a grandparent. She used to call me Jamie which really got my back up. Tom had been right about us carrying on to Malawi and I think we were all glad that we had not upset our plans by staying to be with her.

Now that I have told you about my life prior to Malawi, I hope you have a better understanding of how my early life was to have a profound affect on my future years. Remember that when I arrived in Malawi in 1975 I had no memory of my really father. I had five years of schooling in the UK under the name of Rupert Prickett and this was to continue through my entire educational life; even though my birth certificate and passport (both of which I never saw until I was nineteen years old) had the name James Rupert Moore Wilkey. I know I will say this more than once but masquerading me as Rupert Prickett was illegal and has caused me enormous problems in later life. Only when I took charge of my own life at the age of twenty five was I able to seek employment under my correct and legal name.

One thing I will mention is that although my mother basically ran off with a school boy, they have remained together after almost 55 years. Does that make it right? No I don't believe it does.

With my nanny Mongui and her two boys.

*Me in the garden at the Prince of Wales school in Nairobi with the
historic kikoy*

CHAPTER 1

BACK IN AFRICA

On the 6th of May we landed at Nairobi Airport where we were to change planes. As we waited to board the Air Malawi flight to Malawi, Dick suddenly turned up in the transit lounge. I'm not sure how many strings he pulled but he managed to get through airport security, all-be-it with a police escort but he managed it. I guess it goes to show his standing in Kenya at the time, even then; it would definitely be impossible now. We spent an hour or so with Dick, I knew who he was but only had a memory of seeing him once before when he had visited us on one of his visits to England.

Finally, our flight was called and we said goodbye to Dick and boarded the Air Malawi BAC-111. The only thing I remember of the flight was that the plane was a real bone shaker. The plane looked like it was twisting in flight; over-head lockers rattled and the plane creaked. All this led to me suffering from airsickness and I spent most of the flight being sick in a tiny paper bag that seemed to have been badly designed as even more sick went on me than in the bag. Mother kept saying "don't look out of the window, you'll feel worse" so I can't tell you much about my first impressions of the country from the air.

The plane banked sharply and I did glance out of my window down into the cultivated red-soiled fields below. Kids were looking up from tending their goats and they waved up at the plane. We banked again, suddenly dropped and we were on the ground, I was relieved the plane had finally landed. As we turned round at the end of the runway I remember looking out of the window up the runway and instead of it being level there was a huge dip in it. I later learned that planes had to come in steep to avoid the dip but this left the runway short so stopping the plane before you ran out of runway was a nerve-wracking experience.

The plane taxied and came to a halt in front of a small building that was the airport. African men rushed out to meet the plane like ants. I could see Europeans on the waving base waving towards the plane. As I stepped through the open plane door into the sun I remember being hit by the heat, like a weight was pressing down on my whole body. I also experienced a slight heaviness on my lungs, which I didn't know at the time was because of the altitude of the airport being 779m (2,555ft) above sea-level. Blantyre was 1,039 m (3,409 ft). There was also a different smell in the air and the light was very bright. As we walked across the tarmac the heat started to bounce up off the tarmac, it was hot. Looking back now it seems ridiculous as this was the beginning of May, Malawi's winter season, I'm just glad we hadn't arrived in October, which was known locally as "Suicide Month"!

We were met at Chileka International Airport by John Pitman and he took one look at me and took us upstairs to the "waving base" to get us all a cold drink. "Coke is the best thing for that boy" so coke I had and I did feel much better, which was good because people were starting to make a fuss of me, which I hated. After drinks John drove us back to his house in Blantyre.

It was my first real chance to see what the country looked like. It all seemed very dry and all along the road were, what appeared to me to be, rundown buildings with Coke signs painted on one wall every few hundred yards or so. I remember being shocked to see the Africans dressed in rags and barefoot. There were women carrying large loads on their heads and babies on their backs. There were hundreds of new sights to see but it was hard to catch them all as the car sped along towards Blantyre.

On the way Jim chatted to John about the country and asked a few questions about the school where he would be working.

"So what's Chichiri Secondary School like?" Jim asked.

"No idea, why?" John replied with a bemused look on his face.

"What do you mean you have no idea, you said you were a teacher at the school?"

"I am a teacher at a school, Soche Hill Secondary School. You're not going to work at Chichiri Secondary School; your post is at Soche Hill Secondary".

I guess Mr Pitman was wondering what kind of a teacher Jim would be if he didn't even know which school he was teaching at. Jim was just thinking about the long talk he was going to get from mother based on the way her face had set in the back-seat.

This was Africa I guess and these things happen. As it turned out it didn't seem to bother Mother or Jim as they didn't know where Chichiri or Soche Hill were so it made no odds just as long as there was a job and Jim would be paid.

John Pitman lived in Sunnyside, a well-to-do suburb of Blantyre. The house was set in an immense garden, but no grass grew, instead the garden was filled with huge Eucalyptus Trees or Blue Gums as they were called in Malawi. Beneath them was bare earth, it was like a desert.

After some tea and biscuits John told us that the school had not yet found a house for us to live in yet so for tonight, we would be staying at his house, it would be a bit cramped but the following night the school would pay for us to stay at a local hotel in Blantyre.

I don't really remember much of the sleeping arrangements but it must have been cramped since the house only had four bedrooms and for some reason, I ended up sharing a room with Rowena, Johns eldest and very attractive daughter, who was, I guess, between twenty-two and twenty-five years old. This seems very odd to me now but at the time, when you are eleven you don't question things. All I remember was that her room had two single beds in it and as a kid I obviously went to bed much earlier than the grown-ups, but I was woken by the sound of Rowena coming to bed. As I lay there in the dark it was the first time I had seen a woman naked!

Finally, I forced myself to sleep after that sight, although breakfast the next day was awkward for me as Rowena sat opposite, I think I spent most of it eating my toast and starring at her breasts! Boys eh! I have to say I was very disappointed that afternoon when we loaded our cases into Johns' Peugeot 404 station wagon and drove to the Ryalls Hotel. I was kind of looking forward to staying awake for another night.

Ryalls was an old established hotel which had been there since the pioneer days when it was opened by Mr Ryalls. It had an air of the "old days" even though it was modern. The best thing for me was that it had a swimming pool, fantastic! They were happy days swimming and then having lunch at the "Dugout", the hotels pool bar, named after the canoes that were used on Lake Malawi. Above the entrance to the bar on a large concrete plinth was a real dugout canoe which I thought was very cool as a kid.

When not swimming I would sit at the window in our room and look out onto the streets below, at people going about their daily business. I remember that across the street from the hotel was a long, white building that took almost all of that side of the street as far as I could see. On the outside wall in large coloured letters were the words Farming & Engineering Services. Through the large glass showroom windows, I could see large red tractors inside, all shiny and new. From the height of my window I could look down over the high wall and into the yard that was the workshop where African mechanics had tractors in various stages of repair.

As I watched four-wheel drive vehicles covered in mud would come and go, they looked like they had just completed the Safari Rally. The drivers were all Europeans and suntanned, to me at that age they looked like clothed versions of Tarzan. I would try to imagine the wild places they had driven from, wondered if their farms had wild animals on them, like elephants, buffalo and lions.

It was all very exciting and I spent many hours watching the building, imagining how great and exciting it would be to work at a place like that.

CHAPTER 2

RULES & REGULATIONS

Within days of our arrival we started to hear more about Malawi's strange and strict rules on things like dress code, hair-cuts and other do's and don'ts. To be honest, these were things I don't think we were aware of before we landed in the country.

This will be a lengthy chapter I'm afraid but I make no apology because I think a book about living in Malawi during the 70's and 80's can be written without giving a history of the governing regime at the time.

The country was ruled by Dr Hastings Banda. His official title was *His Excellency, The Life President, Ngwazi, Dr Hastings Kamuzu Banda* - quite a mouthful. Hastings Banda was born near Kasungu in the then British Central Africa as Malawi was then known. His father was Mphonongo Banda and his mother was Akupingamnyama Phiri. The date of his birth is not known for sure, as in those days there wasn't a requirement to register a birth. Most people guess it was around 1898, although his official birthday is stated as May 14, 1906.

He was baptised into the Church of Scotland in 1905 and at that point took the Christian name of Hastings. Sometime between 1915 and 1916, he left home with an uncle called Hanock Msokera Phiri, an "uncle" who had been a teacher at the nearby Livingstonia Mission School, and on foot the two of them walked almost 1,000 miles to Chegutu in Zimbabwe (then Hartley in Southern Rhodesia). Then in 1917, and again on foot, he walked to Johannesburg in South Africa. This was a combined total of over 1,500 miles, quite an incredible feat at that early time where wildlife and disease claimed substantial lives. A cook of mine had done this journey as a boy and he was the only one to reach Johannesburg out of a group of four friends, two were eaten by lions!

In South Africa the young Banda worked at the Witwatersrand Deep Mine on the Transvaal Reef for several years. While he was there, he met Bishop W. T. Vernon of the African Methodist Church (AME). Bishop Vernon offered to pay his tuition at a Methodist school in America if Banda could make his own passage. In 1925, having saved, Banda left for New York.

Banda studied at the Wilberforce Institute, a black AME college (now Central State University) in Wilberforce, Ohio, where he graduated in 1928. After that he enrolled as a premedical student at Indiana University, he then transferred to the University of Chicago. At UC he majored in history, graduating with a B Phil in 1931. While at UC he enjoyed financial support from the Smith family, Mr Douglas Smith had made fortunes in patent medicines and in Pepsodent toothpaste; Banda also received financial help from a member of the Eastman Kodak family.

After graduating Banda, with help from Dr Walter B. Stephenson of the Delta Electric Company, he then moved to Meharry Medical College-Tennessee, where he studied medicine, finally graduating 1937.

In order to practice medicine in African territories of the British Empire, however, he apparently required a second medical degree so he secured a place at the School of Medicine of the Royal College of Physicians and Surgeons of the University of Edinburgh and graduated in 1941. Following his graduation Banda then enrolled for courses in tropical diseases in Liverpool, but was forced to leave when he refused to be conscripted into the British Army as a doctor.

Between 1942 and 1945 he found work as a doctor in North Shields near Newcastle on Tyne at a mission for coloured seamen. Shortly after this he moved to a general practice in London in the suburb of Harlesden.

In 1946, at the behest of Chief Mwase of Kasungu, Banda represented the Nyasaland African Congress at the fifth Pan African Congress held in Manchester. From this point he took an increasingly active interest in his native land, advising the Congress and even providing it with some financial support.

Banda was actively opposed to the efforts of Sir Roy Welensky, premier of Southern Rhodesia, who wanted to form a federation between the three countries of Southern Rhodesia, Northern Rhodesia and Nyasaland. Banda was worried that this federation would result in further withdrawal of rights for the blacks in Nyasaland; he famously referred to it as the "stupid" Federation. The Federation was however formed in 1953.

Banda was due to return to Nyasaland in 1951 but he instead chose to move to the Gold Coast in West Africa. This may have been partly due to a scandal involving his receptionist, Mrs French in his Harlesden practise. Banda was cited as correspondent in the divorce between Major French and his wife. Banda was accused of adultery with Mrs French, who went with him to the Gold Coast. Mrs French died destitute in 1976.

Banda stayed in West Africa until several influential Congress leaders, including Dunduzu Chisiza, Henry Chipembere, T.D.T. Banda (no relation) and Kanyama Chiume pleaded with him to return to Nyasaland. They wanted him to take up the leadership for their struggle for independence. On the 6 July

1958 Banda returned home after almost 42 years. In August of that same year he was acclaimed as Leader of the Congress at a ceremony in Nkhata Bay.

As Leader of Congress he soon began touring the country to speak out against the Central African Federation (also known as the Federation of Rhodesia and Nyasaland). It's interesting to note that Banda was so out of practice in his native Chichewa tongue that he needed an interpreter. The role of his interpreter was performed by none other than John Msonthi and later by John Tembo, who later became Governor of the Reserve Bank of Malawi.

Unrest in Nyasaland was now coming to the surface and Banda was received enthusiastically wherever he spoke. By February 1959, the situation had become serious enough to the British Government that Rhodesian troops were flown into the country to help try and keep order and a state of emergency was declared. On March 3rd, Banda was arrested as part of "Operation Sunrise" along with hundreds of other Africans. Banda was sent to Gwelo Prison in Southern Rhodesia (now Gweru in Zimbabwe). The now vacant seat of the leadership of the Malawi Congress Party (Nyasaland African Congress under a new name) was temporarily taken by Orton Chirwa, who had himself been released from prison in August 1959.

During this time, Britain had been moving towards releasing some of its colonies and when Banda was freed from prison in April 1960, he was immediately invited to London for talks on Nyasaland's future, more importantly its independence from Britain.

Elections were held in August 1961 and Banda nominated as Minister of Land, Natural Resources and Local Government and became Prime Minister of Nyasaland on the 1st of February 1963. To give him credit, he and his fellow MCP ministers quickly expanded secondary education, reformed the so-called

Native Courts, ended certain colonial agricultural tariffs and made other welcomed reforms.

The Federation was ended in December 1962 by Mr R. A. Butler, British Secretary of State for African Affairs. On the 6th of July, 1964, exactly six years after his return to the country, Nyasaland became the independent Commonwealth of Malawi. The name Malawi was chosen by Banda after he had seen it on an old French map as the name of a "Lake Maravi" in the land of the Bororos, He liked the sound and appearance of the word and this became "Malawi".

Within a month after independence, Malawi suffered a cabinet crisis as several of Banda's ministers presented him with proposals designed to limit his powers. He had already been accused of autocratic tendencies. Banda responded swiftly by dismissing four of the ministers, two others resigned in sympathy. The dissidents fled the country, no doubt in fear of their lives.

Banda became the first President of Malawi on 6th of July, 1966. At the same time, he declared that the MCP was to be the only legal party in the country and outlawed any opposition parties. In June 1967 he was awarded an honorary doctorate by the University of Massachusetts.

In 1970, a congress of the MCP declared Banda its president for life and in 1971, the legislature declared Banda President for Life of Malawi as well. It was at this time that he added the name Ngwazi to his title, a Chichewa word meaning "great lion" but can also mean "conqueror". Malawi soon became essentially a police state. Every business building was required to have an official picture of Banda hanging on the wall, and no poster, clock or picture could be higher than his picture.

Before every film at either the cinema or Drive-in, a film clip of Banda waving to the people was shown while the anthem played. This used to amuse us as kids because part way through the anthem a fly would come into shot and buzz around Banda's face before trying to land on his nose and whoever had taken the film clip either hadn't seen the fly or thought to do another take.

His government supervised the people's lives very closely. Early in his rule, Banda instituted a dress code which was rooted in his socially conservative predilections. For women the wearing of trousers was illegal although for some reason trousers could be worn in certain places like up Zomba Mountain, although this right was seldom exercised by the European women. Skirts had to cover the knee, the only exceptions were tennis skirts worn during a tennis game or sports like hockey or netball, but were not to be worn other than to play the game.

Banda argued that the dress code was not instilled to oppress women but to encourage honour and respect for them. This is why also the holding of a Miss Malawi contest was banned since Kamuzu said that ALL his women in Malawi were equally beautiful!

Nonetheless, Banda was very supportive of women's rights compared to other African rulers during his reign. He founded Chitukuko Cha Amai m'Malawi (CCAM) to address the concerns, needs, rights and opportunities for women in Malawi. This institution also motivated women to excel both in education and government and encouraged them to play more active roles in their community, church and family. The foundation's National Advisor was Cecilia Tamanda Kadzamira, the official hostess for the president.

As I have already mentioned beauty contests were irrelevant as "all the Presidents women were equally beautiful". There was nothing sinister in this "ownership". It was simply that when the President gave a speech at a stadium, truckloads of women were brought in from all over the country to sing and dance for him, Malawian women, Europeans were not required to do this thankfully. The women would all wear brightly coloured outfits with the Presidents face printed all over them. When he left the country on official trips the women would be trucked into the airport and would be there again to welcome him back.

Just as a small note the trucks that brought the ladies in were supplied by the farmers throughout the country. One day a few members of the Malawi Young Pioneers (MYP) would arrive at your farm and say that they needed your lorry and driver on a certain given day and you were not allowed to refuse. You had to supply it with a driver and enough fuel to get it back to your farm. There was supposed to be a rota-system of which farms had to supply but it appeared to me to be more of a guide. The women seemed to enjoy the "days out" and they would usually sing all the way to the venue even if it was a six hour drive away. Kamuzu would always say "I am happy to see so many of my ladies here today" and this ownership meant that if you raped a woman in Malawi, the Police actually saw it as you had violated one of Kamuzu's ladies, I guess one of his wives effectively. This meant that in thirteen years I never heard of a case of rape. I think it was one of the only places in the world where a European woman could walk at night and not feel threatened, so there was an upside.

For men platform heels were illegal, as were bell-bottomed trousers, in fact trouser width had to be under a certain size and Police had the power to stop you in the street and measure the cut of your trousers.

A man's hair had to be an inch off the back of his collar. At the airport you would often see an overland back-packer being grabbed by the police and dragged off to a room. The choice was simple, either you had your hair cut in that room by a policeman or they put you on the next flight to the country of the passport you held, simple as that, there were no exceptions. I remember once that there was great excitement when it was announced on local radio and in the press that West Ham Football Club were coming to Malawi to play the National Team. Tickets at Kamuzu Stadium sold like hot-cakes. A huge official welcome for West Ham was prepared at the airport, the Minister of Sport was there, the Minister of Culture, the Press, everyone. The members of the West Ham team stepped off the plane and were immediately detained by the Airport Police due to the length of their hair. The whole Team were held and told that either they had their mullets cut or they could get back on their plane, so they got back on their plane and flew back to London. The game was cancelled and no refunds were given. We never saw another England team ever again. International Rock groups also stayed away for the same reasons.

Beards were also seen as a sign of dissent and although outlawed, this law was seldom enforced.

Pornographic material was highly illegal. Malawi had a strict censorship policy and all films, magazines and books had to be first viewed by the Malawi Censorship Board and edited for content. If a magazine had a photo of a woman in trousers or a short skirt in it then a long dress was drawn in with a thick black marker. The problem was that the magazine was usually closed again before the censorship pen ink had dried and this caused the pages to stick together. Vogue magazine was not worth buying as very few pages escaped the pen!

Movies showing a kissing scene or improper act had that portion cut out. On many occasions the part was cut out and the ends must have fallen on the floor because when the pieces were joined together the end was at the front and the beginning of the movie at the end. It made a film most confusing. Because of these censorship laws, television was illegal in Malawi as the censorship board would have not been able to censor the stream of channels coming in. This was only lifted by the government in 1987 when TV sets for the purpose of playing video tapes were allowed to go on sale. The video tapes were then hacked to death but you could at least watch the back-to-front film in the comfort of your own home! Kissing in public was not allowed.

Churches had to be government sanctioned and the

Church of the Jehovah Witness (Watch Tower Bible and Tract Society - WTBTS) was one church that Banda made illegal. In fact the Jehovah Witnesses were persecuted in Malawi. At an MCP rally at Zomba in September 1972 a green light was given to MCP militants to attack and harass WTBTS members. At least 50, possibly 100 WTBTS members were killed after the Zomba rally. By September 1975 reports of torture of WTBTS members were widespread and in October Dr Banda ordered that all WTBTS members be rounded up and sent to Dzeleka Detention Camp. There were reports of children being separated from their parents and "left to die". By January 1976 up to 5,000 WTBTS members were in Dzeleka. 21,000 members fled Malawi to neighbouring Zambia to escape persecution only to be forcibly returned to Malawi by the Zambian authorities. Its interesting to mention Dzeleka Detention Centre as this was synonymous with brutality and torture. Even as early as January 1965, President Banda addressed the Malawi Parliament and in reference to the new detention camp at Dzeleka:

"I will keep them there and they will rot, they will rot".

Pre-Banda history was discouraged, and many books on these subjects were burned but I think that this really hit out at Colonial History more than anything else. Banda also allegedly persecuted some of the northern tribes (particularly the Tumbuka), banning their language, traditions, dances and books.

Mail was regularly opened and often edited, both going out and coming in so you had to warn family and friends in England not to write anything subversive that could result in them seeing you back in England sooner than they expected.

Telephones were tapped, and conversations were cut off if anyone said a critical word about the government.

Needless to say, speaking out against Banda was prohibited, and could be punished by arrest, deportation or even death.

Opponents were either exiled, like Kanyama Chiume or killed like Dr Attati Mpakati.

The worst and most blatant murders happened on the 18th of May 1983 and became known as the "Mwanza Four", who mysteriously died during the Kamuzu Banda regime. The deaths of the four men were announced in the newspaper and radio as car accidents.

"In the early hours of Sunday morning, a blue Peugeot 504 saloon car carrying four passengers was involved in an accident. The car left the road plunging into a ravine, killing all four occupants who were later identified as Dick Matenje, Twaibu Sangala, Aaron Gadama and David Chiwanga."

Hon. Dick T. Matenje MP was a former Malawian politician, cabinet minister and Secretary-General of the Malawi Congress Party.

Hon. John Twaibu Sangala MP was the Minister of Health for Malawi.

Hon. Aaron E. Gadama MP was a Minister for the Central Region, and Leader of the House. He was also one of the original trustees of Press Trust.

Hon. David Chiwanga was MP for the Chikwawa East.

All four men were known to be critical of aspects of the totalitarian rule of Kamuzu Banda. Three of the dead passengers were ministers who each had their own large black Mercedes and would never "car-pooled" in a Peugeot. It was common knowledge at the time that the passengers were dead before they actually got in the car.

In 1995 former President Kamuzu Banda, John Tembo, former Official Hostess Kadzamira, and three former police officers named as MacDonald Kalemba, Augustino Leston Likaomba and Mcwilliam Lunguzi were arrested for and charged with the murder of the four men. According to court records, Dick Matenje, Twaibu Sangala, Aaron Gadama and David Chiwanga were arrested on the 17th of May along

Zomba-Blantyre road, and taken to the Eastern Region Police Headquarters in Zomba and spent the night at Mikuyu Prison.

They were then transferred to Blantyre the following day where they were brought first to the MCP sub-head office at Chichiri in Blantyre and later to a special branch office in Limbe.

During the night, reports have it that they were hooded, handcuffed and driven to the Mwanza-Thambani back-road which leads south from Mwanza district along the Malawi/Mozambican border, where they were hammered and butchered to death and finally dumped in a blue Peugeot saloon, registration number BF 5343, disguised as if they had perished during a car accident while they were attempting to flee the country into Mozambique.

The court heard that according to the South African Pathologist the Mwanza Four "were killed and died painful deaths as it would appear from their heads were crushed possibly with metal instruments or sledgehammers". She then went on to say that "their skulls looked like shells of broken eggs". All the accused were acquitted due to lack of evidence, as many key witnesses to the assassination of the "Mwanza Four" had since died. I bet they had!

All adult Malawian citizens were required to be members of the MCP. Party cards had to be carried at all times, and had to be presented in random police inspections. The cards were sold, often by Banda's Malawi Youth Pioneers. In some cases, these youths even sold cards to unborn children.

In 1971 the population of an entire village in the Mangochi area was detained at Lilongwe for a number of months, without charges or trial.

Any non-Malawian who broke any of these rules or who committed a crime were "PI'ed" (declared Prohibited Immigrants or Political Immigrants) and deported. The usual practice was that you were simply given 24 hours to pack your things before being escorted to the airport. Non-Malawians were not allowed to be a drain on the country so only Malawians went to Jail!

Some crimes were very obscure. For example, it was illegal to flip a coin in heads or tails at any time, even to start a football game as you were flipping the President. Folding a banknote was hazardous as you didn't want to put a crease down the image of the Presidents face and you never simply crunched up a bank note into your pocket.

An over excited member of the European population set off a firework as the President's motorcade was passing and Fireworks were instantly banned. November the 5th was just a plain old day for us.

March the 3rd was declared Martyrs Day when you remembered the people who had died in the struggle to gain independence from Britain. On this day all forms of entertainment were banned. You were not allowed to play music, play sport, fish, nothing. You were expected to stay at home and think good and hard about the Martyrs and their sacrifice. A group of four European men were caught playing cards on Martyrs Day, they and their families were deported. Police boats would patrol the lake to make sure that you didn't go out with your boat.

Swearing at Malawians was illegal, however if you spoke Chichewa and swore at them in their own language then that was acceptable. Certain books and music were banned. The owning of any Simon and Garfunkel album was illegal. This was since the song Cecilia was about a woman of loose morals and the Presidents official hostess was a lady called Cecilia Tamanda Kadzamira. The President took offence at the lyrics, as he thought they were directed at "Mama" Kadzamira. There was actually a list of all the banned books available in the British Council Library and it made fascinating reading, there were pages of them! To give you an idea the book Africa on Shoestring was banned material. As many of you will know this is the bible for any back-packer travelling through Africa. It was banned as the authors had been critical of the Rules and Regulations that Malawi had. Back-packers would bury their copy in a plastic bag just before the border crossing, travel around Malawi and then dig the book up on their exit again at the border.

The wearing of any type of military clothing was illegal although with the Bush War going on in Rhodesia at the time many ex-Rhodesians who took up farming in Malawi wore their camouflage jackets on the farms. Camouflage jackets were also offered for sale to farmers by entrepreneurial Africans from neighbouring Mozambique where the Rebel War was being fought. I actually bought mine, which I still have, from a soldier at Changalume (Cobbe) Barracks in Zomba!

It goes without saying that firearms without a licence were also banned however many people had them, many from the pre-independence days that they had not handed in. Many farmers also bought a gun from Mozambique's entrepreneurial Africans I have just mentioned, mainly for their own protection in case the Rebel War ever spilled over the border where they were farming. These were mainly AK47 assault rifles, although grenades were often for sale. Blank firing guns including cap guns were also illegal so all track events at school were started with a whistle, although later on in my schooling year I remember our sports teacher getting permission for a starting pistol, although I don't think that they had approved the blank ammunition to go with it.

Indians or Asians were not allowed to live outside city limits. This prevented them from owning farms and meant that they were contained where the President or effectively his Police could watch and control them. In a speech once he said "You are good at running shops, so shops in cities are what you will run. You are not farmers; you cannot feed yourselves in your own country (India) so being shop-keepers is good." It is worth noting that the President chose to have an Asian as his accountant though! Please don't feel sorry for the Asians, they were some of the richest people in Malawi, they were by hook-or-by-crook able to still get money out of the country to buy property in Britain.

When Kamuzu was driven anywhere, people were expected to line the streets. Offices were shut, markets emptied and schools closed. Since my school was on the main road between Blantyre and the airport we were always out when Kamuzu was flying anywhere. The school would be told by the Police that the President would be passing at 11.00am and that we should be out lining the road at least an hour before. By midday Kamuzu had still not past, it was hot, we were in full sun, you could not leave unless you actually passed out. Finally, at about 2pm the Presidents entourage would scream past and we would all be required to slow clap as a sign of our respect. You were not allowed to wave. Once he had gone we would then stream back to our now disrupted lessons. Happy Days!

Some of his journeys were unannounced and you would be quietly driving down a quiet road when suddenly a Police Land Rover would scream up the road towards you on the wrong side of the road with its headlights on. You soon learnt to swerve off the road and jump out and stand beside your car. Within a minute ten Police motorcycles would flash past followed by the Presidents burgundy-red Rolls Royce convertible. You would, as usual and was expected, start your slow clap. When the stream of back-up vehicles, ambulances and army vehicles had passed, you could then get back in your car and continue on your journey.

So that was Malawi in the 70's. Was it a dictatorship? Yes I guess it was but at the end of the day it was their country not ours, we were just visitors and if you obeyed the rules you had a good life, if you didn't you were back in "Blighty" before you could whistle.

Many criticised his policies and his ways but there was a positive side to all this. As I have said women felt safe, without the pornographic element men were not aroused to the level of committing violent acts towards women. As a European you did not commit a crime for fear of being on the next plane out. The short-back and sides hair cut made everyone the same; there certainly wasn't a "biker-culture" element. For the Malawians, hanging was still available punishment for crimes such as treason and multiple murders so that was a huge deterrent.

Banda also did much for the country's infrastructure establishing major roads, airports, hospitals and schools, albeit with loans from Britain that he never paid back. He founded Kamuzu Academy, a school modelling Eton, in which Malawian children were taught Latin and Ancient Greek by expatriate classics teachers, and disciplined if they were caught speaking Chichewa. He was also the only African ruler to establish diplomatic ties with South Africa during apartheid and on one occasion he paid a state visit to South Africa where he met his South African counterparts at Stellenbosch.

Banda only became partially rehabilitated in the eyes of other African leaders after the demise of the apartheid regime in South Africa (many southern African nations traded with South Africa, on which they were economically dependent, but Malawi was the only African nation that recognised South Africa and exchanged embassies with it).

Some families would arrive and see all this and decide that they would not tolerate this and they would leave. I met one family who left after two weeks telling me "there's no TV!" I suppose it was like living in East Berlin, the only difference being that we could leave the country if we didn't like it. Personally, I never had a problem with it.

In 1993 Banda's one-party state was dismantled by a referendum. Soon after this a special assembly stripped him of his title of Life President, along with most of his powers. The whereabouts of the US$320 million in personal assets that Banda was believed to have accumulated is unknown.

Although there were some questions regarding his health, Banda ran in Malawi's first truly democratic election in 1994 but not surprisingly he was thoroughly defeated by Bakili Muluzi, a Yao from the Southern Region. Banda was then allegedly placed under house arrest in his former residence of State House Zomba. If this was in fact true then I think it was a fitting that he would spend the final years of his life within spitting distance of Zomba Prison where many of his enemies had been incarcerated; some even meeting their deaths there. I think that the new regime had found it hard to condemn the "old man" to a life in Zomba Prison although he most certainly deserved it. I suspect that they took the view that State House Zomba was a close enough reminder for Banda of where he could have ended up. He lived there, never leaving the walled grounds until he became gravely ill and was flown to South Africa where he died in hospital in November 1997.

He was laid to rest in the Banda Mausoleum in Lilongwe on the 14th of May 2006. It's interesting to note that his death certificate states him to have been 99 years old but it is rumoured that he was actually 101. The Malawi Congress Party, the party Banda led since taking over from Orton Chirwa in 1960, continued after his death and still remains a major force in Malawi politics today.

An observation worth noting is that since Dr Banda's fall from power in 1993, the population of Malawi has doubled going from from 9.6m to 20m in just twenty-seven years. With this population boom, 3.4 million hectares (8.4 million acres) of predominantly natural forests are being depleted at a rate of 1.8-2.6 percent annually, that's 170,000 acres a year. The deforestation crisis has reached such a level that the army has been called in to protect forested areas. Many in Malawi look back to Dr Banda and a regime that did actually protect the forests.

CHAPTER 3

BULLETS, FISH & SNAKES

Finally, a house was found for us and we said goodbye to the Ryalls Hotel. I was sorry to leave the hotel, having access to the swimming pool was excellent and reminded me of the Safari Park Hotel in Nairobi.

The house was in Kanjedza, just outside Limbe close to Soche Hill where Jim was going to be the woodwork teacher. It was a plain and simple bungalow with a large garden that fell away in front of the house in a series of grassed terraces. Dotted about on the terraces were Frangipani trees and around the house had been planted mother-in-laws tongue. Although there were other houses around, because of the size of the garden you felt very isolated, especially after coming from a terraced block in Harlow!

Within a few days a steady stream of Africans arrived looking for work. Cooks, nannies, gardeners, they all arrived. Finally, a cook and a gardener were hired and we all started to settle down to our new life in Malawi.

Kanjedza Estate is on a hill, at the bottom below the ring road are some trees and past them is Burn Dam. We would often walk from the house to the dam to fish for Black Bass. I would buy a tin can of earthworms from the local African kids for 20 tambala. You would always have to tip the worms into your hand as the clever kids would always place large worms at the top of the tin can and really small ones at the bottom. The fishing was good in numbers but none of the fish were very big.

One weekend we walked down to the dam to find that they had drained it for some reason and the fish lay trapped in shallow pools in the middle and fishing was impossible. So that day we all, as a family, took a leisurely walk round the dam. In the mud around the drained dam all sorts of sticks and objects were protruding from the drying mud. All these things were of interest to a young twelve-year-old boy and I scanned the dry mud methodically. Suddenly out of the mud I saw a bullet, and then another and another, the whole place was littered with them. Jim gently stepped onto the dry mud and retrieved a few of them. They were all .303 rifle rounds.

We guessed that when Malawi had got its independence ten years previously there must have been a European man who had decided to dispose of an unlicensed weapon by throwing the rounds and the rifle into the dam. Jim decided to throw the exposed rounds back into the mud much to my annoyance. I continued to scan the dam to see if I could spot the rifle in the mud but I couldn't so we continued our walk around the dam.

As I walked across the short newly cut grass on the back of the dam something pulled at my right foot, like I had caught my foot in a wire. I looked down at my foot and latched on to the back of my trainer was a snake about a yard long. In panic I kicked and kicked my right leg till eventually the snake flew through the air, landing about six feet from me.

Mother pulled me back from the snake and examined my ankle but there with its' head raised up, watching me. It looked just like a bit of old stick and the top of its head was green like a leaf. This was probably why I had just walked straight over it. Its' camouflage was brilliant.

I later learnt that the snake had been a Vine or Twig Snake (*Thelotornis*), a highly venomous back-fanged snake with no known anti-venom. I was extremely lucky that it had bitten my shoe and not been an inch higher as it would then have bitten into the back of my ankle.

A few weeks later the dam had filled itself and fishing could commence again. By this time, I had made a few friends with other Europeans that lived in Kanjedza; one boy in particular was Nigel Keen.

He was about my age but his family had been in Malawi for some time, a lot longer than me at any rate. His house was at the bottom of the hill and faced the ring road. In his garden he had two very large blue gum trees and his father had run a zip wire between the two trees. Nailed to one tree were some strips of wood that formed a crude ladder up to the wire. Once there you would grab the handle attached to a runner on the wire cable and when you were ready you would launch yourself and fly down the wire.

It was slightly hazardous as by the time you reached the other large blue gum you were going at quite a rate; and you had two choices. Either you could keep hold of the pulley handle, and hit the tree; or you could let go before you hit the tree and face equal injury when you hit the ground. It was great fun and we never seemed to get tired of it.

The other reason I liked Nigel was that in his garage his dad had a glass tank with a small black snake in it. We would spend ages watching the snake through the glass but it never moved and Nigel never wanted to take the lid off the tank and poke the snake, so I could only assume at the time that the snake was really poisonous. I now know that the snake was a Herald Snake (*Crotaphopeltis hotamboeia*), a very common back-fanged species in Malawi. The venom is very weak indeed, something similar to a bee sting.

One day Nigel and I grabbed our fishing rods and headed for

the dam. After we had purchased our 20 tambala tin of worms, we sat down on the grassy bank to soak up the sun and to fish.

After a while I saw a European man and two African men going from one bush after another on the bank that formed the dam wall. They were poking the bushes with sticks and had cloth bags in their hands. Kids being kids we had to go and investigate; so we reeled in our hooks and ran across to the dam wall to see what the men had found.

Without wanting to get told off we stood some distance away from them and watched. The African man was holding a metal pipe in his hand, the end of which was in the bush. The European man was up to his armpit in the bush very close to the pipe. We sat and watched intently.

Suddenly the European man said something to the African in Chichewa, which of course I didn't speak at the time and the African removed the pipe and stood back. The European man then placed his other arm into the bush and a few seconds later produced the largest snake I had ever seen; it must have been at least five-foot-long, bright green and very much alive by the way its tail was lashing around.

A bag was passed to the European guy who then, like a magician, suddenly had the snake in the bag. The three men didn't look at us, let alone talk but moved on to the next bush so we sat patiently.

Within a few minutes another green snake was conjured up and bagged. I was spellbound. I then looked at my watch; it was time to get home so we ran back to our rods and packed up everything. We then gave the remaining worms back to the African boy we had bought them off, and headed home.

Burn Dam has now been filled in and most of the bushes and trees cut down so the snakes have sadly long since departed. Now it's a very sad place indeed.

CHAPTER 4

I THINK WE GET A GOAT

It had only been a few months but we still had not bought a car. Even with vegetable sellers coming to the house on a regular basis, we still had to walk into Limbe every couple of days to do shopping. Even if we just went to Limbe Market it was a round trip of 3 miles, and to the main shops in Limbe it was 6-mile round trip.

Mother finally spoke, "Jim we need a car and quick!"

Jim was on it and within a few days we went to see a car being sold by a Mr Price in Mandala. He was selling up and moving back to the UK and had two cars for sale. One was a 1973 Rover TC 2000 in royal blue with tan leather interior, it was a beautiful car. The other one was a two-door 1968 Triumph Vitesse MK1 2 litre hardtop in ivory with a red interior. I was hoping for the Rover as it was a gorgeous four-seater saloon car, but after a test drive up Kamuzu Highway and back Jim sadly chose the Vitesse.

I think he had misunderstood mother's instruction when she said "we need a car and quick". The Vitesse with its two-litre engine was certainly quick, like a rocket and I think for Jim it was the start of a midlife crises. The straight six-cylinder engine powering such a small car was beyond the capability of most roads in Malawi.

Just trying to get the three of us kids into the back seat was a feat to say the least. With only two doors just getting in and out of the rear seats was like Houdini getting into his chest. Also, the low British sports car was impossible on any dirt roads and felt every pot hole but it did mean an end to having to walk everywhere which was welcomed.

As I said there was some confusion as to which school Jim was actually going to teach at but Mr Pitman was adamant that it was his school, Soche Hill Secondary School, which needed Jim to teach woodwork.

The school was further up the hill at the base of Soche Hill. During the summer holiday we would drive up to the school, park the car in the car park and walk up Soche Hill. We wouldn't go right to the top, mother wasn't up for that, but just as you leave the maize fields and enter the trees there is a very large boulder on the right-hand side of the path and that was our destination, which gave a commanding view of the school below, the Kanjedza Estate in amongst the pine trees, on to Limbe and to the far left you could see Blantyre in the distance.

We had owned the car a little while now and Jim, in his wisdom, decided to book it in for a service at the Datsun dealership on Chelika Road. After a day or two the garage called to say that the car was ready and Jim went off to collect the car.

After a few days however, there was an enormous bang from the back axle and the car came to an abrupt halt. The sad Vitesse was towed back to the garage where it was established that one mechanic had drained the oil in the rear differential and another mechanic had thought that the new oil had already been put in so replaced the plugging bolt. However, no oil had been put in the rear diff. I think it was the first time we heard the phrase "Sorry about that".

Even though it was clearly the fault of the garage there was little we could do. The Vitesse left the family home, never to be seen again and was replaced with a white two door 1970 Ford Escort MK1. It was a slight improvement on the Vitesse in terms of room and ground clearance but again with only two doors getting in and out was a squeeze for me. Interestingly Jim's choice of car was always small. Three kids always packed in the back seat like sardines. In fact, our cars got progressively smaller until I left home, at which point they bought an estate car. I won't take it personally.

One day Jim came home with this really mangy looking dog, it was defiantly a Heinz 57. When I first saw it, I thought it was a goat and even though it was quickly established that it was a dog I am convinced that there was some goat in it somewhere; it even had the floppy ears. Anyway a few weeks later we found out that "the goat" was pregnant and we were going to have baby goats!

The day finally arrived and one afternoon the goat gave birth to six tiny puppies. The strange thing was that there were all black and tan, just like Dobermans and this pleased Jim no end. He even made an appointment with the local vet to have their tails docked in true Doberman fashion. When the day came to have the vet do his business I went along for some reason. I wished I hadn't as it was quite a horrific ordeal. The vet simply tied a bit of gauze tightly around the puppy's tail and then took a pair of heavy-duty scissors and slowly cut through the tail with the puppy yelping at the other end. Once he had eventually cut through the bone joint and the little tail was dropped into a bin, he then painted the raw end with antiseptic and then moved on to the next puppy.

As the vet gnawed through each puppy they all yelped, until he got to one and as he started to cut the little puppy turned its head towards the vet and gave a deep growl.

"I'll keep that one" said Jim with glee.

On the way home I asked if I could have one of the puppies

and Jim agreed. I choose one and called him Tim, for some reason. So that was it, Tim and Wally stayed, the others were sold or given away, I don't really remember.

Timmy was a great dog, mainly because it was my first dog. But as with most things the happy moments didn't last, when a few months later Jim announced that he had agreed to give my dog away to another European family. So that was it, Timmy was gone.

The sight of those puppies having their tails cut off with the over-size scissors is still with me.

ST ANDREWS SECONDARY SCHOOL

BLANTYRE

In the 1920s and 30s there were a few small, private schools being run in Blantyre, Limbe and Zomba. In the 30's the Nyasaland Government requested that the Church of Scotland Mission consider exchanging an area of land "for the purpose of erecting a school". But this was later abandoned.

In 1932, Mr Richard Paterson, Headmaster of the Henry Henderson Institute in the Church of Scotland Mission in Blantyre, appealed to the Mission Council to consider that .... "Today the problem of education of European children gives the country some concern". A year later a committee was formed to "investigate and report" on the problem. But again no progress is made as Government finance was not forthcoming as usual.

In 1935 a new committee was set up. This is due, partly to the fact that Rev. Wratten's private school would soon close. The committee managed to persuade the Government to take a real and practical interest in the opening of a school in Blantyre and within 2 years an agreement was signed between the Church of Scotland Mission and the Nyasaland Government for the establishment of a Primary School for European children, in Blantyre. The Nyasaland Government finally advanced the sum of £2,500, in the form of a loan and The Church of Scotland Mission agreed to give the use of some land, and to build a school.

Building work commenced in 1938 on land just off Chileka Road, that is almost opposite where Nissan Malawi Limited is today, and "St. Andrew's" was selected as the name of the new School. In May the first 14 pupils were enrolled, although where they sat is unknown as the school building wasn't completed until 1939. When it was completed, Mr John C. Abraham, the Provincial Commissioner, performed the Opening Ceremony on the 1st February.

In 1940 the Government agreed to a measure of financial aid in order to open a hostel that would then allow for boarding pupils.

The school was then taken over from the Scottish Mission by the Nyasaland Government in 1947 and then control ceded to the Federal Government in 1953.

By 1955 the site was deemed inadequate and plans are drawn-up for new school at Nyambadwe and construction soon started. Within a year Std 4 & 5 Junior School pupils are moved to new classrooms at Nyambadwe. Kindergarten to Std 3 remained at the old Mission School. In September construction of lower sports field and Science wing started.

On Monday the 28th of January 1957, Senior Classes start and at the same time building work gets underway of the new Junior School in Sunnyside.

In 1958 – St. Andrew's School split into 3 entities and each renamed.

"St. Andrew's KG" and "St. Andrew's Preparatory" at Sunnyside. "St. Andrew's High" at Nyambadwe. (SAHS). On the 11th of July 1959 St. Andrew's Preparatory School in Sunnyside was officially opened. That same year at the High School the swimming pool was built.

With Independence in 1964, the school's control is ceded to

the new Government and in 1965 the name of the school is changed to "St. Andrew's Secondary School" (SASS) after the Malawi Government threatened to close it down for one reason or another.

Today, Saints is an exclusive school and has 520 students from more than 30 nationalities as part of its day and boarding school. The school offers IGCSE, BTEC and A-level qualifications in line with the standard British curriculum. There is a strong emphasis on extra-curricular activities, including sports and a variety of clubs and societies. Most notable amongst these are Football, Rugby, Cricket, Hockey, Swimming, Athletics, Water Polo, Tennis, Squash and the Duke of Edinburgh Award. The school boasts impressive looking grounds, with the school buildings set on a ridge overlooking the sports facilities and adjacent grounds.

Notable alumni are:
- Tapps Bandawe, music producer
- Lillian Koreia Mpatsa
- Billy Abner Mayaya -Theologist, civil rights activist
- Yvonne Mhango - Economist
- Austin Muluzi - Minister of Economic Development
- Kimba Mutanda - Rapper
- Vanessa Nsona - Fashion Designer, entrepreneur
- Joyce Tafatatha - Malawian Olympic Swimmer
- Chapanga (Peter) Wilson - Poet
- Ammara Pinto - Olympic swimmer
- Eve Jardine-Young - Principal Cheltenham Ladies' College

In the late 1970's I did find some old black and white photos while helping to clear out an old store room at Saints. The photos were dated as far back as the late thirties. Some were Group Class Photos and in some of the these sat a Miss Florrie Graham. Many will not know who she was, but she started in the original "Junior" School at the Old Mission School site in the early 1950's and retired from the Saints in the 1990's! Many will of course know her as Mrs Florrie Mullon, whose very name had struck fear into the hearts of kids for decades and in some case generations. Florrie was the teacher with the longest tenure at the School.

For those of you that did attend St Andrews from 1975 to 1980 here are a few other names I'm sure you'll remember:

Bob Prentice, Ian Rudge, Peter Rowe-Roberts, Gwen Evans, Brian Sherry, Tom Brown, Miss Kinniple, Paul McCoy, Mr Jackman, Miss Derisdale, Madame Michelle, Bob Sherwood, Mr Pollard, Mr Kite, Mr Ledsham, Mr Davies, Duncan Auld, Miss Wigg, Mr Watkins, Miss Lynn Grant, Mr Grant, Mr Baker and of course Major Brian Bayly.

CHAPTER 5

DOCTINA HABET ONUS

"WITH EDUCATION COMES RESPONSIBILITY"

Since I had now had my 12th birthday, arrangements had to be made for me to go to school that coming September; and in Malawi there was only one secondary school that European children of my age could go to, and this was St Andrews Secondary, or Saints as it was known.

It wasn't an elitist arrangement it was just that European children were not allowed by the President to attend Malawian schools, it was as simple as that. This meant that every non-Malawian child over the age of eleven went to the one school.

In the nineteen seventies Saints was a harsh place if you didn't tow-the-line. I'm sure that there are still grown men now who shudder at the mention of Mr Watkins. He taught geography but was also the Deputy Head and responsible for caning out discipline at Saints. These were the days of "Black Marks" that could be issued by Prefects for such petty crimes as having one sock down, your hands in your pocket, one shoe-lace undone or the top button behind your tie not fastened.

Other crimes were not standing up when a teacher walked past or not having your shirt tucked in. Those boys who had received three black marks during the previous week had to see

Mr Watkins on a Thursday morning to be caned or getting "cuts" as it was called, as your rear end often bled. The line outside his office regularly went quite a considerable way down the corridor and was usually made up of the same usual faces. Another name to shudder with was Mr Grant, another caning expert!

"First Years" were usually there to be at the beck and call of the seniors and "Skivvies" were often nominated to run errands, or carry books. The straw boater was done away with the year before I arrived, as was the blazer, thankfully. Apart from that the school maintained the "Public School" image well after I had left. Pupils going into town on Saturday mornings were required to wear school uniform up till midday.

All pupils had to be through the school gates by 7.00am, and lessons usually kicked off at 7.30am. On Monday to Thursday the school day ended at 3.30pm, with Thursday afternoon being taken up by Sports/PE. The school closed at 12.00 noon on Fridays unless you were required for detention. In later years Friday afternoon was also set aside for Manual Labour, another form of punishment where students were required to clean ditches, cut grass or paint the school buildings.

Sports were a big part of school life and excelling in one aspect or another of it was usually a one-way-ticket to becoming a prefect. Rugby, football, hockey, cricket, basketball, tennis and squash were all played. The school had its own pool for swimming and water polo. You were also expected to participate in athletics and cross country.

Malawi had its rule on hair length and this was vigorously enforced by the school and your hair had to be an inch above the back of your collar. Girls were not allowed to wear make-up and the only jewellery they were allowed to wear were sleepers in their ears.

Failure to obey any rules was immediately punished and if caning failed, then you could be suspended and persistent offenders could even be expelled. Given that Saints was the only school in Malawi that Europeans could attend, this meant sending your child to a school back in the UK. This rarely happened and I can only recall two pupils ever being asked to leave.

Staff often handed out punishment there and then in the classroom, without involving Mr Watkins. I remember Michael Cane, no pun intended, letting off a stink-bomb in one class and the whole class was held till the culprit admitted his act. When Michael finally stood up and claimed responsibility Mr Evans brought him to the front of the class and caned him three times with a meter-long wooden ruler. Michael may have got more than three "cuts" but the rule snapped on the third stroke so ended the punishment. Girls in the class were even crying at seeing the punishment being delivered.

In one class I saw a teacher slap one seated boy across the face sending him flying from his chair. It was a harsh place where you struggled to avoid being in trouble but I did my best.

I learnt to make elastic garters for my socks to hold them up and I always tied my shoe-laces with a double knot. I learnt to put a stitch in the pockets of my shorts that prevented you from being able to put your hands in them. I also learnt to tuck my shirt into my underpants to prevent it coming out of my shorts, something I still do, to this day - old habits die hard. I remember after one PE lesson getting changed back into my school uniform and automatically tucking my shirt in to my pants. I then grabbed my bag and shoes and headed outside to a bench where we sat to put our shoes on. As I came to the door of the changing room and stepped out, Paul McCoy, the PE teacher asked "where are you going dressed like that?". I looked down and I'd forgotten to put my shorts on. It certainly gave the girls a good laugh for weeks.

A few years ago, when I worked for one of the Colleges at Cambridge University, I met one of the Fellows, a lovely gentleman who was an historian with a passion for colonial Africa. He asked what I'd done in my life and I mentioned that I went to school in Malawi.

"Ah, then you'll have gone to St Andrews then!" he beamed approvingly. We have been friends ever since.

So, this was the "Saints" that I was thrown into on my first day; and by the way I again started this school under the name of Rupert Prickett, not knowing that legally this was not my real name.

I remember nothing of my first day at St Andrews, except the long drive up Brereton Drive with the large sisal plants on each side and the large front gates. I also noticed the small sentry box just inside the gate and the Malawian man in what I took to be a military uniform. It was actually just Khaki shorts and blue jumper although he did wear a beret. Behind the main school buildings, in the distance I could see the silhouette of a large mountain, known locally as Ndirande or "Sleeping Warrior". This was due to the mountains profile looking like a man asleep. I was later to become well acquainted with Ndirande on the many cross-country runs up and down it.

The rest of the day and probably the rest of the week was a blur. I felt that everyone was staring at me, and in fact they were. Having come straight in to the second year, missing the first, it meant that all the other kids in my class had uniforms that were sun bleached and soft after a year of washing. Mine was stiff and dark grey. It was so new I remember that it even had a shine to it. This straightaway identified me as the new boy, I hated that and as far as I could tell the rest of the kids hated me. I stuck out like a sore thumb.

My parents had also insisted in buying me a school bag to carry my books, in the form of a small brown cardboard suit-case. The Indian at the Overseas Silk Emporium, the "official school outfitters" had told them that all the kids had them; however, on my first day I realised that all kids carried their books under one arm and no-one had a stupid suitcase like mine. I proceeded to try and destroy the case as quickly as possible without making the damage look like deliberate abuse. I think the cardboard-case lasted two weeks.

At my pre-start interview with the Headmaster he had automatically assumed that since coming from England I was bright and intelligent; and had therefore placed me in class 2A, the top stream class for the year. What he had failed to comprehend was the huge gaps of schooling years in my life, especially in Kenya when I hadn't gone to school at all.

This all came to a head after a few weeks into the first term in September when it became clear that the school had been over ambitious where my academic ability was concerned. The lesson was English and the teacher was a lovely old lady called Mrs Jones. Her husband, Mr L.G.W.P. Jones taught maths and always wore knee socks, white shorts and white shirt, all neatly starched and pressed. He also had half rimmed glasses and was a delightful chap.

Anyway, Mrs Jones had spent the lesson calling out words and pointing to a child at random for the answer. I had no idea what she was on about. Today I look back and it is of course painfully obvious but at the time they might have well been speaking Japanese.

Slowly she moved around the room from one kid to the next in a random fashion. I sat there praying for the bell to ring and to be saved the torture I was experiencing but I was never lucky. She pointed to me.

"Grief?" she said.

I just looked at her blankly. She repeated the word and again it didn't help me. I couldn't even guess at an answer because I had no idea what the question was. I started to get a pressure on each side of my temples and I started to sweat. The boy behind me leaned over his desk and whispered the answer in my ear.

Hooray, I was saved, so with all confidence and pride I announced the answer I had just been given.

"Griefy" I said and the whole class erupted into laughter.

I sat there expecting to be vindicated by Mrs Jones but of course this never happened, instead she asked me to leave the room and stand outside the classroom door till the end of the lesson as punishment for disrupting the rest of the class. I hadn't given the answer to disrupt the class; I honestly didn't have a clue of what she was talking about.

Of course, the answer she was looking for was Grieve, it's easy now. Glen Rice, the boy who had whispered the word to me, took great delight in calling me "Griefy" for the rest of the term.

Maths, physics, chemistry and biology were all just as bad. The kids in my class were all well ahead of me academically. It was a living hell and I realised that I was in deep trouble. Most of the other kids in class saw me as the class dummy and treated me like one. It was beneath some of them to even talk to me.

I was in hell and in trouble, I needed help - FAST!

The help came in the form of two strokes of luck. The first was that we moved house very soon after starting school to an area called Sunnyside. The house was on Smythe Road and it couldn't have been more different from Kanjedza if you had tried. The area was very up-market. Bank and Diplomatic houses dotted the area. Gardens were huge, well established and manicured. Smythe Road had been named after Mrs Eva Smythe. She was the wife of Edward (Ted) Smythe who had been an employee of the African Trans-Continental Telegraph Company. The Smythe's once lived in what was known as Government Cottage and the only road that led to this cottage was later to become Smythe Road.

The second bit of luck was Richard Terrell, who, as it turned out also lived in Sunnyside on Arnold Road. Richard appeared to be very laid back when it came to his work, he didn't get flustered by homework or studying. He didn't spend hours revising for tests or exams; I guess he was just naturally intelligent.

I told him that I really needed help with some homework that had been given to us and Richard agreed to give me some extra coaching after school. The afternoons at Richards house did help a little but no amount of coaching was going to make up for a few years of poor schooling and in some cases total lack of it and by the end of the first term I was moved down to the "B" stream where I would stay for the rest of my school life, but Richard and I became the best of friends.

Moving to Sunnyside greatly improved my life, with a lot of help from Richard. My only regret about leaving Kanjedza was not being able to go around to Nigel's house and play on his zip wire. We were still friends but his family left Malawi shortly after I went to school so I never got the chance to visit his house again.

So, I made friends with other kids in my year who lived in Sunnyside also, one kid in particular was Alan Fields. Allen actually lived almost behind John Pitman's house where we spent our first night in Malawi. I remember him being dropped off at school by his dad in a 1966 split-screen VW Combi. We soon became good friends and I ended up catching a lift to school with them in the Combi on many occasions.

The other cool thing about the Fields family, was that they also had a zip-wire in their garden; but this was an even more extreme version as the steep incline of the wire and the length enabled you to go even faster.

They also had a large gully at the bottom of their garden caused by a small stream that flowed through the garden eventually joining the Mudi River. The fissure was huge as I say, probably twelve feet at the widest point, nine feet deep and some thirty feet long. We would climb down the fissure onto the bedrock below and turn over rocks to catch freshwater crabs, it was great fun.

In his house Allen had a few small fish tanks with guppies in it and it was him that sparked my interest in these fish. I eventually saved up my pocket money and bought a tank and a pregnant female guppy off him when this family left Malawi shortly afterwards.

Amazingly the off-spring of that one female guppy continued to breed and I still had its descendants in 1988.

CHAPTER 6

A HANGING

Saints was made up of all nationalities and the maximum while I was there was twenty-one different nationalities; with students coming from as far away as Iceland and Korea. The school was basically open to anyone who could afford the fees.

We had a number of Malawian children whose fathers were Army Generals, Police Chiefs, Ambassadors, or Government Ministers. We all got on famously and it didn't even occur to us that we all came from different countries. As far as we were concerned if the kid was good, then he or she was a good kid and that was that. Some kids however, were loathed.

One such kid was Masauko Muwalo; his father was Albert Muwalo-Nqumayo who was one of Dr Banda's most powerful government ministers.

A very large black Mercedes sedan with a red leather interior used to bring and collect Masauko every day with a driver. The number plate was MG3, which gave an indication to the level his father had. MG1 was the president and there wasn't an MG2 as the President said he didn't have a second in command.

So Masauko's dad having MG3 effectively made him second to the President.

Masauko was obnoxious and a bully. He wasn't the brightest kid in the school to say the least but exam results seemed to be brushed aside and he maintained a "B" class seat throughout the years he was there. His favourite phrase was "Don't you know who my father is?" Many a time I would be lined up outside the class room with the other kids and Masauko would kick my feet away from under me and I'd slide down the rough concrete wall grazing the backs of my arms. You just had to take this abuse. He was really the bad apple in the cart and it was only the exceptional nature of the other kids that not all other Malawian students were judged by Masauko's actions.

Even Masauko's "friends" would hide under his shadow for protection and use his clout to bully and harass other students. One guy I remember as a guy called Bert, who used to always hang around with Masauko. It was sad but I guess the fault lies with the parents for letting their kids believe that their father's job was an excuse for such behaviour.

Anyway, this went on for a few years then one day in 1976, Masauko was at school and the next he was gone. No goodbyes, no books handed back, nothing, vanished. Then the story came to light in the papers and on the radio.

There were a lot of rumours going around the school at that time but I was only able to discover the truth while writing this book. Albert Andrew Muwalo Gandale Nqumayo and Focus Martin Gwede, the Presidents Head of Special Branch within the Malawi Police had, it was alleged, conceived, planned and attempted to over-throw President Banda while he was on a trip to London. The attempt had been thwarted by the General's in the Army, namely General Matewere, and by the Chief of Police, a man called Mac J. Kamwana.

Albert Andrew Muwalo Gandale Nqumayo and Focus Martin Gwede were arrested and on Presidents Banda's return were incarcerated in Zomba Prison before being moved to Mikuyu Prison. There was a trial of sorts, but the outcome was inevitable. Firearms and subversive books including George Orwells *Animal Farm* were found in their possession. Both were found guilty and given the death penalty. Focus Martin Gwede was later to have the death sentence reduced to life.

The forty seven year old Albert Muwalo-Nqumayo was not to be so lucky and at 3am on the 27th of August 1977 he was hanged at either Zomba Prison but more likely Mikuyu Prison between Zomba and Lake Chilwa. Mikuyu Prison was where Dr Banda incarcerated political prisoners, many housed in the notorious Block C. The horrors of Mikuyu have only recently emerged, where 47 prisoners were held in cells measuring 3m by 7m. Death must have seemed welcomed for many.

It was a big day in Malawi when the European hangman was flown in from Rhodesia to carry out the execution. Many reading this book will not be aware that Albert Muwalo-Nqumayo was not the first hanging in Malawi. Between May 1972 and August 1973, twenty seven people were hanged. Between December 1973 and September 1975 a further twenty five people were hanged. Dr Banda requested that the "hangman visited Malawi "at intervals of several months...... During each of these visits, usually up to twelve convicts, in groups of three, are executed by hanging."

As a teenager I remember there was an air of excitement and of justice being done. Today there is much debate to whether the two men were actually innocent, and actually framed by other powerful Malawians close to President Banda. There was speculation at the time if the President would make an example of Muwalo-Nqumayo to all his ministers and hang him publicly; possibly choosing to erect gallows outside the Town Hall in Blantyre, where the old fig tree stands. This tree had seen its share of hangings in pre-Malawi times. Thankfully this didn't happen.

I was recently informed that Dr Austin Mkandawire had to be the medical witness at Muwalo's execution. Austin was a good friend of Muwalo and their friendship went back to the 1940's when they were both health workers in Zomba. How awful that must have been for Austin to be present at the execution of his friend. Another evil act by President Banda. Interestingly the records show that Albert Muwalo was executed on the 3rd September 1977 and this is the official date put out by the government on state media at the time. However, Dr Austin Mkandawire stated that he witnessed Muwalo's execution on the 27th of August. My hunch is that when his execution was formally announced Muwalo had already been dead a week.

As a twist of fate, the families of both men were stripped of all processions; homes, cars, bank accounts, everything! They were then banished to their respective villages in Ntcheu District, as they were both of Maseko-Ngoni parentage. Muwalo's family went back to Baleni Village. President Banda decreed that the wives and the children of the two men could never leave their home villages and therefore never hold a job outside that village. He also ordered that their children could never go to school.

Bert left school sometime later and was sent to be educated in South Africa I think. The school was a more peaceful place after that and I was happy. The hanging of Muwalo is a not a pleasant story and looking back now, quite horrific for a thirteen-year-old boy to experience. I think had there been television in Malawi at that time the President would have had no qualms at televising the hanging as a deterrent to any other ministers who had desires of grandeur.

I say, Masauko Muwalo was the exception, the bad apple. Some of my best friends were Malawians, people like Peter Katenga who came to Hugh Watson's fancy dress party dressed as Idi Amin, complete with medals and wearing a single white glove so he "didn't get his hands dirty when he greeted you",

Mada Mangwazu who I will mention next. Clement Mulaba, George Banda, the list goes on. They were great guys with a great sense of humour, and many are still my dearest friends today.

Even now when I drive past Zomba Prison and stare at the high, double wire fence, barbwire and the prison buildings beyond I think of Albert Muwalo-Nqumayo and how my life in Malawi might have been drastically different if his overthrow had been successful. It is now understood that Masauko and his younger brother Chibaya were able to escape Malawi when his father was arrested and lived in exile.

Albert Muwalo-Nqumayo's wife, Linley (Tamula) passed away on the 30th of December 1994.

Focus Martin Gwede spent 18 years in jail and was finally released in 1993 after spending 17 years as a political prisoner in Mikuyu. He died on March 3, 2011.

General Graciano Matewere is remembered not only for being the country's first Malawian army commander but also for his daring rescue mission of a hijacked South African Airways Boeing 727 in 1972. The plane had been hijacked by two Lebanese terrorists who demanded that the pilot fly the plane to the Middle East and threatened to blow up the plane if he did not comply. The pilot managed to convince the terrorists that they needed to land in Malawi to refuel before the flight to could continue to the Middle East. President Banda was due to fly to London in two days time when the SAA plane landed at Chileka. The then Brigadier Matewere was given the task of solving the crisis before the President had to leave, but Kamuzu gave Matewere strict instructions "to solve the drama with no or minimal bloodshed". After two days of fruitless negotiations and pressure mounting from his boss, Matewere decided to scare the hijackers by shooting at the plane, which had no result. The President was now becoming increasingly impatient to get to London and issued Matewere with his final instruction, "use whatever at your disposal!" The terrorists then demanded a sum of cash in US dollars and assurance of a safe passage so Brigadier Matewere told them that he was bringing the cash in a briefcase himself and boldly went aboard the plane. He disarmed the hijackers without firing a shot. A grateful President Banda then flew to London, all thanks to Matewere. It was often suggested that Matewere's brave actions showed he would rather face armed terrorists rather than face the wrath of President Banda. He served thirty three years in the army and was a loyal officer. He died in February 2001 at the age of 74.

Mac J. Kamwana became Commissioner of Police in 1972, retiring in 1982. Sadly he died in 1984. Interestingly Mac J. Kamwana's son Bright Kamwana also went to St Andrews at the same time as young Muwalo. I remember him with fond memories.

CHAPTER 7

CHIMBUZI

Memories of Muwalo soon faded and were replaced by good Malawians who saw everyone as equal and got on with everybody and we got on with them.

Madalitso Mangwazu, or Mada to his friends was one such kid. His father had been a Malawi Ambassador, and had been posted to West Germany, Britain, Belgium, South Africa and the United Nations. Mada remained in Malawi where I guess he had a stable education. He was one of the funniest guys I've ever met at school. Not only could he give it but he could also take it too. He always had a grin on his face and spoke with impeccable English, which enabled him to get away with almost anything. He may have been the target of the teachers' suspicions and questions but deep down they had affection for him.

One teacher who had a great, shall we say affinity, with Mada, was Mr Jackman. The two of them should have had a stage show together. Mada would give the person in the class to give the wrong answer to a question asked just to raise a laugh, he didn't mean to disrupt the class, he just enjoyed making people laugh. Jackman was a bit of a comedian also and appreciated this quality in Mada. The banter between the two of them in a class was thoroughly entertaining if not at times a little close to the edge given Malawi's political climate and intolerance of certain words and suggestions.

On almost the first day in class Jackman had moved Mada from his chosen seat to a desk at the back corner of the room next to the window. Jackman, from then on, referred to Mada's desk position as the "Dark Corner". This may seem racist, which it might have been given today's climate of Political Correctness but I believe at the time nothing was meant by it. Mada even referred to it himself as the "Dark Corner".

I remember once we had been getting ready for the end of term and Jackman had asked a few of us what plans we had for the half term holiday, were we going anywhere, just friendly chat. He had bypassed Mada as he went from child to child round the room as if knowing this would raise a reaction from Mada, it was like a game of chess with them I think. Anyway Mada put his hand up, "aren't you going to ask me where I'm going for my holidays?" he asked.

"What was that? Did I hear something from the peanut gallery? Ok, where are you going Mangwazu?" Jackman took the bait.

"I'm going to the Lake, Sir." Mada answered with a huge grin.

"The Lake eh? Why are you going to the Lake, to get a suntan?" Jackman asked, quick as a flash. The class fell into laughter.

"Oh, good one Sir!" replied Mada, also laughing.

During one lesson Mada asked if he could be excused to go the "toilet". Jackman looked up and said "Toilet? Don't you mean Chimbuzi?" with perfect Chichewa pronunciation.

Although Jackman was a geography teacher he knew a lot about a lot of things. I think he had been in a Japanese concentration camp in the war, or at least he spoke Japanese and often came out with scraps of history in his geography class from the

Second World War. One day he told us how a border was disputed and was moved following the outcome of a certain guerrilla war in the Far East. Straight away he looked towards the "Dark Corner" and said,

"Gorilla warfare, something you'd be good at hey Mangwazu?" with that twinkle in his eye, emphasising the pronunciation of gorilla.

Jackman continually turned to Mada when he referred to Ox-BOW-lakes, Jungles, local tribes, and other geographical references that he could use to refer to Mada's ethnic background. Mada always took it in the humour it was intended. We were all well aware that all it would have taken was a single telephone call from Mada to his father and Jackman could have found himself deported out of the country but I think they were both knew that no harm was ever meant by it and that they were both sad when Mada left at the end of the 5th Form.

I saw Mada a few years ago in the Capital Hotel, in Lilongwe. He now runs a successful Taxi and Mini-bus business both in Malawi and Zambia.

Mr Jackman retired to Durban, South Africa where he continues to play his beloved game of golf but I think he would be proud of Mada.

It's worth noting that Mada's father was in fact Timon Sam Mangwazu! Timon died on the 17th of October 2012 at Kamuzu Central Hospital in Lilongwe at the age of 79. While we were at school we never really knew who Mada's father was and how important he was. Turns out that Mr Mangwazu was one of the first five ambassadors chosen by President Kamuzu Banda when he came to power in 1964. Mr Mangwazu was the longest serving ambassador in Malawi history finally stepping down in 1989.

On hearing of Mr Mangwazu's death, the Vice President Khumbo Kachali paid tribute to late Timon Sam Mangwazu describing him as a "dedicated nationalist and well-known figure in Malawi's history".

In his short eulogy, the Vice President said the "passing on of Mangwazu was a greater loss to government than it was to his family and the people of Kasungu...........Through the death of Mangwazu, government has lost more than has done to his family because he was source of wisdom to us in government," mourned Kachali.

He said President Joyce Banda, was equally saddened with the death of Mangwazu, adding the president acknowledged the contribution the deceased made to the development of the country in his lifetime. Important people at the funeral were country's Defence Minister, Minister of Youth and Sports Enock Chihana, and even former Government Hostess for the late Dr. Hastings Kamuzu Banda, Mama Cecelia Tamanda Kadzamira,

It turned out that Mada's father was the Chairman of Press Holdings Ltd between 1978 and 1982. He also served as cabinet minister in the United Democratic Front (UDF) regime of former President Bakili Muluzi and was eventually president of the Malawi National Democratic Party (MNDP).

Even as I write this a shiver goes through my spine at the jokes that were directed at Mada by Mr Jackman. In Malawi at that time it would have just taken one call to his father and Mada would have had Mr Jackman on the next flight out of Malawi. It just shows the character of Mada and I am proud to call him a friend.

I was sad to learn that Mada passed away in 1997.

CHAPTER 8

NO, BUT YOU WILL

You always get your characters at every school and we certainly had ours. The list is long but I am going to try and keep it short, with a few well-chosen stories. Some of the characters were individuals, one offs. Others were characters that came from a family of characters, much to the dismay of teachers that had been at school many years. For these few teachers, their lives had become haunted by family names and that is where I shall start.

It was the first day of a new term and Mr Jackman is taking register, calling out the names and they pupils replying with "here Sir" or just "Sir".

Suddenly he stops and stares at his list and then throws his hands to his head and mournfully says "Oh, God NO, not another one?" The class is silent. Mr Jackman removes his hands from his head and searches the faces, like an eagle searching for its prey, studying the little faces. Finally, he calls out the next name on the list and looks up.

A little kid across the room says "Sir" and Jackman flashes his eyes towards the unsuspecting kid who hasn't the foggiest idea what's going on. In three large strides Jackman is at the kids' desk.

"You're John? Any relation to Stuart and Amanda?" Jackman demands.

"Yes sir, they're my brother and sister."

"Thought so…." Says Jackman and grabs the kid by the back of the shirt and lifts him out of his chair and carries him to the back of the room where the coat hooks are and literally hangs the kid by the back of his shirt on a hook.

"But Sir, I haven't done anything yet." Pleads the young boy, as his legs dangle a foot off the floor.

"No….but you WILL!" says Jackman who walks back to his desk and continues with his register. John stayed there for the remainder of the lesson.

Mr Jackman had a similar seizure when a "George" joined his class. His family were infamous and Jackman's first question to the latest edition of this family was to ask "Just tell me one thing, are there any more of you coming to this school? Please say you're the last one!"

"No, my younger brother will be coming next year".

"Oh God, remind me to hand in for early retirement before then, now take your desk outside." Jackman made George sit outside the classroom for the rest of that first day.

Mr Jackman could easily be wound up, just the simple shout of "Camel" or the yelling of "Burrrrrrrrrr" was enough to have Jackman searching the corridors for the source. I never found out why these two things got to him so much, but it was like a red rag to a bull and never failed to get a response.

One story that still has me amused happened on weekend while Mr Jackman was enjoying a quiet weekend at his home on the ITG Estate in Limbe. Three boys were John, George and one whose name I cannot remember but I shall call "C", decided to cycle to the Jackman Residence with the aim of disturbing his peace. The plan was that they would each cycle past his gate shouting Burrrrrrrrrrr!

John went first, shouting at the top of his voice. Jackman is now alerted!

George was next and zooms past the gate yelling. Jackman is now out of his front door.

Next up is "C" yelling "Burrrrrrrr!" as he passes the gate, then peddles hell-for-leather down the road in pursuit of his comrades.

Jackman is now at the gate to see the back of kid "C" disappearing up the road and his face drops with disappointment as justice evades him. Just then kid "C"'s chain comes off and jams his back wheel solid.

Jackman's face changes from sadness into a vicious grin as he welcomes the change of luck. In a few bounds he has the unlucky "C" by the scruff of the neck.

It was the last time they ventured anywhere near Mr Jackman's house again.

CHAPTER 9

PALS FOREVER

As I have already said, Richard and I became friends during my first year at Saints. While helping me with my homework Richard asked if I was doing anything at the weekend and invited me to go down the river with him. I had no idea what the river was but agreed to meet up at his house the coming Saturday morning to find out. I envied Richard, he had been born in Malawi and therefore knew everything about the animals, which fruits you could eat, and he also spoke Chichewa. His father had come to what was then Nyasaland and remembered a buffalo being shot at the bridge on the Dundudzu Road below Limbe Market, which gives you an idea of how the country must have been in those days.

The week dragged by but finally the Saturday morning arrived. I told my mother I was off to Richards for the day, there was no way I was going to tell her we were off to the "River", she might know more about it than me and not let me go.

"Make sure you're back before dark, 5.30pm at the latest!" she insisted and so I headed off to Richards house.

Richard lived on the other side of Sunnyside to me, on the edge of the residential area, in fact at the bottom of Richard's garden was the road then after that it was trees and overgrown bushes interspersed with African cultivated fields. I had looked at it often but it always seemed like a forbidden place, where the only thing that was missing was a sign saying "Here be dragons". The "River" turned out to be the Mudi River that ran through town, across the Blantyre Sports Club and then on past Richards house, through the trees and fields and finally joined the Shire River after many, many miles.

Richard came out of his house and together we crossed the tarmac road and took a small dirt path going off to the side and into the trees. I noticed that there was a light blue PE bag pushed into the back of Richard's shorts. I meant to ask him what it was for but as we walked, I never really got level with him to ask so I saved my question for a later time. As we walked along this path, we lost sight of the houses and you soon forgot you were still in "town". The occasional dog barked and reminded us that just through the trees were houses. Further down the path we went when suddenly we came out on the bank of the river, an old tree leaned out over the bend and scattered in the river were large boulders. Richard leapt from the bank and grabbed an overhanging branch and swung out into the middle of the river and let go, dropping onto a large boulder in the river. He steadied himself for a second then leapt to the next stone and finally landed on the opposite back.

"Come on, follow me!" he yelled and I awkwardly fumbled my way across the river with none of the grace Richard had shown but more like a hippo in tap shoes.

On the other bank the path turned left and followed the river. On the right side of the path were African fields growing cassava, and maize and where the land was level sugar cane grew almost down to the water's edge. The river was not fast moving and the sluggish waters were brown with mud. Richard suddenly stopped walking and looked across to the far bank where some bushes had grown so large that their branches almost touched the water.

"There" he pointed to the bush, "can you see it?" I followed his finger and looked into the bush.

"What is it? I can't see anything".

"It's a snake." He said with a smile like a kid who had just seen the shop keeper turn his back on an open sweet jar on the counter.

Again, I gazed into the bush, then suddenly I saw it. A green snake, so green it was almost electric in the bright sunshine. It was curled up on one of the low branches and was motionless.

"Wow!" was about all I could say. "Is it dangerous?"

"No, it's a Spotted Bush Snake, harmless. The place is full of them, it takes a few minutes to see the first one but once you see one, you get your eye in and you can then see them all over the place. They catch frogs on the river bank."

I would have been quite happy to just have sat there and watched it but Richard had already made a grab for it from our side of the river but the snake had seen him coming and uncoiled and headed up to the higher branches of the bush. Richard was not going to give up and made a final lunge and managed to catch hold of its tail before it got too high up. The snake, seeing that it was being held back, turned around and struck forward and down towards Richards hand.

"Look out!" I yelled but Richard had seen it coming and avoided the open gape of the snake while still maintaining his grip on the tail.

Slowly he managed to "jiggle" the snake out of the bush and held it by the tail out in front of him and moved to some open ground at the edge of a field. He then lowered the snakes head to the ground while still holding the tail in the air and using a broken twig he pressed the snakes head to the ground and let go of its tail. As quick as a flash he then caught the snakes head securely and stood up holding his prize.

I was speechless. "Here touch it, I've got its head, it can't bite you."

It felt strange, warm, and not cold and although it was so shiny it was dry. I felt excited, I think because to me there was a danger involved, and that made my adrenalin pump around my body.

Richard then reached behind him and pulled the PE bag from his shorts. He then fed the snakes body into the bag then with one last action threw and let go of the snakes' head into the bag and folded the neck of the bag over and tied it.

Before I could find any words to say Richard said "Come on, let's find some more".

As we walked along the river, we ate Guavas and Passion Fruits that grew here and there. Saints, homework, the family were a million miles away and I never wanted the day to end. By the end of the day we must have had twelve or fourteen snakes of various sizes; most were Spotted Bush Snakes but we had one or two Brown Water Snakes too.

"What are you going to do with the snakes now?" I asked

"Probably keep them for a few days then let them go down the river and then catch some more. Do you want to come down here again tomorrow?"

"Yeah, sure, that's great." I said with great enthusiasm.

And so was my first introduction to snakes and the start of my friendship with Richard. We spent almost every weekend and most afternoons after school down the river over the next five years. I never kept a log of the amount of snakes we caught over that time but we used to catch about fifty snakes a week so with slim days and off weekends I estimate the total to be close to 6,500 snakes, sure with our "catch & release" we obviously caught the same snakes more than once but for such a small river there were an enormous amount of snakes.

CHAPTER 10

A COBRA IN OUR SCHOOL BAG

Richard and I would spend every available moment down the river. It was only a matter of time before one or two of our recent catches were taken in to school. Taking snakes to school was of course totally forbidden; although there were no written rules to say such as far as I knew so Richard and I always said we would state this in our defence.

We would take the snake to school in a snake bag then just before class we would slip the snake into the opening between the buttons of our shirt and let the snake sit inside our shirt. It was dark and the snake settled down thinking night had come early. If the snake did move you could feel it against your skin and check on it.

One particular lesson I was sat next to a girl called Anna Pantallionie, a fiery Italian girl. We were well into the lesson when she let out an almighty squeal and yelled "SNAKE".

I was dead excited at the thought of a snake in the classroom and replied "Where?", hoping to catch it.

I then realised she was pointing at my waist. When I looked down there was the bright green head of my pet Bush Snake protruding from the gaping hole between my shirt buttons, its bright golden eyes shining. I quickly tapped his nose and his head shot back into my shirt.

There was a brief investigation by the maths teacher but I managed to convince the teacher that Anna must have been seeing things as no person in their right mind would have a snake in their shirt. Anna was told off for interrupting the lesson and thankfully my snake did not make another appearance.

At the end of the lesson I was one of the last to gather their books up and leave the classroom. Anna was waiting for me outside. Before I had time to explain she gave me an almighty slap across one side of my face.

"Don't you ever make me look stupid again, you and your snakes are disgusting!" and she stormed off. I got a round of applause from the other kids, who thought it was all very funny.

One afternoon I was cycling around the garden on my bike weaving in and out of the flower beds and around trees. There was no particular reason, it was just one of those things that boy's do I guess. As I passed between a large blue gum stump that we had and a flower bed I felt some water hit my left thigh. I didn't stop peddling but wiped my leg with my hand and yes it was wet so I glanced up at the blue cloudless sky.

"That's odd," I said to myself, and continued to complete another circuit of the garden.

When I reached the same spot between the old stump and the flower bed on the second lap there dead in front of me was a cobra rearing up looking at me. Things all happened very quickly; I leapt off the bike before I got to the snake, while at the same time realising that the water on my leg was in fact venom from the cobra that it had spat at me as I rode past.

The cobra wasn't very big, possibly a foot or so long, reddish brown above and the hood which was actually its throat was a salmon pink with some thick black bars lower down. I quickly identified it as a young Mozambique Spitting Cobra (*Naja mossambica*) a highly venomous front fixed fanged snake, very common in Malawi but the first I had seen. I raced up to the house to get my stick and bag.

"What you running for?" my mother asked as I flew through the lounge.

"There is a small cobra in the garden, I'm just getting a bag" I said without thinking as I disappeared through the room.

My mother muttered something which I didn't quite catch and I didn't have time to ask her to repeat.

By the time I had collected a snake bag and my stick from the bedroom and got back onto the veranda I could see my mother with the garden boy and the cook at the spot where I had left the cobra.

"Don't disturb it!" I yelled and ran down the garden.

Before I got there, I could see by looking at the three of them what had happened. There was no point in me running so I walked the rest of the way. There on the grass was the mutilated body of the young cobra. My mother said something but I didn't hear her voice. I knelt down to examine the poor little snake. I wasn't crying but inside I was heartbroken. I picked the snake up by the tail and carried its limp lifeless body to the garage where I picked up a hoe and then headed down to the bottom of the garden to bury it. But before I did, I got my tape measure out of my pocket, it measured 43cm in length.

I then replaced the hoe in the garage and headed off to Richard's house to moan at him about my stupid family.

I imagine that being a young and inexperienced cobra it had been attracted to the peddling movement of my legs rather than my eyes, which was lucky for me. A few weeks later I was running back from Richards along Smythe Road. It was already dark, way past the 5.30pm curfew time for me to be in. As I ran some rustling in the leaves at the side of the road caught my attention and I stopped to investigate. As I peered into the darkness where the rustling had come from there was a faint noise like escaping air and some liquid hit me in the right eye. There was immediate pain, burning pain, like shampoo in your eye only ten times worse. I knew straight away what it was - a Spitting Cobra!

I clasped my hand over my eye and took a few steps back into the middle of the road. I wanted to get away from the snake, as it was dark and now I was blind in one eye, not the best circumstances for tackling a highly venomous snake like a cobra. I wiped my eye with my hand then wiped my hand on my shorts to remove what venom I could. Then I spat in my hand and rubbed the spit into my eye over and over again.

It was helping a bit to dilute the venom but I needed to get home quick so ran the seventy or so remaining yards to the house and crept into the kitchen via the back door and washed my face and eye under the running tap.

Mother heard the water running and came into the kitchen.

"What time do you call this, you're late!" she said.

"Sorry I was on my way home when a bug flew in my eye and its stinging, I have been trying to get it out" I said and turned around to show her the evidence.

"It does look very red, are you sure it's out?"

"Yes, I think so" I said returning my eye to the running tap. There was no way I was going to tell her it was a Spitting Cobra. Next morning my eye was much better, a bit weepy and red but it didn't burn anymore.

At school a few days later, Richard found me on the corridor between lessons.

"Hey you have got to see what I have in this bag" he said holding up a blue Adidas shoulder bag and stepped into an empty classroom. He placed the bag on a desk and unzipped the bag. "Look inside!"

I parted the opening and there sitting in the bottom of the bag, reared up at me was a baby Mozambique Spitting Cobra about 20cm long. I let go of the bag and reeled back shielding my eyes.

"What you doing?" Richard asked, like I was some kind of idiot.

"Hey you saw my eye, I don't want another dose!" I said delicately peering into the bag. Richard then zipped up the bag and put it over his shoulder.

"Isn't it cute? See you after school" he said as he skipped down the corridor.

If only the school had seen what he had in his bag they would have gone nuts!

CHAPTER 11

OWLS IN THE BEDROOM

Growing up in Malawi made you soon realise that all fauna was edible as far as Malawians were concerned.

A sack being carried by a Malawian usual meant that inside the sack was an animal that was destined for the pot that evening. Richard and I would always stop the African and ask him what he was carrying in the sack. Since we were children, we did not pose a threat to the African and they were usually happy to open the sack and show off their prize. More often than not Richard and I would make an offer for the animal being held captive and, in this way, we obtained everything from kittens to Pangolins, and on one particular occasion three baby owls.

The owls were really cute creatures, little balls of grey fluff with big eyes. I decided to take ownership of one of them and Richard took the other two. We fed them on meat from the market mixed with cotton wool to substitute fur to clean their stomachs. My baby owl was soon standing on its legs and waddling around like a penguin. Its wing feathers had not yet developed so it was a long-time off flying.

I housed him in the garage and after school I would take him out onto the lawn to walk around and investigate the garden while I lay down on the lawn and read a book in the sun. One afternoon while I lay on my side propped up by one arm reading, and watching the baby owl waddle round the garden like a penguin, an eagle flew over-head. The baby owl let out the shrillest shriek and ran up the garden as fast as its little legs would carry it. It ran straight for me and hid under my arm-pit and there it stayed till it was sure the eagle had gone. I guess it saw me as its mother and looked to me for protection when danger appeared. Richard's two owls grew up equally fast and soon associated him with food and protection.

One morning Richards's mother went into his bedroom and was hit by an awful smell. She couldn't quite place what the smell was but set about to locate the source. She looked under the bed and through the cupboard but found nothing. She then opened the two bottom doors of the wardrobe and had a good look but couldn't find the cause of the stench but it definitely smelt stronger around the wardrobe. She then looked up at the two top doors and decided she would need a chair to stand on to reach them so headed off to the dining room to fetch a chair.

On her return she stood on the chair and opened the two doors and got the shock of her life. As she looked into the dark four very large eyes looked back at her, then a loud shriek was emitted as the owls realised that the face looking in was not Richard with food but an intruder who as far as they were concerned was pretty dangerous. The effect was total shock to all parties. Mrs Terrell almost fell backwards off the chair and slammed the doors shut. When Richard got back home, he was told that the owls were to be banished from the bedroom.

After some weeks the owls did develop their flight feathers and it was only when they had their adult plumage that we discovered they were Spotted Eagle Owls (*Bubo africanus*).

We were able to train them to catch live rats that we "liberated" from the zoo and soon the owls were ready to be released back into the wild. We used to visit the area to see how they were doing on a regular basis and they would often come to the fist when called for food. I think Mrs Terrell was pleased to see them go.

Three young Black-shouldered Kites (*Elanus axillaris*) were also rescued from the supper pot and we successfully returned these to the wild also.

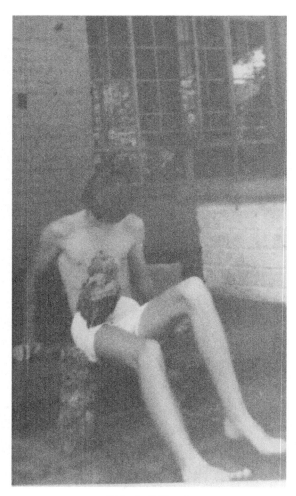

Richard with his owls

There were many routes down to the Mudi River from the house and we didn't always go the same way: there was never a specified plan of which route we were going to take, we would just leave the house, get into conversation and the route just seemed to happen.

One Saturday morning Richard came to call on me and once I grabbed the snake bags and my knife, off we went. On the particular route we came across a troop of Vervet Monkeys playing in the trees at the side of the road so we stopped to watch them. Within a few minutes that had moved from the trees to the electricity poles that ran down one side of the road and were swinging on the cables like a scene out of Jungle Book.

Suddenly there was a loud crack and sparks as one monkey tried to cross from one cable to the other. All the other monkeys leapt back into the safety of the trees leaving the electrocuted and singed body of the monkey suspended between the two cables.

Monkeys being monkeys, it didn't take them long to pluck up the courage and become inquisitive to what had happened to their colleague. Slowly they left the trees and ventured back onto the poles and cables.

Well it was only a matter of time before another monkey completed the circuit between two cables with its tail and there was another loud crack and sparks and another monkey lay amongst the cables, smouldering. Again, the rest of the troop dashed for the trees.

It had been a quite entertaining but sad at the same time and we were glad that after the second short-circuit, the troop left the cables as a bad idea and disappeared into the trees. The local electricity supply company, ESCOM, would come round doing regular maintenance on the cables and remove decomposing wildlife that had been killed on the cables. On one occasion I happened to be walking along the road when the chaps from ESCOM were about to remove the chameleon. After a quick chat with them I was able to get them to remove it in one piece; now this might seem gruesome and disgusting but there was reason in my madness. Maggots had eaten away all the flesh from inside the chameleon but the hard-thick skin had dried so fast in the African sun that it had been left whole. So, what you had was a dry, hollow chameleon, preserved and in perfect condition; it was every school boys dream, well mine anyway. Since the chameleon was completely dry there was no smell to it at all. I had the chameleon for many years until it was thrown out in a house move by my mother.

Rabies was rife in Malawi and any dog running free was a worry. After an afternoon down the Mudi River with Richard catching snakes I was returning home along Smythe Road when I saw a Malawian with a metal pole with a wire noose at the end of it leaning over into the storm drain at the side of the road. At first I thought he was catching snakes so stopped to chat with him. He explained that he was catching a "wild" dog that was hiding in the drain. As I was in no particular hurry, I sat under a nearby tree to watch. After a few minutes the man pulled the dog from the culvert and dragged it up onto the road. The dog didn't look rabid to me, cross and angry at having a wired noose choking its neck yes. Its eyes were bulging and its tongue was hanging out of the side of its mouth and I was upset to see a dog being treated in this way. Without much feeling for the dog the man forced the end of the pole onto the ground so that the dog was almost lying on the road.

He then produced a small hand-gun from his waist and placed the end of the barrel against the top of the dog's head and pulled the trigger. This all happened so quickly that I was unable to look away. I was horrified and shocked. He then pulled the gun away from the now dead dog and as he did I saw that coming out of the end of the barrel was a long metal bolt and it was this, and not a bullet that had gone into the dogs' skull. While he cleaned the gun, the dog lay bleeding from its mouth nose and ears.

I was shacking when I got up and staggered the rest of the way home. I didn't tell my parents about it but I cried myself to sleep for that poor dog and I had nightmares for months. I always remember the fear in its eyes.

A few weeks later I heard that were were going to the Lake for the first time to a place called Davey's Cottage at Nkhudzi Bay. The weekend had been arranged by Linda and Geoff Kenyon who were family friends. Geoff worked at David Whitehead and his wife ran the Blantyre Dog Kennels in Chichiri. Geoff was ok, I guess, but he used to tease me endlessly and I nicknamed him "the mouth", because he always had something to say towards me. All I remember about this weekend was the heat and the loneliness really. There was a large iron boat that had run aground many years ago and was now a rusty skeleton. I would spend much of my time sitting on this wreak thinking. I was glad to get back to Blantyre.

CHAPTER 13

MAD DOGS & ENGLISHMEN

I
n 1977 my grandparents, Gan and Dick, came down from Kenya to stay with us for two weeks. I remember there were some huge family discussions between Mother and Jim prior to their arrival. Mother had never got on with Jim's parents and she was going to lay down some ground rules. I now find this totally bizarre, given all the support they had given her when she walked out on my father.

As the days got closer to their arrival mother got tenser and more stressed, till finally the day came when Jim went off to Chileka to pick them up. I had not seen Gan and Dick since they visited us in Harlow and then when we saw Dick at Nairobi airport in May 1975. They both burst through the door demanding the hugs and kisses, which was something we weren't really used to in our house but we gave in. Then Gan proceeded to dish out presents and I was really happy with my Kenyan T-shirt. Amy and Isabel were less enthused with theirs as I remember.

Dick had arrived with quite a list of things he wanted to do and see. Malawi is famed for its Nyala and Greater Kudu and seeing both these majestic antelope were high on his list, luckily both of these can be found just south of Blantyre in Lengwe National Park in the Lower Shire. The park was designated a game reserve in 1928 and was originally twice the size it is today. However, due to the pressures on making money for the colonial government the reserve was halved and later this became a National Park.

Finally it was arranged that Jim would take Dick down to Lengwe, while Gan stayed at the house with mother. It was the lesser of two evils for mother but there was no way she was going to a Game Park with Dick. Seeing as the house was being divided into boys and girls, I got to go to Lengwe too, which I was glad about.

The drive down to Lengwe is a short drive down the escarpment and into the Lower Shire Valley. It makes no real odds when you go because it's always like an oven and added to this was the obvious tension in the car between Dick and Jim. I don't remember what was said in the car but it wasn't a lot.

Finally, we signed in at the gate and parked up at the designated car park area. From there it is a very short walk to the main hide which over-looks a waterhole. We settled ourselves in the hide and waited for animals to arrive, which they did after a few minutes. Dick was excited to get his first glimpse of a number of Nyala and a few female Kudu that had come to drink and his camera clicked away almost every few seconds. Eventually Dick had had enough and spoke.

"John I'm not happy about the angle of the photos from up here, I need to be at ground level to get some more realistic photos!" he said and got up off the wooden bench.

"I'm gonna take some photos from the ground." he said.

"But you're not allowed to be anywhere else but this hide" Jim replied, but it was too late, Dick was already out of the door and down the stairs muttering something in a combination of Cumbrian and Swahili that I didn't understand.

Jim was already muttering to himself and when I asked

where Dick was off to, there wasn't much of an answer from him.

"He's going to sit under the hide and take some photos at ground level or something" he muttered and we both turned to the narrow window and watched the animals in silence. Nothing more was said, until Jim shattered the silence.

"Bloody typical!" he said. I never really heard Jim swear so I knew something was up.

As I looked across to where Jim's eyes were fixed on the right-hand side of the water hole I gave a little chuckle. There was Dick on his belly, shuffling along between the trees heading for the far side of the waterhole.

"It's not funny!" Jim snapped so I tried to control my sniggers.

As we watched Dick crawled silently to within a few feet of where the Nyala were drinking. Satisfied that his angle was now perfect he slowly brought his camera into position and began taking his photos.

Just when Jim thought his day couldn't get any worse we heard the faint sound of voices coming along the track towards the hide. Within minutes a group of Japanese tourists climbed the steps and settled themselves down in the hut between Jim and I. Jim's face was a picture.

It didn't take long for one keen-eyed Japanese gentleman to spot Dick and the whole hut descended into a mass of whispering and pointing Japanese. Jim pretended that he had no connection with the man lying on his belly beside a tree and this went well until Dick, now satisfied with his pictures, shuffled back and returned to the hide.

"John, I think I got some super photo there. Those bull Nyala are beautiful beasts."

All the Japanese looked at Jim, who abruptly got up and ushered us out of the hide. Jim stormed up the track and I had to almost trot to keep up. Dick was bringing up the rear. After a few yards I turned around to see if Dick was keeping up but he was gone.

"Jim, Dick's gone!" I said.

"Now where's the idiot gone?" he said and we headed back to look for Dick. It didn't take long for Jim to see where Dick had broken away off the track and after a minute or so we managed to pick up sight of Dick in the thicket bush.

"What's he doing?" I asked.

"Who knows? Let's just wait here".

After a few minutes Dick returned to the path and pointed to some tracks in the dust.

"Leopard, it was walking here then went off to the left but I think its old spoor."

I don't think Jim spoke another word all the way home. I just sat in the back of the car thinking what a great day this had been.

Dick did manage to take some amazing photos at Lengwe but during his stay he would take one of the very few photos of the whole family together.

After their two weeks were up Gan and Dick headed home and they would never visit us again. In fact, my mother would never see the two of them again, although she and Jim were quick to contact Dick for money when they wanted to buy a business in South Africa in 1987/88. Jim would never see his mother again before she passed away 1990 and only see his father once more before Dick passed away in 2003. It was extremely sad. I would not see Gan again before she died and was taken aback when I heard she had left me £1,000 in her will. I went out to visit Dick a few times before he passed away and we spent many an evening siting on his veranda chatting about the "old days" in Kenya. He was a good man.

The rare photo of the family taken by Dick

CHAPTER 14

THE MAJOR ARRIVES

The teachers at Saints were of both extremes. We had Mrs Florrie Mullon, whose very name had struck fear into the hearts of kids for decades and in some case generations. Florrie was the teacher with the longest tenure at the School, having started in the original "junior" school at the Old Mission School site as Miss Graham in the early 1950's and retired from the Saints in the 1990's! Many a pupil caught chewing gum were ordered to put it in their hair till the end of the lesson.

Then we had the other end of the spectrum in the form of Mr Ledsham who taught both Metalwork and Technical Drawing; and Mr Davies who taught Woodwork. The two of them went well together, their workshops were even next to each other. Mr Ledsham would fall asleep at his desk during lessons, and Mr Davies would often spend an entire lesson marching around the class doing military drill with a broom. We had Mr Evans who would often go to his classroom cupboard and take a crafty swig from a bottle of methylated spirits! Madam Michele who taught us french, and drove a red Triumph TR4 sports car and would, by the end of the lesson, be sobbing at her desk. I never knew what caused this because I used to sit at the back of the class and as she started to write on the board I would open the window and climb out and spend the whole lesson sitting in the sun looking across the playing field towards Ndirande; then just before the end of the lesson I would climb back in. I did this for a year, I just couldn't understand why we were learning french in Africa when we should be learning something useful like Chichewa.

However, in 1976 all this was about to change. We had a new Headmaster arrive and we realised very quickly that things were going to change at Saints. Major Bryan Bayly was a no-nonsense, ex-British Army Officer who certainly came in with a new broom. At over six-foot-tall with a booming voice he quickly instilled discipline to "his" standard. He was always accompanied by his golden Labrador on his rounds.

His reforms were on three fronts. First St Andrews Secondary School was made a Government School under the auspices of the 'Designated School's Board' and the school crest was changed.

Secondarily between 1976 and 1983 he obtained funding from the Biet Trust to undertake an enormous building programme at the school. In fact, the number of school build-ings almost doubled with the addition of a new library, the science block and numerous other classroom blocks. The House rooms of Laws, Sharpe and Henderson were also built and a squash court was constructed.

Thirdly he put more emphasis on sport. He established the awarding School Colours for outstanding sportsmen and women. There was a standing joke amongst pupils that if you wanted to become a school prefect then all you had to do was play cricket! I don't think it was that bad but the majority of prefects were on the school sports teams.

He was fast to act to a problem and didn't dilly-dally about anything; I admired that.

It wasn't long after the Major arrived that one day, out of the blue, Jim announced that he was leaving Soche Hill Secondary School and coming to Saints to replace Mr Ledsham who was retiring due to ill health. As you can imagine this "thrilled me no end". No other pupil had their family working at their school but I was not in a position to do anything about it. It was a case of like it or lump it!

It was around this time that I got my first and only caning. I was basically set up and done for "handling stolen property". The thief denied all knowledge and the blame was landed squarely at my feet.

After a few weeks of questioning I realised that the other school boy was not going to come clean, and I was on my own. During a science lesson one of the Malawian messengers knocked at the door and had a quiet word with the teacher.

"Rupert, can you go with Joshua please" the teacher informed me and I followed Joshua out of the class and up to the Headmaster's office, where I was summoned inside by the Majors booming voice of "COME IN!"

"Rupert, thing is, I don't know if you took the calculator or not, I think you probably didn't but I have to punish someone. Do you understand?" the Major paused.

"Yes Sir." I say, not really finding any other words to say at the time.

The Major then pulled a wooden chair out from under a table and reaches for a long and twisted cane.

"Bend over the seat of this chair with your knees under the seat and hold on to the legs the other side." I then get six of the best; in typical Major fashion and boy did it hurt.

At the time I didn't know I was going to get six so braced myself for this going on all day! After the final lashing he told me to stand up and put the chair back under the table. I then stood there in front of him.

"My advice is, choose your friends with a little more care next time, that'll be all." He said in a low voice.

"Thank you, Sir." And I left to go back to my class, but not until I'd checked my backside in a nearby loo. There were large red welts across my backside and it was hurting like mad.

I never spoke to the boy who set me up again and he never spoke to me. I had learnt my lesson. Later this episode would cost me being made a prefect and that probably hurt more.

I knew what happened regarding the stolen item and I think from his words so did the Major. Was I upset that he had to cane someone and I was the candidate? No not really, in a way and this is going to sound strange and weird, it felt like the Head Master was in a jam. The kids father demanding the school find out who had stolen the item even though his son now had it back.

I imagine that the Major hated caning me but he had to. I wasn't upset, I felt like I was helping him out in a way, like he was asking for a volunteer and I was stepping forward to say, here, cane me.

In 1987, when I wrote to the Major and asked him for a reference for the British Army he wrote:

"Rupert is thoroughly dependable, level-headed and a practical young man of sensible disposition. He passed through the school with much personal credit. Throughout his school career Rupert impressed by his maturity and dependability, and the thoroughness with which he undertook his work or any duty or activity. His behaviour was beyond reproach and he left school with an enviable record."

"He is a pleasant young man: cheerful, loyal and in every way reliable. I recommend him most strongly, and would be prepared to entirely rely upon him in any eventuality."

I think his words say everything he couldn't on that day as he caned me. He had relied on me to take the caning that day to put an end to the day and save his face with the father. I was quite emotional when I read the reference.

CHAPTER 15

RICHARD GETS BITTEN

S ince I'd first met Richard, we continued to catch snakes and soon our growing collection was becoming hard to accommodate at our houses. By 1977, both our parents were tolerating the snakes but there was a limit. Richard then had the idea of the vacant Snake House at the Blantyre Zoo. It was a purpose-built snake house that had last been used when Gray Bowden had used it to house his snakes some years ago. I was dubious that we would get permission to put our snakes in it but Richard was confident so I wasn't going to argue.

The Zoo was owned by the City Council but as far as everyone was concerned Paul Taylor ran the place, he was also the Headmaster at St Andrews Primary School so off we headed for the school to talk to Mr Taylor.

All I knew about Mr Taylor was stories I had heard from my sister when she was a pupil there. He had a heavy hand and kids who misbehaved were hit with a slipper, even as young as seven. Richard didn't seem to be put off by this, probably since he had been a pupil at the primary school and knew Paul Taylor better than I did; so into Paul's office we strolled.

Richard did all the talking, there were some rules and conditions but at the end of the chat we had got our Snake House. I was shocked as I was only fourteen years old and Richard had just turned fifteen, but we were both very happy.

One of the conditions was that we opened the snake house at weekends to the public, which didn't seem a problem to me. It was the first responsibility I had been given and I felt a sense of pride at being trusted to take care of poisonous snakes in a public environment. We still kept a few snakes at home, which I think secretly pleased our parents because in all the years in Malawi, neither of our houses was ever broken into! One of our first jobs was to clean up the over-grown "snake-pit" that was outside. This pit was about eight meters by four meters in size. It had been dug into the ground and then a wall built round it about a meter high, so you were able to stand at the wall, and look over into the pit whose ground level was about 2 meters below you. Inside the pit were boulders and trees to make it as natural as possible. The vegetation in the pit had become over-grown from years of neglect and we needed to give it a good pruning ready to be re-stocked within a variety of snakes. It had been a few years since Gray Bowden had been in charge of the snakes at the zoo so we didn't expect there to be any snakes still in the pit. We were wrong!

On moving some small rocks in one corner we found a baby Puff Adder! I obviously have a love for snakes so make no apology for saying that it was the most beautiful looking little snake. It was a Puff Adder so we gave it the utmost respect during capture even though it was a baby and only about 25cm in length. We placed it in one of the glass fronted cages in the snake house and admired our first exhibit.

"I wonder when it last ate, I'll go and get it a baby rat" I said and headed off to the zoo's white rat pen and returned a few minutes later with a small white rat.

The live baby rat was then placed in the cage with the baby Puff Adder and we sat back and waited to see if the snake was hungry. We watched because you should never leave live rodents with snakes as sometimes the rodents can attack the snake and may even kill it.

We didn't have to wait long. The baby rat came within about 10cm of the snake and the Puff Adder struck out at the rat with lightning speed. Now keep in mind that the cage was only about 30cm high. The young rat gave a shriek and leapt up into the air, it hit the roof of the cage and then fell back to the floor of the cage, stone DEAD!

Richard and I looked at each other in shock and simultaneously said "Shit!"

We knew about snakes and their poisons but the time between strike and dead rat was no more than a second and half, and we had just been handling the bloody snake! It was time to investigate so we gingerly opened the cage door and removed the dead rat with some long forceps and slammed the cage door closed before our young Puff Adder decided to give our hands another demonstration of its fire-power!

On closer inspection it became clear that one fang had gone straight through the skull of the rat and into its brain, this together with possible shock had caused a near instant death for the rat. We were slightly relieved and replaced the rat into the cage. After about half a minute the snake uncoiled from its strike position and proceeded to eat the rat.

A few months later we had caught a medium size Puff Adder and Richard had held it for a photo. On releasing the snake into it's new cage I think Richard must not have let go of the head and pulled his hand away quick enough because he just said "Ouch!" and looked at his hand.

"You ok?" I asked

"It got me I think." He then put his knuckle to his lips to suck at a spot of blood.

He then pulled at something with his teeth. As he opened his mouth and turned to me, he was holding a large fang between his teeth. He didn't say anything, just stared at me unemotionally.

"Shit, it definitely got you then!" I said, stating the obvious.

We had no anti-venom and Malawi Doctors were next to useless when it came to snake bite. Richard just calmly walked to the door and stepped outside into the sunshine, I quickly followed. He then went and laid down on the wall of the tortoise pit and lit a cigarette and smoked it slowly starring up at the clear blue sky.

"Do you want to go to hospital?" I asked.

"No not really, let's just see what happens, no need to worry just yet, hey? It might be a dry bite."

"Oh you wish! Remember that baby rat!" I said without really thinking of how my comment would be taken.

"Rupert you're not being much help, but if I do die then I don't want to be buried ok? I want to be left in the bush where my body can be eaten by lions ok? Promise me!"

"I promise. Not sure what your mother will have to say about that but I'll give it a shot."

The minutes ticked by and when he had finished his cigarette Richard looked down at his knuckle. "There's no swelling so I guess I'm fine. You want a coke, I'm thirsty?" and he leapt off the wall and we headed for the main gate to get a coke.

We could only assume that the fang that went into his knuckle was an old fang that was being replaced. Snakes shed their fangs on a regular basis, the front one being lost and replaced by the one directly behind it. When a snake is due to shed a fang the venom duct is shut off to the old fang and redirected to the replacement fang. This is what must have happened in Richard's case. I kept the fang as a memento for many years but sadly this went out in one of my mother's many clean-ups.

We had many happy years running the Snake House and

they were good times. Thankfully that was the only time Richard came close to a serious bite.

It's funny, as Ive said the Snake House had been empty for a few years before Richard and I took control of it in 1977. We ran it until 1979 when Richard left Malawi to do his A-levels in the UK. Yet it always astounds me how many people I bump into that claim to have "worked" at the Snake House during that period. At last count it was seven people. It always makes me laugh.

Paul Taylor finally left Malawi in 2019 and currently lives in England. He is eighty nine years old and still going strong.

Richard holding the Puff Adder that gave him a bite

CHAPTER 16

PET MONKEY

The zoo had a number of large wire mesh enclosures where they kept the monkeys. One enclosure had Yellow Baboons (*Papio cynocephalus*) in it, another had a single De Brazza's Monkey (*Cercopithecus neglectus*), and another had a Samango Monkey (*Cercopithecus albogularis*). The final enclosure had a young Vervet Monkey (*Chlorocebus pygerythrus*).

I loved the Vervet Monkeys, with their hazel brown eyes and little hands, they were wonderful little monkeys. One little Vervet took an instant shine to me and whenever I passed by the enclosure it would run up to the mesh and push the side of its body against it and wait for me to give him a scratch. If I stopped it would push its little arms through the holes in the mesh and prompt me to continue.

Slowly over the weeks I got to the stage of grooming the monkey then placing my head against the mesh to allow it to groom me. The monkey would eagerly search through my hair looking for fleas; luckily for me it never found a meal.

It was still a very young monkey, probably less than a year old so I decided one feeding time to take the tray of vegetables and fruit into the enclosure instead of pushing it through the mesh. Vervet's have large canine teeth but over the weeks it had never made any attempt to bite me so I was not too worried.

As soon as I came through the door of the enclosure the little monkey came running at me. I thought this is either make or break time; it will either be a happy reunion or I will be torn to bits!

I needn't have worried; the little monkey ran straight up my legs and up my body and came to rest on my shoulder where it proceeded to eat a large carrot.

The little monkey became quite attached to me and I would often sit in the enclosure for hours with it sat on my shoulder rummaging through my hair. When it felt it had done a sufficient service it would almost drop off my shoulder into my lap where it would lay sprawled out with its arms and legs at all angles waiting for the favour to be returned. I would have to make the little lip noises it used to make otherwise it would look up at me as if to say "you are not doing it right".

If I stopped before it felt that his time was up he would again look up at me and scratch its back as if to say "come on, like this, keep doing it" and I would have to begin searching for fleas, ticks or flakes of skin. When it was ready it would leap off but then the games would begin.

I usually wore a hat and the monkey would snatch the hat off my head and run off with it behind a tree. There it would pop its head round the tree to see if I was coming to get my hat. As I went round one side of the tree it would dive round the other side. The more I chased it the faster it ran, clutching my hat. I usually tired out long before it did and I would slump down against the side of the enclosure catching my breath. When the monkey realised it had won it would trot over to me and place the hat back on my head and then lay down next to me like a little dog would.

Sometimes I would just go into the enclosure to read a book

in the sun which all went well until the cheeky monkey would grab the book and run off for a game of hide and seek crossed with catch. It was like a little person with the intelligence to match. One Saturday I was in the Snake House with Richard doing something or other when we heard a commotion going on outside. We went out to see what was going on and it appeared that "my" little monkey had managed to get out of its enclosure and was now being chased by the zoo staff as they made a vain attempt to catch it.

Richard and I just broke down in laughter as they were unable to catch the monkey, it was far too quick. Suddenly the little monkey saw me from almost 100 yards off, stopped and then tore towards me at full sprint. From about six feet away it made a leap and landed on my shoulder, grabbing a small handful of hair to steady itself. From there it looked back in the direction of the staff as if to say "I'm safe now, you can't touch me".

I simply walked back to its enclosure, opened the door, it jumped off my shoulder into its pen and I simply closed the door; job done. Richard gave a round of applause. I turned to the staff "and that gentlemen, is how it's done" I said with a flourish.

A few weeks later another kid who had seen me inside the enclosure decided to take a tray of food in to the monkey one feeding time. The baby Vervet leapt on the boy pulling great handfuls of hair out of his head. I heard the screams and ran to his aid. As soon as the baby monkey saw me it leapt from the boy onto my shoulder where it sat displaying its teeth at the boy and making threatening noises. The kid was never seen at the zoo again.

In time I used to take the monkey from its cage and we would go for walks. It would walk a few yards in front but at the first sign of danger, a dog or a car it would be on my shoulder baring its teeth at the threat.

CHAPTER 17

I MOVE OUT

The house at Sunnyside was a great house, it was close to Richard, the Mudi River and the Zoo; but there was something wrong.

I was never really sure what it was at the time but I felt that there was a social ladder in the house and that I was certainly at the bottom of it. I always felt like an outsider, not really part of the family. My sisters could get away with murder. This social ladder must have been obvious to both of them as they used it to their advantage.

I'd be in the garden somewhere, oblivious to all this. Jim or my mother would rush to Amy's aid and examine the red fingers and yell "Rupert, come here!"

I would hear the summons and go up to the house where I would get hauled into lounge to answer for "what I had done" and made to say sorry for the non-existent crime. I would then be sent to my room for the rest of the day to think about what I had done. This happened on a regular basis.

My sisters would smash my Airfix planes and nothing would happen. I was very upset by the injustice of it all, to the point that I took a sheet of A4 paper and wrote THE UNLICKED

BOY on it and stuck it to the outside of my bedroom door. What I actually meant to write was unliked but the spelling mistake and humiliation that followed at my inability to spell just forced me deeper into depression.

I was now getting home after school, dropping my books in my room and disappearing down the river every day till 5.30pm. At weekends Richard and I would be at the Zoo. I was hardly spending any time at home but this still wasn't enough, I wanted to exclude myself more from the house.

The kitchen had a back door that led out onto a small back veranda. At the far end of this veranda was another door that led to a laundry room. This room was never used since our Cook did all the washing of clothes in the bath.

The laundry room was about six-foot square with a single window. I suddenly saw the potential of this room as a bedroom; I would be away from the family and I would also have direct access to the garden. It would certainly give me the solitude that I wanted from the family.

The only problem was that in the far corner of the laundry room was a large concrete block built into the wall that was about a foot high. No matter how you positioned a bed it would not fit because of this block; the block would have to go.

I spoke to Richard about my "change of address" and my dilemma of the concrete block. He was quick to come up with a suggestion.

"I could come over one weekend and with a hammer and chisel we could chip the block out".

Maybe he was right, so the next weekend he turned up and between us we had the block broken into rubble by the end of the day. Sure, the finish was not brilliant but with luck I could hide this under the bed. We then set about sweeping the room and getting rid of the brick dust from our demolition. After a couple of coats of white wash to the interior walls the room was habitable so Richard and I moved my single bed from my old bedroom into my new "apartment".

We then put up a couple of wooden planks on angle brackets and painted these white also. The transformation was complete. I was one happy young lad.

This room was brilliant. Since its door opened directly outside it was already fitted with a mortice lock so I could lock it when I was inside or when I left it to go out. This was to keep Amy out rather than thieves since in all the time we were in Malawi our house was never broken into; I think the fact that I was well known to the Africans as the boy who caught snakes, they didn't want to risk crossing the threshold in case they came face to face with cobras or Puff Adders. Even the milk boy would shout from the road and would not come down the drive until the cook had told him it was safe.

In the mornings when the Cook arrived to open up the kitchen, he would boil the kettle, then there would be a knock at my door and he would place a cup of coffee on my bedside table.

I was able to lie on my bed during the day, listening to my music cassettes or the local radio with James "Uncle Jimmy" Chimera, or if the prevailing winds were favourable, I could catch Capital Radio 604 that broadcast from Port St John in South Africa. I could also read my snake books without being disturbed. I just wish that I had thought of this idea sooner.

CHAPTER 18

SNAKE MAN

To stock the Snake House with snakes required a lot of time searching the bush in and around Blantyre. Not all species could be found within the area but since we were still at school it was almost impossible for us to get out further into the "wilds" of Malawi to collect regional species. Lucky for us we had a secret weapon, the "Snake Man"!

The "Snake Man" was an old Malawian gentleman who didn't speak a word of English, probably in his late sixties, but nobody knew his age, least of all him. He was small, around 5feet tall and had a large scar across the right side of his forehead where an African axe blade had come out of the wooden axe and landed on his head when he was cutting firewood.

In all the years that we knew him he appeared to wear the same clothes, well I say clothes, they probably were shirt and trousers at one point in their lives but now just looked like rags. He was always barefoot.

He didn't have a job and his only income was collecting snakes for us for which we paid him from our pocket money. He had a great knowledge of snakes and an even greater knowledge of what they were worth to Richard and I! Since we were his only customers, I have no idea how he worked out the prices but the rarer the snake, the bigger the price. Whether he actually charged us mileage or just simply knew that a particular snake was rare I'll never know.

He had not gone unscathed through his years of catching and handling snakes. His thumb on his right hand was highly deformed from a Puff Adder bite that he had not treated. His arms and legs bore the scars of other bites. He claimed that he had some kind of African medicine but never divulged the secret of what it was. He did, however, have a piece of stick that he hung around his neck and he did say that for the bites of some species he would chew on the stick and that would then suppress the symptoms of the poison.

Some sceptics may brush aside his claims but on one occasion I saw him receive a very serious bite. He had come to the Snake House one Saturday afternoon with his little sack of goodies. The sack was writhing with snakes and as usual it was always exciting for me to sit there and watch him dip his hand into the sack and rummage around and pull a snake out, because you never knew what he had and he would never tell you first.

He had pulled out two female Boomslangs and had transferred them to his left hand while he delved into the bag to find another snake. As he rummaged around, I suddenly noticed that one of the Boomslangs in his left hand was now chewing on his thumb and by the amount of blood that was flowing from its jaws it had been latched on for some time.

"Hey, the snake is biting you!" I said in Chichewa.

"Ah stupid." He said looking down at the snake chewing on his thumb. He then prised the snake off his thumb and then continued to rummage around in the sack.

"Hey, look, that's a Boomslang; we need to get you to Hospital!" I said thinking that possibly he was not aware of its deadly venom.

"No don't worry bwana, I'll be fine." He assured me as he continued to empty his sack of snakes. No amount of pleading would get him to come with me to the hospital or even allow me to clean the wound or even dress it.

Since the only Boomslang anti-venom is held in South Africa, it needs to be flown in at special request. Basically, your body starts to bleed internally and blood oozes from all old scars, ears, nose, mouth and eyes. It's a horrid situation and death is slow. By the late afternoon I had managed to get him to promise that he come back to the Zoo the following day for me to check on his health and then he headed off to his home.

The next day he appeared again and showed no symptoms at all and even had another sack of snakes that he had caught that morning. I made him again promise to visit my house the next day so I could check on him. After about a week he still had not developed any symptoms and the bite had all but healed up. The snake had been chewing for a good one to two minutes so venom had definitely been injected. He said he was protected by his African medicine and I have to say that I believe him.

He once came to my house in Sunnyside with a very large Mozambique Spitting Cobra to show me. When I agreed to buy it he simply released it at his feet, and had another rummage in his old snake sack! The cobra instantly reared up, spread a hood and faced the Snake Man, who didn't flinch. He just looked at the reared cobra and spat at it. The cobra instantly fell to the ground, and lay there motionless while he showed me the rest of the sack's contents.

Make of it what you will but to be around this man and to see him work was like watching magic. He certainly had a way with snakes that I have never seen with anyone else. Sure there are snake handlers in Kenya that "free handle" Black Mambas, but they never appeared to have the control over the snake like the Snake Man did.

CHAPTER 19

COME HOME PIGEONS

J im had always kept pigeons for as long as I could remember. We had them in Kenya and in Harlow, so it was no surprise when he built a pigeon "loft" in the garage and started breeding pigeons.

His fascination was to breed a homing pigeon and this turned to obsession. Homing pigeons are very different form your "common-or-garden" pigeon, they have a very distinct white wattle on the top of the beak.

The true homing pigeon is a variety of domestic pigeon (*Columba livia domestica*) derived from the wild Rock Dove. This was selectively bred for its ability to find its way home over extremely long distances. Flights as long as 1,800 km (1,100 miles) have been recorded by birds in competitive pigeon races. Their average flying speed over a moderate 965 km (600 miles) distance is around 97 km/h (60 miles per hour). In 3000 BC, Egypt was using homing pigeons to send messages so it has a long history.

Anyway, Jim would often be seen scouting the markets and street for likely ancestors of these ancient "homing pigeons".

He'd regularly come home with some moth-eaten bird to breed the "homing genes" from.

One day he announced "eureka", one of his latest hatchings possessed the qualities need for a good homer! So after a few weeks of growth and training he decided that his pigeons were ready for the big test, and we all got into the car. Jim chose two prize "homers" from his flock and once they were boxed up we all headed off to Zomba Plateau on Sunday.

Zomba Plateau was only forty miles from Blantyre and an easy run for us, and we were there in less than an hour. It was agreed that once Jim had released his pigeons we would do a spot of trout fishing and then have a picnic, before heading home in the late afternoon.

Jim decided to release the two pigeons at Chagwa Dam, well away from people, so the box was ceremonially brought from the boot and Jim proudly lifted the first pigeon out and and like a scene from the Lion King launched it skyward. The bird took to the air and landed on the ground about a hundred yards away. Undeterred, Jim launched the second bird, which flew and joined the first bird on the ground.

"They are just getting their bearings." he said knowledgeably, followed by a few cutting comments from mother.

I started to unpack my fly rod and headed along one of the streams to fish. After an hour or so I retraced my steps back to the dam and sat down on a blanket to have lunch. The pigeons were still on the ground, pecking and walking round the dams edge.

Mother had continued her sarcastic remarks and Jim was getting more and more angry. After a few more hours of fishing it was time to head home and as we drove away from the dam we all looked back towards the two pigeons.

"They're still walking around" said Amy.

"Yes, thanks, I can see that!" snapped Jim.

Not much was said on the drive home, although Jim did say

that he thought "they would wait till the car had left then fly up, circle, get their bearings and probably be home before us".

Much to mothers glee the two pigeons were not at the house when we got home and Jim was forlorn. Every day he after work he would go to the garage expecting to see "Tweedle Dee and Tweedle Dum" as we were now calling them, but they never returned. There was a dark cloud over the house that week.

The following weekend it was announced that "we were off to Zomba again to look for his bloody pigeons", so again we all climbed into the car. This time the journey was silent, as we all knew Jim was in no mood for jokes.

As we drove down the dirt track and Chagwa Dam came into view there were Jims two pigeons walking along the road, pecking at the ground; but the funniest thing was that they had been joined by two ravens, common on Zomba. Well the car erupted in laughter. Jim was steaming and brought the car to a halt.

We had lunch, watching the, now four birds, walk around the dam. Jim had brought a bag of seed and threw handfuls out towards the pigeons, who ran up to him to be fed. After lunch Jim went to the car and collected his large butterfly net and proceed to try and catch the two pigeons in the net. I just couldn't watch any longer and went off to fish. Needless to say Jim finally caught the two "Tweedles" and they were returned to their box for the drive home.

At least they'd had a nice holiday on Zomba for a week. We never took any pigeons to Zomba again, and as I recall Jim never realised his dream of breeding homing pigeons.

CHAPTER 20

THE TEMPLE OF DOOM

One Saturday morning we unlocked the Snake House as usual as we had always done every weekend. As I turned down by some cages, I felt something hit my neck. Initially I thought Richard had thrown something at me so I turned expecting to see Richard trying to get my attention about something. Instead there at eye level, sitting on top of its cage was a large Boomslang less than 30cm from my face. Its neck was inflated and its head was swaying. It was not a happy snake.

I froze and tried to call to Richard, trying not to shout but realising that it would have to be louder than a whisper. The snake just kept its position, watching me. Finally, I managed to get Richards attention, by using the movement of his hand he was able to distract the snake's attention onto himself allowing me to get out of striking distance.

I felt my neck and looked at my hand to see if the snake had drawn blood but couldn't see any. Richard had by now captured the snake and holding it in one hand had a look at my neck.

"There's no mark, you're fine." He said thankfully.

Before I could thank him, my eyes caught sight of something

moving at the back of the snake house, then something moving above us. As I looked around the place was crawling with snakes, they were everywhere, all loose! It was like the Temple of Doom from an Indiana Jones movie.

We both froze. As our eyes slowly scanned the room and we saw that the glass fronted cages had all been smashed and doors prised open. We were in serious trouble. We were now facing a number of Spitting Cobras, a few Puff Adders, and a Forest Cobra, plus two more Boomslangs and a handful of Vine Snakes. Slowly we moved back towards the front door and stepped outside for a breather and to make a plan of action.

To cut a long story short, we recaptured all the snakes, bagged them and then deposited them into the outside snake pit while we repaired the broken cages.

We then found where the person or persons had shinned up the drainpipe and broken in through the roof so now, we just had to find out who. We didn't have to wait long for the culprit to brag about his act at school a few days later. I wont name the kid, but he was a regular visitor to the zoo so the next time he paid the zoo a visit Richard and I cornered him in a quiet area of the zoo and gave him a good thrashing! He ran home and blubbered to his mother, who was then on the phone to my mother saying how her little boy couldn't ever do such a thing and how Richard and I were beasts for setting upon her son. A few weeks later she rang my mother to apologise, having found a leather snake glove in his bedroom stamped inside with "Property of Blantyre Zoo".

The next near miss was due to African information. A Malawian came running into the zoo saying that he had just seen a snake near his house and would we go and catch it. We had always made it known locally that if anyone saw a snake, they must not kill it but call us and we would catch it and if it was a rare species, we would pay them for the information. The

African lived nearby so we grabbed our snake sticks and bag and headed off.

On arrival at his house, the man pointed to a sheet of corrugated iron or wriggly-tin as it was called by the locals, lying on a patch of waste ground near his front door.

"The snake went under there." He said confidently.

"What kind of snake was it?" asked Richard.

The man did not know, but it was black and very small. This was unusual as most Africans exaggerate the size of the snake, so for him to say it was small must mean that he had a good view of the snake and it must be small. The colouration was no surprise as all snakes are either black or green; being either Black Mambas or Green Mambas.

A good crowd had by now arrived to watch the spectacle of the two Mzungus who were going to catch the snake. There were kids, men, women, grandparents, the lot, they had all arrived. Richard got ready with his stick and bag and I took hold of the end of the iron sheet.

As I lifted it five Mozambique Spitting Cobras, all about one and a half meters in length dashed out from under the iron sheet in all directions.

The Africans screamed and scattered. Some leapt through windows into the house, kids scrambled up trees, others just ran. Richard and I just froze as cobras went in all directions; one went between both our legs. I just stood there and looked at Richard, we both knew if we made a sudden movement that the snakes would be inclined to strike out. Richard looked at me with a look of "oh this is bloody typical" and said "Bloody idiot!" in the direction of the African man who had seen the "small snake". After about 30 minutes we had four of the five cobras bagged. The last one had disappeared down a hole and would require some digging but after another twenty minutes we had the snake securely captured. I held the snake for the African man to inspect.

He pointed to the cobras' dark tail and said "That's what I saw go under the iron sheet!" trying to redeem himself.

With all the snakes now in bags we headed back to the Zoo. As we looked back towards the house Africans were starting to re-emerge from doorways and out of trees, it was a laughable sight. I bet they were telling this story for months.

CHAPTER 21

IF IT BITES YOU, YOU WILL DIE

My Grandfather, Tom Moore, had come out from England to stay with us for a few weeks. It was the first time he had been to Africa and with his thirst for knowledge he was in his element with everything African.

I had been suffering from Malaria and was bed ridden when there was a knock at my bedroom door.

"The snake man is here to see you" the cook said.

I opened my bedroom door and propped myself up in bed so that I could talk to the Snake Man. He said he had some snakes for me so I was all for inviting him into my bedroom so I could see the snakes but my mother quickly intervened, there was no way she was letting this "lunatic" into my bedroom to show me what he had for sale. She insisted that the "sale" be conducted with me in bed and the snake man safely in the garden.

Tom was immediately on the scene to watch the afternoon's entertainment. He was enthralled by the Snake Man, and the Snake Man soaked up the extra attention, he could be a real performer when he wanted to be.

The Snake Man opened up his sack and plunged his hand in up to his arm-pit and searched for his first snake to pull out.

"Vine Snake" the snake man shouted in my general direction, quickly followed by another shout of "Vine Snake" and another.

Tom was hypnotised. Using our cook as interpreter Tom asked the Snake Man if the three writhing snakes he was holding with his bare hands were dangerous. The Snake Man then came out with the classic line of:

"No Bwana, they are not dangerous" he replied, "but if they bite you, you will die".

I think that put snakes into perspective as far as the Snake Man was concerned. Snakes were only dangerous if they bite you.

From my bed I was blind to all this but heard my grandfather shout "By Jingo!" and take a few steps away from the Snake Man, who had just run out of hands to hold the Vine snakes and had just placed three of them in his mouth, holding them mid-body between his teeth. My grandfather said later that the snakes were dangling from the Snake Man's mouth like lengths of rope, with their tongues' flickering in and out and their gaze fixed on my grandfather, which he found rather worrying.

Vine Snakes are back-fanged like the Boomslang and their venom is very similar in action. The only difference is that for the Vine Snake there is no anti-venom. Even Boomslang anti-venom is not effective against its bite. The bite can only be treated by numerous blood transfusions, so handling it is highly risky. It is not as docile as the Boomslang and is always quick to inflate its neck and strike when disturbed.

I negotiated the prices from my bed and asked the Snake Man to leave the snakes in one of my snake bags and hang it in the woodshed out of the sun, where Richard would then collect it after school.

Tom took almost a whole roll of film that day with the Snake Man; sadly, the complete roll was ruined by the X-ray machine at Chileka International Airport.

Snakes eventually won against the Snake Man who died

following a bite from a large Forest Cobra on the slopes of Mt Mulanje in the mid 1990's, but he must have been at least in his late eighties by then, if not more.

For those of you who find the subjects of African Magic, "Black Magic" or Witch Doctors too hard to believe then let me just recount the story of "Gwalila Caesar". Anyone who has lived in Malawi will have heard about him, he is a national celebrity, the "Hercules of Malawi". He is just your average Joe but has amazing strength, superhuman even.

His favourite trick was to punch a 6" nail into a tree with his fist and then pull it out with his teeth. Someone bet him that he couldn't carry ten bags of cement from Blantyre to Zomba, so he did, that's over 40 miles. Since he had borrowed the bags of cement to undertake the challenge, he had to return them so carried them back to Blantyre.

Pulling trains, trucks or lifting cows across his shoulders was just daily entertainment for his fans. He attributed his strength to his grandmother, who was a Witch Doctor and had mixed up a potion, cast a few spells and hey presto, he could punch nails into trees with his fists.

It's up to you to believe it or not but I think that there is more unknown than known in the world. Modern athletes and Strong Men take a cocktail of drugs and steroids to improve performance, what are these drugs except commercial alternatives to herbs and plant products that grow wild in the forests of the world. Maybe Old Grandmother Caesar knew a plant that when boiled and drunk gave the body phenomenal strength and a higher pain threshold then any commercial drug on the market.

In Africa I find it is easier to keep an open mind on all subjects; however the fire-breathing dragon that the Africans are convinced lives on a certain hill in southern Malawi and eats dogs, will, of course need a full investigation and for the witnesses who claim to have seen it, a full drugs test!

Anyway back to my grandfather Tom. I did not grow up with many family role-models but I did look up to my grandfather Moore. He always treated me on a level and I always loved listening to his stories and memories.

His father William had been a renowned naturalist in Yorkshire being a founder member of the Greetland Naturalist Society and a member of the Yorkshire Naturalist Association and this gave Tom a keen interest in the natural world. Tom was born on the 26th of September 1908 in Greetland, a small village on the edge of the mill town of Halifax. His great, great grandfather was born in southern Ireland in 1806, coming over to England and settling in Yorkshire in the early 1800's. Tom had joined the South Yorkshire Police Force as Police Constable No. 552 (Sheffield City Police) on the 21st of April 1932, which almost didn't happen.

As a young boy Tom and a few of his mates had acquired a rifle from somewhere. One Sunday morning down at a large works in Halifax they took shots at one of the large warehouse doors. Suddenly a man ran out of the building shouting that they had just killed someone. It turned out that the two men were working in the warehouse out of hours and Tom's bullet had gone clean through the door and killed one of the men stone dead. Tom was on a murder charge but the judge said that it had been a terrible accident and seeing as the two men were not supposed to be there on Sunday the case was dropped. Tom's application was not hampered by the killing. Tom did however continue his love of guns, going on to shoot both rifles and pistols making the City of Sheffield Rifle Team, the Yorkshire Rifle Team, Yorkshire Pistol Team, and the British Short-Range Team winning the championship in 1936. He was also part of the record-breaking Yorkshire Team that won the Queen Alexandra's Cup at Bisley in 1949.

He was a no-nonsense old-style policeman, who believed that what criminals needed was the strong right-hand of the law, rather than a jail term; and standing well over six foot he was easily able to deliver it to those in need. He had a gift for languages, speaking Welsh, and translating for the police in Hindi, Punjabi and Urdu. He quickly rose through the ranks to Detective Sergeant No. 67 in the CID before finally retiring on the 30th of July 1959.

After his service in the police he became a game-keeper, working at Blenheim Palace in Oxfordshire for the Duke of Marlborough.

Although I was to spend time with my grandfather Moore later in life it was his visit to Malawi and that day with the Snake Man that is my lasting memory of him.

CHAPTER 22

CALL ME ASAP

At this time in Malawi there weren't any televisions or videos, let alone DVD's so the only entertainment was either the cinema or the Drive-in.

The normal rule of thumb was that on Saturday morning us kids would walk into town and meet up at the tiny coffee shop, upstairs in the PTC. The coffee shop had a small balcony with tables, chairs and parasols and we would congregate there soaking up the sun and drinking coke floats.

If there was a movie that we fancied seeing we would then all go across the road to the Apollo Vistararma, which was the only cinema in Blantyre at that time. We would usually watch comedy films like "I'm for the hippopotamus" with Terrence Hill and Bud Spencer. Bud Spencer never said anything in the movies and Terrance Hill was the brains of the outfit but we found them hilarious. The Pink Panther movies with Peter Sellers were another hit; tears would stream down our faces as we laughed.

The paper screen had been repaired when a touring group of Chinese acrobats had fallen through the screen and the Indian cinema owners had repaired the damage with tape. But apart from this it was clean and tidy.

The shows usually finished just before lunch so afterwards we would go to the Ice Cream Parlour where we would have burger and chips and yet more coke floats. Then we would head down the road to the Central Bookshop, the best bookshop in Malawi at the time. There we would search the shelves for new snake books.

Then it was down to the Blantyre Sports Club where most friends would spend the rest of the afternoon; however Richard and I would then walk across the golf course back to Sunnyside, stopping at his house to pick up snake bags and either head down the river to catch snakes or to the Zoo to check on the Snake House.

The other option was less of a friend's thing and more of a family thing. If there was a film that mother and Jim didn't mind watching then we would all pile into the car and go to the Drive-in one evening. For us it was only a short drive from the house down the Chikwawa Road.

The slight problem with watching films at the Drive-in was that the projectionists never matched the image to the size of the huge billboard that formed the screen. This meant that you never got to see the edges of the film, which wasn't normally too bad as most of the action was in the middle of the picture. However, it did affect the title and opening credits; for years I thought First Blood was irst Bloo starring ylvester Stallon after seeing it at the Drive-in in 1982!

Most evenings the film would snap where they had censored it by cutting bits out then sticking it back together.

To be honest we seemed to entertain ourselves without the need for films and I never ever missed TV. The days were busy and full, and the mornings early so the thought of a TV never really crossed my mind.

It was on one such evening after watching a movie at the Drive-in that we came home to find a glass jam-jar sitting in the middle of the dining table with a note under it.

The note read:

To Rupert.

Two kids from Moir have been bitten by this snake.

Been to hospital.

Now going back to school.

Call me ASAP.

It was signed by one of the male teachers that lived on the school grounds. I then picked up the small glass jar and looked at the small worm length black snake inside; it was tiny, about the thickness of a match. How could such a small snake have bitten a person? I then unscrewed the metal lid and peered inside.

Laying there in the bottom of the jar was what we called at the time a Burrowing Adder, although now they are called Southern Stiletto Snakes (*Atractaspis bibronii*) and this one must have been a newly hatched baby.

The Stiletto Snake has the largest fangs of any snake for the size of the head. They are so long that the snake cannot actually open its mouth to bite, but has to slide its lower jaw to one side, where the fang then drops down and the snake jabs it's head driving the fang into the victim or prey. This was how such a small snake had been able to "bite" the two boys. But how they had both been bitten was a mystery so I rang the number on the note.

It turned out that the two kids were both playing with the snake in the toilet, in the dark. One of them got bitten on the hand causing him to drop the snake; the other boy picked up the snake to place it in the jar and he got bitten too on the hand.

The teacher said that both boys had extensive swelling so I decided to get over there to take a look and made arrangements with Jim.

When I walked into the room and looked at the two boys. One was Kenny Dawson and the other was Jess Nyman. I was amazed at how much swelling there was from such a small snake. They were both worried and so was the teacher.

"What happened at the hospital?" I asked as I drew an ink line where the swelling had reached and the time on each boys arm. Kenny was quick to give his version of events.

"We turned up at the hospital and we had to wait in this line with all the other emergencies. The Doctor gives an injection to a local and then calls us in. As I explain what happened he starts to clean the needle and syringe that he used on the previous patient in a washing up bowl of soapy water. He then reassembles it and grabs the anti-venom from the fridge. I said to him that wasn't he going to use a new needle but he didn't seem too bothered".

"What happened then, you didn't let him inject you did you?" I asked nervously.

"No chance, I told him he must be bloody mad and I grabbed Jess and we left!"

I think it just shows how hospitals don't have much idea about snake bite since antivenin is not recommended for bites from this species and it could have done far more harm than good. The less said about the syringe hygiene the better.

After another look at the arms I said my goodnights and went home, leaving instructions that if things got worse, they were to call me.

The next morning at school I went to check on the two boys, the swelling had eased and they felt much better. By the end of the week they were back in classes but convinced that I had saved their lives, which I hadn't.

The snake measured just 15cm in length and was therefore only a few days old. There was no way we could feed such a small snake due to its selective diet so I decided to free the snake in a patch of bush near the zoo.

CHAPTER 23

The rains had just started and we were all sitting in the lounge listening to the rain, as you do in Africa when there isn't a TV. Isabel had been asleep in her room for about an hour when suddenly she stared crying. Since she was only three years old at the time this was not unusual.

"I'll go and see her" Jim said and went off towards the corridor that led to the bedrooms.

He had just gone through into the corridor when he yelled "Snake" at the top of his voice then there was a bang as he hit against the corridor door slamming it shut.

I leapt up from the sofa thinking what we were all thinking and that was that she had been bitten by a snake. By this time Jim had opened the corridor again and I was able to get into the corridor expecting to be facing a six-foot cobra.

Instead, wriggling towards me was a small, foot long, Brown House Snake (*Lamprophis fuliginosus*), completely harmless. My first thought was that maybe there were two snakes in the house so I quickly gathered up the House Snake and Jim went through into my sisters bedroom. There was no second snake, she had simply woken up and cried at the same time as the little Brown House Snake had entered the house via the badly fitting back bathroom door seeking shelter from the rain.

Jim was shaken but the only damage was a bruised elbow from hitting the door in his retreat from the snake. He decided to take the rubbish out to the dustbin before turning in himself.

No sooner had he gone out to the dustbin than there was another shriek of "Snake" from Jim and then the noise of a dustbin lid crashing onto the concrete floor of the veranda.

Again, I leapt out of the chair and dashed outside. Jim was already at the kitchen door white as a sheet and shaking.

"Where is it?" I asked.

"It came out of the dustbin! I lifted the lid and this snake, about three-foot-long flowed out of the bin on to the ground around my feet" he said.

A few yards from the dustbin I retrieved another Brown House Snake but this was a monster, well over a yard long. I quickly bagged this snake as well. But what I couldn't understand was how the snake had got into the bin in the first place. The riddle was unravelled the next morning.

The gardener had come across the snake while I was at school and in the circumstances, he had decided to kill the snake and then dispose of it in the dustbin, thus hiding the evidence! The cook had agreed to place some kitchen waste over the dead snake to conceal it in the hope that I would never find out about their dastardly deed.

This would have all worked to plan if they had in fact killed the snake. But obviously it was merely suffering a concussion. When Jim lifted the lid, the snake saw its chance to escape and rolled out of the bin.

I am not sure who gave the garden boy more of a tongue lashing, me for him trying to kill the snake or Jim for him having failed.

The snake was a bit the worse for wear but recovered fully and went into our collection at the zoo. It measured 135cm, the largest we ever caught.

CHAPTER 24

CLIST-MAS

Christmas times were odd events in Malawi, well in Africa in general. They would decorate the supermarkets with Christmas decorations and play carols but it would be bright sunshine and baking hot outside. It never really felt like Christmas even when the carol singers came around to the house.

We would usually hear them some way off while they played at another house. You could never hear the words but the base would boom for miles.

These singers were not your conventional carol singers as you would know them. They were a small group of African youngsters, probably four or five in number and their ages would range from seven to about seventeen.

They had a base which was an old tea chest turned upside down. Attached to the tea chest was a length of thick string, the other end of which was attached to the end of a wooden broom handle. The broom could then be used to alter the tension on the string and therefore the tone of the base. This was usually played by the eldest and tallest youth, oh yes and the name of the band was painted on the sides of the tea chest, things like

Mudi River Boys Band, Clistmas Boogie Boys or Sunnyside Jazz.

One of the small kids would have a tin full of gravel to act as a shaker. Another would have a guitar made out of an old, one-gallon oil tin. It usually only had three strings but he could get quite a tune out of it.

Then two or three other very small kids would be dancing and singing. If you think back to the early Jackson 5, that's what they were like, except they were filthy and dressed in rags. They were excellent musicians although their song writing skills were a little lacking at times and more often than not the chorus would soon be repeated and repeated. One year they came and announced that the next song would be "Mary, she's a beautiful girl"; what they didn't tell us was that those were the only lyrics!

On another occasion the song was far from Christmassy; being a song about an old man who got drunk in the local bar and lost all his wages and when he got home his wife beat him.

After the band had played the first song they would stop and you would have to clap. Then they would move on to the next song. When they had played through all the songs from their "current album" one of the smallest kids would produce a tin and you would place money in it as payment.

Some bands were better than others. Some just did a few plinks on the tin guitar and then came around with the tin. The other thing was that you never seemed to get the same bands the following year.

I wasn't really a big fan of Christmas; they were awkward times for me. As I didn't really get much pocket money, I had no way of buying presents. This was made even worse by the fact that Jim usually didn't have any money either as mother controlled all the finances; so, where most fathers would take the kids out to town and say "come on, let's get something for mum" this didn't happen in our house. Looking back now it was extremely sad but I guess the family just didn't know how to act or interact.

I usually just raced to get the day over with, and tried to get out of the house as quickly as possible, either down to the zoo or the river to escape the humiliation of it all. I still hate Christmas today after all these years. I prefer to lock myself away, and hope that it will pass me by.

CHAPTER 25

SNAKE WRESTLING

I
t was another evening of rain, which made a hell of a racket on the corrugated iron roof of the house, but it was welcomed. I never got tired of the rain in Africa; the smell of the earth after rain was fantastic. The other side to it raining was it always brought out the snakes!

This particular evening Jim went out to put the car in the garage; it was always a risk leaving the car outside as you may find all the wheels gone in the morning, but as I have said before we never had a single break-in while in Malawi. My snakes made sure of that.

I had heard the car start, and then drive into the garage, the garage doors shut, and then there was a pause as Jim dashed back to the house dodging the rain. Then all of a sudden, we heard Jim's familiar "Snake!"

In one move I leapt up and dashed out of the lounge doors and onto the veranda. At that moment Jim appeared out of the darkness, landing a few feet from me on the veranda. He could be quite agile when it came to getting out of striking distance of a snake.

"It's in the culvert by the side of the house" he said pointing down off the edge of the veranda.

Africa is usually as black as the ace of spades at night and I wasn't about to try and tackle an unknown snake in the dark so shouted to mother for a torch.

Now with the light I ran around to the side of the house and there in the culvert was a white snake. It took me by surprise, like I was dreaming. I stood there for a minute looking at it before it dawned on me what I was looking at.

It was a Cape File Snake (*Gonionotophis [Mehelya] capensis capensis*) about a foot and a half long. I shouted to Jim that I had found it and that it was harmless. Jim then appeared at my shoulder.

"I think it's a File Snake, this is the first one I've seen." I said "I will not take any chances till I know for sure what it is".

With that I pinned the snakes head with a stick and grabbed it firmly behind the head and transferred it to my snake bag. I wasn't taking any chances with this snake as I had never seen one before, it was dark, and it was raining. My rule of thumb was to treat it as venomous until you have identified it.

The next morning, I examined the contents of the snake bag. It was a Cape File Snake and therefore totally harmless; it is actually one of Africa's most docile species. It was a good size too, 69cm in length. The species was not rare in Malawi, it was just rarely seen; in fact, in 13 years this was the only one I ever saw.

I eagerly awaited Richards' arrival at the house to show off my prize but before I had time to even return the handsome snake to its bag the garden boy came and said that he had found a snake. I guess he was trying to redeem himself for earlier trying to despatch the large House Snake with a broom and hiding it in the dustbin.

I quickly tied up the bag and followed the garden boy out into the front garden. We had some large trees that formed the boundary of the property on the Smythe Road side of the house and the garden boy pointed into the top of one of these trees.

A number of Common Bulbuls (*Pycnonotus barbatus*) were mobbing a clump of branches high up in the tree and making a hell of a noise so I guessed that was where the garden boy was pointing. Birds will always mob snakes as they see them as a danger to themselves and their young.

As I walked around the tree trying to get an unobstructed view, I suddenly saw what the commotion was about. There in amongst the branches was a large Vine Snake (*Thelotornis*) some thirty feet off the ground.

This was not going be to the easiest capture since there was no way of getting up this large tree and even if I could, the other branches where the snake was would not hold my weight. I had to quickly make a plan.

I sent the garden boy off to bring me a few lengths of bamboo poles that we used for constructing the grass fence around the house while I ran inside the house to find a ball of string. We both met at the base of the trees.

We then lashed the bamboo poles together, end to end on the ground and I then fixed a wire hook on the end of the pole. With great difficulty we lifted the pole combination up into the tree. It was bending and swaying about and the slightest move-ment on the ground caused the tip of the pole to thrash about like a whippy ariel. As we guided the pole into the tree, we realised that we were about eight feet short of the snakes' posi-tion so the whole contraption had to be lowered to the ground and another two poles added which only made the thing even more unwieldy.

Again, we gently lifted the pole up into the tree and this time it was long enough. My hope was that I would be able to guide the wire hook up to the snake and lift it out of the tree and then lower the pole with the snake on the end to the ground.

By this time a small crowd of passers-by had gathered on the road thanks to the garden boy telling them that the Mzungu kid was going to catch a large snake in the tree. This only increased the pressure on me to deliver his promise. My arms were starting to ache from holding the pole and my stomach muscles were burning as I tried to counter the lever effect of the long pole sections.

I knew that I was going to have to lower the pole to the ground very soon just to rest my arms and made one last attempt to hook the snake.

Success! The snake was gently lifted from its branch and curled around the end of the pole. I think it was just glad to get away from the Bulbuls who continued to mob the snake on its descent.

As I lowered the pole it soon became clear that the Vine Snake was a lot bigger than I had assumed from being thirty feet below it; also, most of its body had been hidden amongst leaves. To bring the pole to the ground I had to walk back away from the tree, which meant that when the snake actually touched the ground, I was some thirty feet away from it. I didn't want it making a dash for cover once it was on the ground, especially with the even larger crowd that had gathered and were now peering over the fence to get a better view of the impending death of the Mzungu Boy.

Just as the snake touched the ground I dropped the pole and ran forward to close off is escape. I needn't have worried though, because as soon as the snake saw me coming towards it, it just stood its ground, raised its head and inflated its throat in a normal threat posture. I called for the garden boy to bring me a stick to pin the snakes head down with.

The garden boy quickly produced a stick about a yard long. At that point I realised that the snake was a monster, almost six feet long, or twice as long as the stick I was hoping to pin it with.

I stopped to gather my breath and make sure that the

strength had come back to my arms. I then stepped forward in the snakes' arena and instantly the chatter of the watching crowd went silent, it was just me and the snake. I am sure crowd were placing bets but I tried to concentrate.

When you tackle a snake like this you both move around, trying to anticipate the others move; waiting for the right moment to make your move and strike. You wait to strike and pin the head to the ground and the snake waits to strike and pin your fingers with its fangs. We danced for a good minute or two when finally I made my move and pinned the snakes head to the ground and placed my index finger on the top of its head and my thumb and middle finger on each side of its head, behind the jaw line so I was well out of reach of its fangs.

I had it, but the problem was that the body was immense and strong and coils immediately lashed around my arms. I stood up holding the snake in both hands and the crowd cheered and screamed. The Mzungu had beaten the snake.

Yes, I finally had the snake under control - just, but it was not happy at being removed from its slumber and used all its body strength to pull my two arms together. That's when I noticed that it was actually looking at my left hand and was pulling it towards its mouth with a look that said "just another few inches and I will be able to clamp my jaws down on those fingers". It was the only time that I had seen a snake consciously work out a plan of action. I tried to unravel my left hand out of the coils and to stop my hand being pulled towards the waiting jaws. It was just a case of who tired first.

"Get my snake bag" I yelled to the garden boy.

While he retrieved my bag from the ground, I slowly coiled the snake up, while maintaining my grip on its head and after a few minutes of trying to re-house a jack-in-a-box, the snake was in the bag. I was dripping with sweat and I breathed a sigh of relief.

A few minutes later Richard arrived. "Looks like you have

had a busy morning" he said as he looked the perspiration flowing down my face and a writhing bag of angry snake in my hand.

"You have no idea!" I said and handed him the bagged Cape File Snake. The Vine Snake stayed in its bag, I wasn't going through all that again.

Later at the zoo we checked the length of the Vine Snake, it measured a colossal 198.5cm, just over six feet! The previous Malawi record was 140cm, some four feet seven inches. We were the happiest kids in Malawi!

CHAPTER 26

RAIN FROGS

Whenever we went down the river, we always used to carry a panga or a knife of some sort. It wasn't for protection or anything sinister like that; this was Malawi and then, in those years, you were perfectly safe.

We carried knives for a few reasons. We would use the knives to cut the sugarcane we would buy as we walked down to the river. Also carrying knives made us feel grown up, like real men. Often if we were having a bad day catching snakes, we would just find a place to stop and we would lounge around on the large boulders and talk about stuff. As we talked, we would practice knife throwing into the loose sand at the water's edge. I used to enjoy our trips down the river. Now and again we would raid a sugar cane field; although we only ever took one stem which we would share as we walked. Other times we would catch grasshoppers and dare each other to eat them. They were happy days.

On one particular occasion I had decided to take a knife from the garage that Jim had just finished making. I "borrowed" it because it was new and since Jim had just finished sharpening it, it would slice through the sugar cane like butter. We had been walking for a few hours and had gone further than we normally would go. We came to a point in the river where there were high banks on each side, some six or seven foot high. On one of the banks grew a large Malombo tree, its solid trunk growing tall, straight and smooth for some fifty or sixty feet until it branched out into a mass of green leaves. It certainly was a monster of a tree.

We sat against the great trunk of the tree, it was almost midday and we were grateful for the shade. As we chatted about this and that Richard began to dig a small hole in the soil with his knife. It wasn't long before he stopped digging and lent forward looking into his dug hole. Conversation suddenly stopped.

"What is it?" I asked.

"I think I can see a frog" he replied, and gently started to move the soil away with his hand.

Within a few seconds, in his cupped hand was a small frog, which he handed to me. He then continued to dig with his hands and within another few seconds he handed me another frog. This went on for some time until we had fourteen little frogs of various sizes, the largest was about 1 ½ inches long.

They were charcoal grey in colour with bright yellow running down from under the eye to the front of its armpit. Its mouth did not run horizontally from its nostrils to the eye like in a normal frog, but followed the contour of the chin which gave it a real down in the mouth, glum look. When you touched them, they inflated their little bodies and stood up on all fours. On the ground they didn't hop or jump but walked so we assumed they were toads and not frogs.

After a few minutes being entertained by these delightful and comical little toads we replaced them in their sandy hole and covered them up again.

Once the toads had been discussed we then started throwing our knives into the dry bank below the huge Malombo tree which entertained us for a while. Then things progressed to throwing the knives into the base of the tree, however we were not having much luck and with each throw the knife would hit handle first no matter how I regulated the throw. It didn't take long before I lost my patience with the knife and threw it as hard and as high as I could aiming for the mass of leaves some sixty feet from the ground.

The knife flew up the tree, turning handle over point as it went before burying itself point first into the trunk at least thirty or forty feet above me.

"Oh, you've got to be bloody having a joke." I said aloud as I gazed up at Jim's knife. Richard just rolled with laughter.

"It's not funny! Of all the luck. It wouldn't bloody stick in when I wanted it to and now look at it!" I yelled angrily.

I was really annoyed. I looked up at the smooth branchless trunk; it was totally impossible to climb. I had to get the knife down, there was just no way could I leave it there, Jim would go mad when I got home.

"Richard, throw your knife up there and see if you can knock it out of the tree" I demanded.

"Not a chance mate! What and get my knife stuck up there with yours? Not a hope!"

I turned back towards the river and searched for a few good cricket-ball sized pebbles to throw at the knife. Now imagine trying to hit a knife with a stone a few feet away, well now try it thirty odd feet in the air. The danger was that the pebbles would hit the tree, then bounce off and head back down in our direction; more than once did we just dive for cover to prevent ourselves being knocked unconscious by our own stones.

The hours passed until finally a lucky stone finally hit the knife and it moved slightly. We were almost there. After a few more attempts we hit the knife again and both stone and knife plummeted to earth sending us running for safety.

I retrieved the knife from the dry earth at the base of the tree and we headed for home. The knife went straight back into the garage and in future I only took my knives to the river.

On looking through my book on Malawi Amphibians, the little frogs turned out to be Mozambique Rain Frogs (Breviceps mossambicus). They burrow into loose soil or sand where they wait till the arrival of rain, when they then dig their way to the surface to feed. They are the most delightful little creatures and with their down-turned mouths they have a comical face.

We were to find many of these frogs over the years and the novelty of their comical features never wore off.

Shortly after the "knife in the tree" incident I decided I needed my own knife so over a few weekends I used the school metalwork shop to create myself a "boot knife".

I cut the blade from a circular saw blade that I softened by heating and letting it cool slowly. Once the blade had been cut and shaped, I then re-heated the metal and quenched it in oil to harden it again. The hilt of the knife was made from a piece of aircraft aluminium from a crashed plane at Chileka Airport. I was really happy with the finished knife and had it for many years. As with most things it eventually got lost in endless house moves over the years.

CHAPTER 27

TOKOLOSHE

One morning Richard arrived at the house on a red and white Moto Guzzi 125 scrambler. His dad had purchased it as a box of bits from an Italian Priest and one way or another it had all been there and was put back together. It was a great machine and got us to areas that were too far on foot. Richard didn't have a bike licence and neither of us had helmets but that just meant we had to take a few detours through maize fields when we saw a Police Land Rover coming up the road.

One of the places that little bike used to take us was Soche Hill. We never found many snakes there but it was always a good day out and from the summit the view of Limbe and Blantyre was amazing. On the walk up the hill there is a section about half way up of almost tropical rainforest (although it's not). At this point on the right there is a large cave and we would often stop here to play with Ant-lion larvae, whose conical pits covered the cave floor. When we had captured a few of these ferocious looking insects we would continue up the mountain.

It was quiet up on the top and we would spend hours on the

large boulder where the lightning conductor point is and talk, planning all the things that young boys dream about doing. We would talk about the places we would go and things we would do. We dreamed of how we would buy two canoes and circumnavigate Lake Malawi, coming ashore in the late afternoon to make camp and go snake hunting. How we would buy an old Land Rover and drive up to Mzuzu and catch Gaboon Vipers and be the first people in nearly forty years to find one in Malawi.

Some of our plans were outside Malawi's borders. We both made plans for when we left school. These were either to enlist in the Rhodesian Army where we would join the SAS or Selous Scouts. If we didn't do that then we were going to work in the Game Department. Richard said he wanted to be a Game Warden in some remote park that nobody wanted to work in. All he would want was a house, a Land Rover and enough money for cigarettes. Our heroes were George Adamson and C. J. P. Ionides. If we could have had their lives, we would have been happy.

Sometimes we would find a Baboon Spiders hole in the ground and then build an arena around the hole with stones and soil about eight inches radius around the hole. We would then go off and find a Stink Ant (*Paltothyreus tarsatus*). These large black ants are about an inch long and give off a real pungent smell when molested. They are scavengers and raiders so when the ant is placed in the area it doesn't take long before the spider emerges from its burrow and a fight ensues. As we watched the fight, which the spider always won, we would talk about life and the universe.

Richard again talked of death and again how he wanted to be left in the bush somewhere to be eaten by lions and hyenas. He said he didn't want people to have a grave to mourn over; he just wanted the animals of Africa to feed on his body so that no evidence would be left.

Up on the top of Soche Hill we would watch the eagles circle the summit, sometimes they were so close to us that we could almost reach out and touch them. From our vantage point on the summit we could look down onto the undisturbed forest on the southern side of Soche Hill, where Vervet Monkeys would climb about in the tops of the trees. We felt like we were in a small aircraft flying low over the treetops.

On one afternoon spent on the top of Soche Hill a strange thing happened. I tell the story because Richard and I saw it. We have no explanation and all that we know is we saw what we saw. It was probably about two o'clock, we had just been sitting around on the rocks on the summit, chatting and enjoying the rest after the climb up.

Out of the forest on the southern side of the hill where the Vervet monkeys would climb about the trees came a man. He was walking towards the large boulders that we were sitting on. He looked at us, so we greeted him in Chichewa but he did not answer, just lifted his chin and raised his eye-brows to us in a way Africans will greet each other without a word being spoken. Richard and I returned the gesture and left him to his "business". He was not a tall man, probably less than five feet tall, and quite elderly. He was extremely thin; you could almost see all his bones and he had a slight hunch to his back. He was naked except for a short brown cloth round his waist made from a heavy material like a cross between canvas and hessian. He walked with the aid of a long staff. The thing that was strange about him was the shape of his head. He had an enormous forehead that sloped backwards. The back of his head sloped backward following the same angle as his forehead. The distance between his eye-brows and the top of his head was twice that of the distance from his eye-brows to his chin. He carried nothing else about his person except his staff.

The summit on Soche Hill is an enormous white rock probably seventy-foot-high, in the shape of an egg. Anyone looking across at Soche Hill from Limbe or Blantyre can see this rock, it's huge. On the south-western side of the rock is a narrow ledge no more than a foot wide, the edge of which is a sheer drop probably fifty feet down into the forest canopy below and another fifteen or twenty feet further to the ground. The ledge stops abruptly halfway round and there is no exit other than for you to retrace your steps backwards the way you have come. Richard and I had inched along it many times to get a view across to Blantyre and Sanjeka Palace to the west.

The old man walked past us and headed for the ledge. I turned and whispered to Richard "where the hell does he think he is going?"

"Maybe he is going to pray?" Richard suggested, and I agreed, he did have the look of a Holy Man or Sharman.

We were curious to see what he was up to but didn't want to disturb him or invade his solitude so we just swivelled around on our bottoms and faced the entry to the ledge. From where we were sitting, we could see both the left side of the rock and the right side. The time ticked by and the old man did not reappear and finally Richard's curiosity got the better of him,

"I'm going to have a look, stay here." And he inched himself along the ledge and disappeared from view. After about half a minute he was back. "He's gone!" he said with a look of horror on his face.

"What do you mean he's gone?"

"Gone, disappeared, vanished!"

"He can't have, did he jump?" I asked trying to find a logical explanation.

Richard was having none of it, "Are you nuts, have you seen the drop at the end? It's well over seventy feet to the ground if the tree branches don't smash him to bits before that! Did you see him come around the other way?"

"Now you're bloody nuts, what is he, Spiderman? No he

didn't come round the other side. Here, let me have a look." I said.

I went along the ledge to see for myself, but Richard was right, the old man had vanished. I gazed down into the forest a good fifty feet below the ledge. There was nothing, no broken branches, nothing. I looked up at the rock face above me to see if there was anyway a man could climb that, but if he had, he would have come into view on the summit of the rock. Also carrying a long staff in one hand was going to hamper his climbing ability to say the least. I came back along the ledge.

"Well?" Richard asked.

I looked worriedly at Richard, "He's gone!"

"Told you" he said. We both then scrambled down the path where the old man had come from and then right through the forest to the place where the old man would have landed below the rock, had he jumped. We couldn't see any broken branches, leaves, indentations or foot prints.

Richard turned to me and said "Maybe he was a ghost?"

"How could he have been a ghost; I saw him too."

"Well where the hell did he go then?"

Neither of us had any explanation. We both took a piece of paper and drew the old man that we had seen without letting the other see; our memory of the man was identical.

As I say I had no explanation then and I don't have one now. Anyone who has been to the top of Soche Hill will know that from that ledge there is no way out, not forward, down or up. Where he went I don't know. Make of it what you will. Malawi is famed for its Tokoloshe or Little People, mischievous forest-mountain dwellers who are only a few feet tall. Tokoloshe are, I guess, a spirit people, real enough to the Africans, who see them when the Tokoloshe want to be seen and are real.

The man on Soche Hill that vanished.

CHAPTER 28

DEATH ON THE MOUNTAIN

I t was a Saturday morning and I was just coming out of Kandodo in Blantyre when I bumped into another pupil at Saints.

"Did you hear the news? Steve Younger has died!" they said.

They didn't have too many facts and right at this moment I didn't really believe them, since the story that they had was a little too unbelievable, something about him falling down a cliff-face on Mulanje. This was Martyrs Day weekend so it seemed a little far-fetched.

As I walked home from Kandodo I took the usual short-cut through the Blantyre Sports Club and met some other kids from school. They had heard the news too and the whole place was buzzing about it.

Monday was back to school and we all went into the hall for our usual morning assembly. There was a buzz with everyone talking to each other about the accident. The Head Master stood up and announced that Steve had indeed been killed on Mulanje. As he spoke about the great loss of a student at the "dawn of his life", (we were just about to sit our C.S.E.'s) there was an outburst of tears from the girl side of the hall as Belinda collapsed in tears, she was Steve's girlfriend.

It was shocking news for the entire school. Sure, Steve was far from a model student and had spent more time in trouble with the Deputy Head than most but deep down he was not a bad kid. I had got to know him quite well through the Solar Energy Club that we were press-ganged into joining along with Stuart, who I guess was Steve's best friend. It was through Stuart that I found out exactly what had happened.

Steve and his family had been spending the Martyr Day weekend up on Mulanje around the area of Chambe Peak. Steve and his younger brother had decided to climb up Chambe Peak alone while his mother and dad stayed down at the Forest Hut at the base of the peak. Chambe Peak is a huge monolith of a rock that stands tall in front of the Chambe Forest Hut and rises straight up almost 600 feet into the clouds. The other side of the peak falls dramatically to the plains below, almost a 1000 feet; it's a very imposing rock. I have never climbed up Chambe, no particular reason, just never got around to doing it, so I cannot say directly what it's like to climb, so I will just have to tell you what I have heard. The path up the rock is very narrow indeed, in places, just wide enough for a single person to walk. With a drop of hundreds of feet to your right as you go up the path it is not for the faint hearted. Steve and his young brother who was only in his early teens were about halfway up when Steve either lost his footing or a portion of the rocky path gave way under his feet, either way Steve fell.

Luckily, he managed to grab hold of the ledge of the path and prevented himself falling but his grip was not good and he held up one hand towards his brother and asked for him to pull him back up. His brother grabbed Steve's hand and tried to pull him up, but Steve was a big kid and his young brother just hadn't got the strength in his young arms to pull Steve up. Slowly Steve's hand began to slip through his brothers' grip, and there was nothing the young brother could do. Eventually Steve slipped from the hand of his young brother and plummeted almost 400 feet to the ground below.

The young brother turned around and made his way to the bottom of the cliff face to his brothers' body, who, miraculously was still alive. The young brother then ran the mile or so to the Hut to call the father who then ran to Steve. Steve was still alive when his dad got there but died shortly afterwards.

I can only imagine the feelings for the family as they carried Steve's body down the mountain, it must have been hell. Mr Younger was a priest so I can only imagine that his faith in God held the family together. Steve was buried in Blantyre a few days later at a quiet funeral. But a strange thing happened, as they were lowering the coffin into the grave one of the ropes gave way and one end of the coffin crashed to the bottom of the grave. It sent a shiver round the congregation.

Steve's death was very sad but it is incomprehensible to imagine how the young brother must have felt as it was his hands that couldn't hold Steve's weight and he had to watch his big brother fall with his own eyes. We all felt sorry for the small kid and we all looked out for him at school, like big brothers to him as Steve would have looked after him if he had been there.

CHAPTER 29

HE WEARS GIRL PANTS

It was shortly after Steve's death that my problems seem to double when my mother announced one day that "We are going to have a little boy stay with us for a while, his name is Tommy" she said.

Tommy? I was a little confused to say the least, who the hell is Tommy? Mother tried to lay on the sob story about this little boy.

"His mother works at the Primary School and she is having some problems so Tommy will be staying with us for a while".

"A while, how long is a while?" I asked, but there was little reply.

So, Tommy came to stay and it quickly became apparent to me that he was getting away with stuff I would never have been allowed to do. Everything "was for Tommy"; "don't drink that, it's Tommy's" etc. I really began to resent the kid. However, it wasn't long before Tommy's mother turned up and I really didn't like her one bit!

To top it all his mother Freda appeared to have a boyfriend who everyone thought was the "cat's whatsits". His name was Shane Arthur, however today I more inclined to think that was not his real name but we will never know. He was a tobacco farmer up in Mzuzu in the north of the country. He must have been over six-foot tall and wore the smallest shorts you ever saw, even by Malawi's standards. He would arrive at the house every second weekend, usually in a different four-wheel drive vehicle and the house got a little crowded to say the least.

One day I was at the garage watching him and Jim off-load a motorbike off Shane's latest vehicle and in the struggle to get the bike off the truck Shane's shirt rode up slightly exposing some lovely frilly ladies' knickers protruding above the waist band of his shorts.

"That's odd" I thought but I guess as a kid you don't really grasp the situation fully.

However, a few weeks later, after Shane had finished his evening bath, he came into the lounge wearing nothing but a pink frilly ladies' nightie.

"Rupert - BED!" my mother yelled and I quickly excused myself to my room.

A few days later Tommy and Freda were gone without any goodbyes and I never saw any of them again. The house returned to normal - or as normal as it used to be at any rate.

Shortly after Tommy, Freda and Shane had vacated the house, I started to take a greater interest in wildlife and the environment as a whole. This was sparked mostly by one of the teachers at the school call Brian Sherry. He had established the "Ecology Club" and I soon became a member. The club would have some classroom based work but usually we would head out to Michiru Mountain, located about 5 miles north of Blantyre. There we would be met by a man called John Hugh if my memory serves me correctly. He was a British guy who was studying the wildlife of the mountain and both he and Brian were our tutors. We were each given a square meter on the ground to study and catalogue the species of flora and fauna within our square meter of bush. This work fascinated me and led to me doing some detailed insect paintings of the species that I found on Michiru.

Brian Sherry would also organise trips down to Lengwe and when possible I would join these trips. Brian always carried a pocket full of raisins and nuts, constantly eating these throughout the day, a trick he said he had picked up in Rhodesia. Everyone like Brian Sherry, he was a real role model to many of us.

CHAPTER 30

MOUNTAIN GUIDES

Richard and I had been playing squash together for a few years. His parents were members of the Blantyre Sports Club so I was able to play at the courts there as Richards guest. He was a far better player than me; in fact, he always made the school team, I never did, so that says a lot about my squash skills.

A place had become free at the Squash Club at school which I quickly applied for and got, this enabled me to play on Thursday afternoons at a squash court on the Chileka Road towards the airport. The club was run by Mr Tom Brown, my geography teacher and every Thursday we would pile into his Rover TC 2000 followed by a few more of us in the schools Renault 4 driven by the school's Malawian driver called James.

On one occasion James was called back to school which meant not all of us could squeeze into the old Rover, so Richard and I offered to run the few miles back to school. Mr Brown thought this extremely sporting and agreed instantly so off we dashed back to school.

We had run in during PE lessons and even cross-country up Ndirande and back so running was not a new thing, but that day something happened and after that we were running everywhere.

I would run to school and back, then at lunchtime on Friday after we had finished school we would run down to the airport, a distance of just over ten miles. There we would have a sandwich lunch then get the airport bus back to town; it would drop us at the Mount Soche Hotel and we would walk home to Sunnyside.

At least once a week we would run the cross-country course; some 5 miles up Ndirande and back, plus we would have at least two PE lessons. We would of course play squash and I would play water polo one afternoon a week also for the school team. This did not take into account the trips down the river after school or the walking to the zoo.

I recently calculated the weekly miles that we ran:

Sunnyside to school and back per day, five days a week = 33

School to top of Ndirande and back, once per week = 5

School to Chileka Airport every Friday afternoon = 10

1500 m track run a couple of lunch times a week = 2

It came to a staggering 50 miles per week. No wonder I was like a rake! It did help me get a 1500m running time of 4 mins 26 seconds which I'm still proud about. Remember this was at an altitude of 3,409 ft. The current Senior Boys 1500m record is 4:24.5 held by C. Saillez in 1987.

Our Fifth Form year at Saints did offer Richard and I a few perks, one being that we were made "Mountain Guides" for all trips to Mt Mulanje by lower forms. Our job was to escort the group and be assistants to staff. This was a responsible role for us, Mt Mulanje had an eyrie reputation of claiming lives and we therefore took our position very seriously. The first European to report seeing Mt Mulanje or "the Massif" as its sometimes known was David Livingstone in 1859, but archaeological investigations have revealed evidence of human visits to the mountain from the Stone Age. The first recorded people to live around Mulanje were the Batwa or Akafula, who were related to the southern African San Bushmen. Recently the Catholic University has unearthed tool-making sites along the Thuchila shelf dating back to the Middle Stone Age, some 100,000 years ago. The highest peak of the Massif is Sapitwa peak at 3,002 m (9,849 ft). Sapitwa is actually Kosapitidwa and translates as unreachable, no go zone or don't go there, which just about says it all. It is rumoured that it was first climbed in 1894, but this has not been confirmed.

Mulanje is steeped in superstition and legends. Various creatures are believed to live there, including a flying serpent called "Napolo" who floats around in the sky creating the misty conditions that envelop the mountain's upper reaches. Tokoloshe are believed to inhabit the peaks of Mulanje. There are good and evil Tokoloshe; some leave bananas and other tasty meals on the summits to help out weary travellers, though they kidnap those who refuse their offerings. There are beliefs that a kindly old woman sits by a waterfall blessing new born infants with long life in return for food. Recently the Blantyre Water Board proposed to take water from the mountain but elders in the Mulanje District sabotaged these plans as they said "taking water from the Dziwe la Nkhalamba (Pool of the Elders) would anger the spirit ancestors and BWB shelved plans. All in all, it is a mystical place, inhabited by the ancestors and I always feel a presence when I'm up on the mountain.

Over the years there have been many fatalities on the mountain; Fred France (1949), Steve Younger (1970's). Gabriel Buchmann (2009), Tasiyana Chipala (2018), Martin Jerenje (2019), Abel Nyondo (2019) and probably countless Malawians who have simply "not returned home." You certainly have to tread with respect and caution.

Richard and I had been up Mulanje many times via different routes so we were familiar with any area of the mountain that the school party were being taken to. It was a hard job, as while you were leading the group you also had to maintain an eye on the members of the party bringing up the rear. The paths on Mulanje are very narrow in places so the group would be stretched out like a line of ants and you had to keep running up and down the line checking on the progress. The staff, while maintaining a form of discipline, had no real idea of the mountain, hazards, weather, flora and fauna and least of all snakes. So, Richard and I were there to advise on all that.

At Mulanje's height the weather was extremely unpredictable, thick mist could come down in minutes, causing you to be only able to see a few feet in front of you. Rain falling on one side of the mountain would cause rivers to swell causing tranquil rivers below blue skies to flash-flood unexpectedly. A honeymooning couple had both been swept to their deaths in this way. Mulanje always had an atmosphere about it, like it was just waiting for you to make a mistake; you certainly had to keep your wits about you up there, oh and always be on your guard for Tokoloshe!

We would travel to the base of the mountain in the school bus from Blantyre, a distance of about forty miles. At the base we were met by a group of porters that had been pre-booked. They would then collect all food items, usually boxed and sealed to prevent thieving. The porters were used to the steep ascent and would set off at a run to the designated hut, leaving us to arrive some hours later with the group. The "kids" were given the option of handing their rucksacks to the porters too at the start, which the majority usually did. Some staff too "whimped" out and went for travelling light. I have to say Richard and I always carried our own rucksacks as a matter of principle. Richard would always say "If you can't carry it, then you shouldn't take it!"

Some kids who had elected to carry their own rucksacks often regretted their decision after a few hours and would simply sit down at the side of the path and burst into tears. If the kid was just "giving up" we would give him a good kick up the backside. Kids who were genuinely near collapse were allowed to rest and take on water and if need be Richard and I would take their packs in addition to our own.

I remember on one 4-hour trip down from Chambe I was carrying my own rucksack on my back, another slung over my left shoulder and another over my right. Richard was carrying three in the same way. We were exhausted by the time we arrived at the waiting bus but at least the four kids were able to make it down the mountain and we made the bus on time. We never complained, "Character Building" Richard called it.

Accommodation while on the mountain was provided by the numerous mountain huts maintained by the Mulanje Mountain Club. These log-cabin style huts had a kitchen, lounge and sleeping area. Some of the more remote high huts were very basic.

These trips were, I guess, our first taste of adult life for when the "Kids" had gone to bed Richard and I were able to sit and chat with the staff not only about the day, the plans for tomorrows hike, the route plan but also just chat generally with the staff who were not teachers anymore but were asking our advice. Sitting around the log fire in those wooden huts surrounded by the hiss of the Tilly lamps made us feel like adults and not kids.

Although these trips were very serious and people's lives were in your hands, we still found room for a laugh. On one trip I remember Richard was suffering from an upset stomach and was constantly stopping to relieve himself. The opportunity was too good to miss so at each stop I added a small rock to his rucksack. He noticed that his pack seemed to be getting heavier but put it down to his upset stomach weakening him. It wasn't till we got to the hut that evening after a five hour hike up the mountain that he unpacked his rucksack to find he had carried "half the bloody mountain" up there with him!

Although we were not able to use the trips to go looking for snakes, they always seemed to cross our paths and we collected some locally occurring species on these trips, like a Snouted Night Adder that was almost stood on by one of the accompanying lady teachers. I'm not sure if her screams brought us rushing to her aid or the aid of the snake, she was hysterical!

On one of our trips as "Mountain Guides" we were crossing an area of heath high up on the plateaux area and we came across a small Chameleon unlike anything we had ever seen before. It was about 10cm in length but almost deformed in appearance, with an extremely short and stumpy tail. The back was so arched that you would have thought that it had swallowed a penny. We both brought our reptile books out of our rucksacks and sat down in the tussock grass to identify the little chameleon without any success. It wasn't in any of our books.

I turned to Richard, "What do you want to do with it?"

"If it's a new species the museum will kill it. Then there will be hordes of people up here searching for more. Let's just let him go. Leave him to be found by someone else." Richard said.

"Yeah you're right, poor thing." And I let him step off my hand onto the tussock grass we had found him on. "There goes your chance of having an animal named after you." I said to Richard.

"Another time maybe, eh?" he said with a smile.

I continue to search regularly through reference books but still haven't seen it mentioned in any of them, so for now the Chameleon *Terrellii Wilkeyii* still plods around on Mulanje in peace.

CHAPTER 31

THE MAJOR PULLS RANK

I remember being awarded the Form Prize for the year in 1978/79, which was a great shock to me. Jim was then my metalwork teacher and had not awarded the metalwork prize to anyone.

The Major summoned Jim to his office.

"Why have you not given a Metalwork prize this year?" he demanded.

Jim said that the only person who deserved the prize was me and seeing as I was his "son" he didn't want the rumour of favouritism to be attached to the award and therefore he thought it better not to make any award that year. This was very much Jim all over, anything for a quiet life and not standing by his convictions. Sometimes he worried too much about what other people might think. Anyway, the Major acted!

"Right, if Rupert deserves the prize then Rupert will jolly well get it man, do I make myself clear? I will award him the prize myself and let anyone question the recipient and by god they will have me to deal with. I will be giving the Form Prize to boot. Understood? Dismissed!" he bellowed and Jim left his office before there was any further dressing down.

So that year I was awarded the Form Prize and the Metal-work Prize, thanks to the Major. The prize was always a book, and I was invited, along with all the other prize winners to go along to the school library and choose a new book from the prize table. The book would then be put aside and given to us on the day. Books were of different values and we were given a budget. I chose Innocent Killers by Hugo & Jane van Lawick-Goodall, which was my full budget for the two prizes. I did feel immensely proud at the prize giving evening as I walked up to the stage to receive my book. In the presentation note inside it is actually signed by him, so he was leaving no doubt to the giver of the prize.

Neither of them should have worried because not a single fellow pupil said anything to me or questioned me about getting it. I still have the book and it sits proudly on my book shelf.

I cannot say whether my place on the school water polo team affected the Major's decision or not! Strangely it was Jane van Lawick-Goodall who had named her son Grub and caused me to be called Totty all those years ago in Kenya.

There is one other story that I feel I must tell and the reason will come clear later in the book. One lunch time the tranquillity of the school is disturbed by the arrival of a couple of Greek farmers in a blue Toyota Land Cruiser. These two guys used to turn up on a regular basis on the pretext of meeting their cousins who were still pupils at the school, however we knew that they were actually coming to charm up a few of the senior girls. The younger one we nick-named John Travolta, the other one was a short, older guy with stubble and always appeared to be smiling. Either way we didn't like them too much as they were trying to make a move on "our girls", even though the girls were completely out of our league!

What made this visit different and why it was drawing so much attention was that the Land Cruiser didn't have an exhaust pipe. This was really amusing the two Greek drivers who were revving the guts out of this vehicle. Well it didn't take the Major long to get up from his desk and come outside to find out what all the noise was about.

"...your transportation doesn't even have an exhaust!" he stated to the Greek driver.

"Oh yes it does" came the quick reply from the short guy, "It's here in the back!" he said pointing to a rusty length of exhaust pipe laying in the back of his truck.

With this the Major exploded. "Get off my premises now!" he bellowed drawing himself up to his full height of over six foot something, as only a former major of the British Army can. The two Greeks climbed into the vehicle and fled up the drive and out of the gate.

～

The Major was the Headmaster at Saints from 1976 to 1983 before he retired to Portugal. Sadly, Major Bryan Bayly died in Coimbra Hospital, Portugal, on 9th March 2008, just six days short of his 89th birthday. He'd been admitted to Hospital in February and underwent surgery to pin a broken femur after a fall at his home. His passing was peaceful, according to staff at the hospital. He was cremated in Porto on 14th March 2008. His ashes were brought to the UK to be scattered in the Malvern Hills, according to his wishes. I corresponded with him regularly over the years and we both enjoyed reminiscing about those school days at Saints.

CHAPTER 32

NIGHT SWIMMING IN THE LAKE

I
t was my final year in the Fifth Form and the end of the
school year; my CSE exams were approaching. I had not
given them a lot of thought or preparation. My life so far
had been just living each day as it came and any thought of my
"future" was a million miles away.

I had no idea what I wanted to do with my life when I left
school. Richard and I had talked about many things and usually
our future employment usually contained working with animals
or the army. I still felt too young to think about working for a
living. I envied the kids who knew from an early age that they
wanted to be a pilot, a mechanic or a lawyer, they were lucky. I
never had any real desire for anything in the real world. I still
don't really.

Come what may I had exams to revise for and there was no
escaping that. My parents never really sat me down and
explained the importance of this time in my life; so when I had
the chance to go to the lake for a week with Don Cromar when
I should have been revising for my exams they didn't really set
me straight so off to the lake I went.

Don owned Petroleum Services in Blantyre and was a

167

respected business person in Malawi and very much liked. He had made money, lots of it. He wore a gold Submariner Rolex and ordered his new Mercedes from Germany and then went to the factory to pick it up. I guess at that age I looked up to him. He had a cottage at Cape Maclear and had invited me to stay with him and his kids. Dani Britz was there with his kids too.

We spent the week either fishing with Don or Dani or water-skiing. Don's neighbours were very keen fisherman, so much so, that in the evenings they would set up their rods on the beach to catch Catfish or Barbel as it is known locally. They would cast out their baits and leaving their rods on rod-rests, they would retire to the veranda with their beers to wait for the fish to take the bait then rush down to the rods. One night we decided to swim out into the lake and collect the hook and bait and give it a pull to watch them run out of the house. It was most entertaining; we had them in and out of the house like yo-yos for at least an hour before we got cold. The next night we swam out and tied the end of their lines to a small sapling that was half submerged in the lake about 20 meters off-shore. When it was tied, we gave the line a good yank. The reel ratchet clicked and we heard beers being hastily placed on tables and doors swinging open as they rushed out of the house towards the beach. The two blokes grabbed their rods and started to reel in. Once the slack had been taken up, they made no head-way against the sapling but it was too far out into the darkness for them to see.

"God it's a bloody monster! I'm not getting any line in, how you doing with yours?" we heard one of them say.

"Mine's big as well, we are going to have a fight on our hands!"

We just sat there in the lake, in the dark, treading water, trying to control our laughter. They fought their "fish" for ages. As they fought, we would give the line an occasional tug so they didn't rumble that it wasn't a fish. After a while we swam quietly back to the shore and snuck back to our cottage, dried off and sat on the veranda to watch the fishermen.

Finally, after some thirty minutes one of them called back to his wife at the house for a flashlight, which she brought. As he shone the light out into the lake and the two men saw the sapling swaying about but luckily for us, they assumed that the huge monsters they hooked had got caught around the tree. So as not to lose their prize or pride one of them waded out into the lake to the sapling. He of course found their lines "tied" around the trunk and the fish gone. His cursing was something to behold. So were the two men's assumptions of the size of the fish, we heard them debating the monster fish story for days. Needless to say, I did very little revising.

While Richard sat his "O" levels and I sat my C.S.E's. I hadn't really studied and had spent most of my revision time "snaking down the Mudi River" but managed to get seven passes and I was quite pleased by that. My parents thought I had more in me and they approached Mr Baker, the Deputy Head, to see if I could go back for another year and take my "O" levels.

Mr Baker and I never really hit it off but he finally agreed to let me join the Upper 5th the coming September. I was happy because it gave me another year at school with Richard and our snakes.

A few weeks later Richard called round the house and by his face I knew something was wrong.

"My parents have decided that I am going to do my "A" levels in England. After I've done them, they are going to make me go to University there too". I was devastated and felt as sick as Richard looked. There wasn't a lot we could do about it. If I'm honest Richard hated England more than he thought he would. He missed Malawi, the snakes, the Bush and didn't really care to much for the plans of going to University either. But for whatever reason he went along with it and after his exams at Saints went off to England. All I can say is, it was a sad day.

We didn't really say goodbye to each other, there was no last day down the Mudi River. The only thing we did have to do was close the Snake House down at the zoo. I wasn't prepared to run it without Richard; it just wouldn't be the same so one day we went to the zoo for the last time. We bagged up all the snakes and went off for the day to let them loose. I was quite emotional and choked up, I realised that our childhood was soon coming to an end.

Afterwards we cleaned all the cages and swept the room down and handed the keys back to Paul Taylor. We were done and Richard headed off to his school in England.

Richard often wrote from England telling me about the school he was at and how bored he was. In one letter he said that "the only highlight of the term was that the school nearly burnt down".

I felt sorry for him.

I guess, like every child does, that we thought our days of running around the bush, catching snakes, eating wild fruits, and messing about like boys would last forever. But suddenly, before we realised it, it was all gone, over.

I remembered Mr Brown with his wise words "a second lost now is lost forever, you will never get it back".

Sadly Don Cromar has passed away. Dani Britz was killed in a tragic accident at his lake resort at Palm Beach on the 6th of July 2019.

CHAPTER 33

I GET A SCHOOL RECORD

In September 1979 I went back to school to join the Upper 5th. Things weren't really the same without Richard being there. The days of the Snake House were now over and there was a void in my life.

This void did allow me to concentrate on my studies as I realised that I couldn't mess around, and that work had to be done. I had ten months to learn enough to sit my "O" levels so it was not going to be easy.

I had done miserably in my Maths CSE and decided that at the end of year I would re-sit the maths CSE again and would not take Maths as an "O" level. To bring the subject numbers back up I decided to sit Art "O" level although I had not done it as a CSE subject. Because of my timetable I had no time to fit art lessons into my week, so after much pleading with the Headmaster it was finally agreed that I would do the course work in my own time and then sit the art exam at the end of the year without having to take a lesson. I thought I was fairly artistic so this seemed feasible.

A month into the Upper 5th, it was announced in the school assembly that I was being made a House Monitor, which was a step down from Prefect, but you didn't get to wear a blue shirt. My "black-mark" was slowly being rubbed out. This gave me access to Sharpe House Common Room and allowed me to reprimand pupils for the standard of their dress, running in corridors, all the usual things that a prefect did, except hand out Manual Labour!

Now Richard was no longer at Saints I became firm friends with Kanghoon Lee (a Korean whose father worked for the Mazda dealership in Lilongwe), Andrew Mather (a Rhodesian/South African) and Mike Robinson (an English kid, whose parents lived in the Copper Belt in Zambia). All three were boarders at Saints. Richard and I had been friends with them the previous year but the bond seemed to firm up while I was in the Upper 5th.

Lee, Mike, Andrew and I would spend weekends camping up on Zomba. They were good days, climbing the high peaks and chatting, very much the way Richard and I had but not to the same level. We also did a lot of trout fishing; in fact, it was on this trip that I caught two of my biggest trout from the pool below Williams Falls; they were 17 inches long and a good pound and a half each.

Evenings cooking around the camp fire were always a laugh with Mike. We always had a small tape-player and even now I can't listen to Abba, Pink Floyd or the Commodores without thinking of those days on Zomba. We were all fit lads then and running down the "Potato Path" to Zomba Township to buy provisions and then back up to the campsite was just "fun". If I tried it now it would probably kill me! We had some real good times together and there are a lot of good memories.

The exams finally came and this time I did some serious revision and felt confident as I sat each exam. I even felt quietly confident as I went into the art exam. I had chosen Textile Design, not really my thing but I had decided to use my batik skill to create an abstract pattern based on a cheese plant leaf.

The following day I handed in my folio of course work that I had done in my own time to the art teacher and I felt happy with what I done. I just had to wait for the results to come back from the UK, which would be August/September time.

During one of our House assemblies, the Head of House, Mike Stevens, made an announcement about the upcoming Swimming Gala.

"Guys as you know the swimming gala is this Saturday and sadly "so and so" has come down with malaria so we are looking for someone to take his place in the 100m backstroke. Can I have a volunteer please?"

Mike then paused and gazed out across the room but was met by a deathly silence. Being a House Monitor I was also stood at the front of the room next to Mike and I could see the lack of enthusiasm from our chaps.

"Anyone? Come on guys, we can win this gala if we make a bit of effort!"

Again, there was a silence.

Since I was in both the House and School water polo teams and clearly no one else was going to step forward I said "Mike, I'll do it".

"Good man, well done Rupert, thanks" Mike said and moved on to the next item on the agenda.

So that was it, I was going to be swimming in my first Swimming Gala in my schooling career and it was less than four days away. The situation did not really phase me as I was only making up numbers so nobody would expect much out of me and were certainly not asking me to train like a demon over the next four days, right? So, I just carried on with my normal week of running to school, lessons and then running home again.

Finally, the Saturday arrived and there was the usual buzz and the stands at the pool started to fill up with pupils and parents. Still at this point I was not worried, why should I be? Programmes were handed out with the approximate times of each event and since mine was not till the afternoon I sat back and relaxed to watch the other events. The highlight for me and most of the other boys was the girls diving – eyes would stare full of private thoughts as girls like Julie R. and Susanna B. prepared themselves on the 3m high board. That is not to say watching Poppy T. climb out of the pool in a wet costume didn't send all kinds of thoughts through a young boys' mind!

Eventually the 100m backstroke race was called and I jumped into the water and prepared myself for the four lengths of the pool. As the starter pistol went off, I launched myself off the wall and started to swim. I have to say I wasn't really working hard at it, as it seemed I was just there to make up numbers. On the fourth length, and the home run I remember looking back down the pool and noticed that there were a lot of boys behind me but thought nothing of it. I finally hit the wall and the race was over.

As other boys finished, they turned to me and asked who had won but I had no idea. Then Mike came down to the pool side as House Captain and congratulated me on winning.

"What are you joking?" I gasped.

After a few minutes the time was announced and it was a new school record! How about that? Makes me wonder what time I could have done if I had really tried or trained.

As was usual with sporting achievers at Saints along with winning races came attention from the girls and I have to say my winning the race and breaking the school record did bring the very welcomed attention of a lovely girl called Poppy, although I was far too shy to act on it and wrongly she soon assumed that I wasn't interested. Oh, to have my time again!

My 100m backstroke was broken a year or two later by Martin Motjeld. The school record for this event currently stands at 1:09.37 held by A. Scordis in 2010.

The current British record holder is Liam Tancock with a time of 00:52.73

CHAPTER 34

I BECOME AN "OLD BOY"

Near the end of term, we had a leavers disco for the kids who were leaving that year. I have to say I didn't much care for discos; I love music but I can't dance for toffee and always felt uneasy about "letting my hair down" and looking a fool. I think in my whole school life I had only been to one other disco but decided to make an appearance at this one as it was the final "Goodbye" disco.

I don't even think I got too dressed up, mainly because I didn't have "disco type clothes". I had my school uniform and I had my short-sleeved shirts, my t-shirts and my shorts, that was it. I managed to dig out a pair of almost unworn jeans and a colourful shirt. I put it on and felt uncomfortable but it was all I had. I arrived very late hoping to drift in quietly without anyone really seeing me and if I was seen I would claim that I had been there for ages.

As I walked through the doors into the dark of the hall where the disco was, I couldn't really see anything or anyone. The coloured lights were flashing and the music was loud.

Almost immediately a hand came out of the darkness, held mine and pulled me to the edge of the dance floor. I knew it was a girl but who? I went with the hand to the dance floor and even though a fast disco song was playing the girl just held me close and swayed out of time with the music. That's my type of dancing I thought and held her back, swaying in time with her. Soon my eyes became accustomed to the darkness and I realised that the girl was Luksheni Rodrego, Richards ex. I felt ok, she missed Richard and so did I. Together we held each other for most of the night and talked about Richard and ourselves.

Part way through the evening Luksheni told me that before Richard had left to go to school in England she had asked him for a keepsake, something for her to hold dear to her heart to remind her of Richard. She had asked for something that was important to him. Richard had never mentioned to me that he had given her anything so I was curious.

"What did he give you?"

"A shed snake skin of a Spitting Cobra, errrr yuk!" she wrinkled her face up.

I laughed. "What you laughing at?" she asked.

"Well to Richard that snake skin WAS important and dear to him."

Saints had the tradition of shirt signing on a kid's last day at school. I suspect other schools have this tradition but at Saints it was a strong tradition. Since it was the last day for the whole year it seemed that the whole school was signing shirts. Kids who I didn't really know that well were coming up to sign their name on my shirt, or write a poem or a humorous comment. With each signature the hours were ticking away to the sound of that final bell. I still have that old school shirt and take it out now and again to read the names, remember faces and good times.

If I'm honest I didn't want to leave school. They were the happiest times of my life. I had no bills, no tax, no mortgage or insurance. Life was easy. But I realised that it was my friends that had made school such a great place and with my friends gone school would not have been the same. We all had to move on, it was life and whether we liked it or not our time was done and we were being thrown out into the outside world to make our own lives.

As I left school for the last time, I walked up the school drive past the Beit Library I glanced to my left at a small brick wall about three feet high and four feet long. I had seen it before many times but today it caused me to stop. I always called it the "Wall of Death" and it had been put there at the request of the Major to honour all the kids that had died since he had been Headmaster. Sorry, that makes it sound like he was responsible for their deaths, he wasn't.

I looked at the brass plates that were fixed to the brick wall. Steve Younger's name was there, so too were the three kids that had died from rabies after being bitten by that small hedgehog. There was the name of the kid that had been killed by a hippo while at the lake for the weekend with his family.

I looked at the names and the cause of death. I thought about all the crazy and mad things Richard and I had done and we had both escaped the "Wall". Looking back, it was five years of my life and with a school of just six hundred pupils it was shocking how many pupils had actually died in that time.

I turned and began jogging up to the school gates for the run back to Sunnyside for the last time. We don't need no education by Pink Floyd plays in my head. I wondered if we would both be as lucky in the outside world. Time would tell.

Saints has in some ways changed a lot, but in other ways it has changed very little. On one recent visit to Malawi I dropped into the school to show my face and the team and prefect photos from my time at Saints are still on display either side on the hall entrance. It was good to see Richard in the cricket, tennis and squash team photos. There has been very little building work since the Major's huge facelift. But there have been some changes. The school became an independently financed "International School", under the "Council for International Schools" in 1981 and the name was then changed to "St. Andrew's International High School" (SAintS), which I think has made it lose its sense of history.

In 1989 an alternative 6th Form 'Business Studies Course' was started and the school uniform was changed at that time. The 'Owen Room', (named after Bill Owen), which had been used as an Audio-Visual Aids room was converted in 1996 by Headmaster John Taylor, into the School's first Information Technology room, a real sign of the times. Another forceful drag into the 21st century was when satellite TV was installed at the School in 1997. Kamuzu would be turning in his grave!

In 1998 the school celebrated its 40th Anniversary of the change of name of the school to "High" School, and 60 years since being founded. On the 1st of May 2001 Saints went into the Guinness Book of World Records for the longest non-stop lesson - 25 hours of PE and History!

In 2005 "The Federal Saints" was formed by Ian "Witty" Whitfield in Pretoria South Africa. This brought together all ex-Saints, (pupils and staff), from the Federal period. It also published a monthly Newsletter. On January the 27th/28th 2007 Federal Saints in South Africa and Australia celebrated the 50th Anniversary of the start of Senior Classes.

I am very proud of being an Old Boy, or is that too sexiest in today's climate. Maybe Old Andrian is more apt. I'm proud either way.

I left school with seven CSE's and seven O-levels, sadly they were all in the name of "Prickett" and not my legal name of Wilkey, but that was unbeknown to me at the time and more on that later.

CHAPTER 35

NOW WHAT?

Just after the end of term Mike, Lee, his brother and I decided to go camping up Zomba. The weather at that time of year wasn't brilliant up the mountain where in July it could be pretty wet, misty and cold up there but we decided to brave it. It was the usual fun of exploring the streams of the Mulunguzi and climbing to the fire-lookout above Ku Chawe.

Nula FitzSimons was also staying up the mountain at the Army Cottage with her mother Betty. The Army Cottage was an old large colonial house set amongst the pine trees that was owned by the Malawi Army, but it was possible to rent it from them if it was available. I have stayed there many times and it's a great cottage, very secluded and being there was like stepping back to the 1920's. Nuala and I went back many years as our two families were good friends so Nuala tagged along with us boys most days. In the evenings she would join us as we attempted to cheat at Lee's Korean version of rummy.

One afternoon Betty FitzSimons pulled into the campsite with her large portable radio in her hand. As her husband was the Irish Consul in Malawi, politics were important to her. For some reason she thought that us kids should listen to the news that was unfolding over the radio. Rhodesia was having its elections and the white Rhodesians were set to lose the country.

We listened intently as the results came in over the radio. Betty was right, this did affect me and the rest of the listening group in a number of ways.

First, we had a lot of school friends at Saints whose fathers ran farms in Rhodesia and there was a possibility that the new Black Government might seize these farms from the white population without any form of compensation. We would just have to wait and see how Mr Banana, the president elect, was going to play it.

The second way it affected me and quite a number of kids at school was that going to Rhodesia and joining the army was an option that many of us were strongly contemplating.

The war was against "terrorists" or "Freedom fighters" as they wanted to be known who were launching attacks on Rhodesia from their bases in Zambia, and Mozambique and to some extent Angola. The terrorists were supported militarily by the Soviet Union who sent advisors and instructors to the bases to train the Freedom Fighters.

For Rhodesia to have lasted so many years fighting a guerrilla Bush War on three borders while being sanctioned by the western world shows the determination and resolve of the white Rhodesians. Their army was a hell of a fighting force.

Many students had left Saints to fight for Rhodesia. A student called George had a brother who had lost a leg in Rhodesia. A number of us had talked about going to fight in Rhodesia including Richard, Stuart and myself. Now with the war ended that was not going to be an option and I would have to think of another line of work.

In late August my parents received an envelope with my exam results. The bad news was that my result for the Maths

CSE retake was worse than the first time....god knows, don't ask!

I had passed all the other subjects at grade C or above. I had even got a C in Art, which I was slightly disappointed about but a pass is a pass.

Just as a note on the art subject. The following year when I'd left Saints Jim who was still a teacher there was going through some boxes in a cupboard in the art block and in one of the boxes was all my preparation work for the textile GCE exam, the still life drawing of the Cheese Plant, the drawings showing the development of my idea from plant through to fabric design. It was all in the cupboard, the bloody Art teacher hadn't sent it off to the UK as part of my exam, so all the UK examining board got was a piece of Batik fabric with some shapes on it. So, no wonder I only got a C grade, it was a miracle I got that. I'd like to give a huge bloody thanks to Brian K. wherever you are. BASTARD!

I still had no idea what I wanted to do with my life but suggested to mother and Jim that I would like to join the British Army, since going to Rhodesia was now not an option.

"No son of mine is going to bloody Northern Ireland to get himself killed!" she said and that was that.

I went down the Mudi River on my own to contemplate my life and the direction it should take but the truth was I had no idea at all. If I was honest all I wanted to do was to catch snakes on this river with Richard till we were both old men.

CHAPTER 36

TOO YOUNG TO DRINK

Shortly after getting my exam results, I had an invitation to go up to Lilongwe to stay with Lee and his family. I had not been to the Capital before and was excited to see what it looked like.

Lilongwe had been undisturbed bush till a few years previous but then the President had chosen to make his new capital city there and the bush had been cleared. The City had been designed on a grid system very much like some American cities. The grids formed areas, each numbered and allocated for a different purpose. The residential areas were also made into blocks, some just for Asian housing, some for only African homes and some where only Europeans could live. Unlike Apartheid in South Africa where the world kicked up against this form of segregation, Malawi's "Apartheid" went unchallenged by the rest of the world. For the residents of Lilongwe, the designated areas were not an issue and it was as normal to have to live in a certain grid as having to drive on a certain side of the street.

Since it was school holidays, I was pleased to hear that Richard had come back to Malawi for the summer and I went to visit him at his house in Area 10. Just outside the back door near the carport was a large wooden crate and in it was a load of bits from a motorbike. As I looked through the bits, I realised that it was the old red and white Moto Guzzi that Richard and I had so much fun on over the years.

"Hey, the old bike, what happened to it?" I asked.

"It started its life in bits in a box and it's ended its life in bits in a box." Richard replied very philosophical with a shrug of his shoulders.

If I had the money then I would have bought it off Richard but sadly you never have the money for these things when you need it. We had some good times on that bike and it would be nice to have had it now.

After that Richard and I went to the Capital Hotel to meet up with Lee and have a few cokes and a chat. Lee and I had always talked about going up to Mzuzu at some point, just as Richard and I had talked about it. With the three of us together again the subject of Mzuzu soon came around. I guess with kids time goes slowly and you always think you have all the time in the world and there was no sense of urgency to get up to Mzuzu. This was due in no small part to the fact that Lee's parents had offered to drop us all off at Salima and pick us up again a week or so later. So with the offer of transport Mzuzu was shelved for the moment in favour of Salima. So, with a few days to kill before the trip to Salima, we entertained ourselves around Lilongwe with a trip to The Sanctuary, a small reserve within the city limits. We also spent a few days at the Lilongwe Golf Club (LGC) where Richards's mother was secretary. We messed about on the golf course and played snooker.

As with most things, idle hands and all that, someone brought their newly acquired motorbike to the LGC to show off. This kid was our instant hero, I didn't care if I didn't know him from Adam, and he had a motorbike! The only thing young boys were really interested in was how fast could it go. Obviously, the proud owner was understandably reluctant to "open her up" but there were plenty of willing "friends" to help him out. I really can't remember whose bike it was or even what his name was.

As you come off the main road and turn into the LGC there is a barrier with a gateman who supposedly checks your membership pass and opens the barrier although I never saw him. The drive is then straight for a few hundred meters where it then comes into the car park. The Club house is straight ahead of you as you come into the car park. We had decided to take it in turns to cruise to the barrier then on the given signal accelerate down the straight and into the car park. The watch would be stopped as the bike entered the car park. The quickest time wins, simple. When you have a motorbike, it is not hard to find quite a gathering of like-minded boys and soon there was about fifteen of us gathered in the car park.

Four or five kids had had their turn when it came to the go of a kid called Mark Lee. I didn't know him at all but Richard did as he also went to school in England and was just out for the holidays. We all stood at the car park end of the road and listened to Mark revving the bike up at the barrier. One kid waved his hand and Mark tore up the drive towards us. We all knew that this was going to be quick but as he neared the point where previous riders had started to ease off Mark didn't so we knew this was going to be a cracking time. As Mark came past us like a bullet the time keeper pressed the stopwatch and yelled out the time. We all heard it but we were all looking at the quickly disappearing Mark who had failed to slow down.

"He's going to brake any second" said one knowledgeable character.

Mark didn't brake.

"What the hell is he doing?" someone yelled.

Before there was an answer Mark drove straight into the two swing doors that were the entrance to the club house. One door broke off its hinges and there was the shattering of glass. Mark disappeared through the doors. We all ran towards the club house.

Mrs Terrell, who had been sitting in her office with her door open, heard the crash and looked up to see a motorbike shoot past her door heading for the bar. There was another crash as Mark and bike went through the saloon style doors of the main bar and another crash as the two of them hit the front bar. By the time we got over the broken front door Mrs Terrell was on her feet and at her door. Richard slowed down to try and explain but then realised that he couldn't so ran past with the rest of us and into the bar.

There was the bike smashed against the bar and Mark in a heap next to it. The engine was still revving and the back-wheel spinning, the noise was deafening. Either side of the revving bike sitting on their bar stools were two elderly gentlemen with their beers still in their hands. As we got there one elderly man looked down at Mark and said as calmly as you like, "You're too young to drink in here young man" and then went back to sipping his beer.

Mrs Terrell had been trained as a nurse and her first concern was that Mark had broken some bones and while one of us "killed" the bike and dragged it out of the bar she checked Mark over. Luckily nothing was broken but Mark was clearly shaken.

Mrs Terrell looked around and said "Richard, get a large brandy for Mark, quick, he's shaking!"

"Brandy? heck, if I knew he was going to get a free drink I'd have crashed through the doors myself!"

Mark was then given time to recover in Mrs Terrell's office and drink his brandy. It was some time before he emerged into the car park to the cheers of the "expectant crowd".

We all wanted to ask Mark questions but decided to let the owner of the bike ask the first question. It only seemed right.

"What the bloody hell did you think you were doing? You have wrecked my bike, my dad's going to kill me!" he fumed.

Mark then explained that at some point along the road from the barrier he had tried to ease off the accelerator but it had stuck. In his panic he had not thought to pull the clutch in. Mark said as he screamed past us in the car park he looked to his right and remembered seeing the wording on the pool bar wall, the pool bar was called "Hazards", he thought "No Shit?" as he headed for the swing doors.

"Why didn't you just jump off before the doors?" a smart kid asked.

"What? Are you out of your mind?"

The bike owner continued to whinge about his wreck but we explained that the throttle could have stuck while he was on the main road and he would have probably ended up under a truck and actually he should be grateful to Mark for saving his life! Unconvinced the kid pushed his crumpled heap of a bike home and frankly we were happy to see him go. Stuntman Mark was our new hero of the moment.

I found the time to talk to Richard about my future although if I'm honest he wasn't much help. Not that he didn't have any ideas, he did, thing was that they were just so "far out" that I had no idea where to start.

Lucky for me the trip to Salima soon arrived and we all piled into Mr Lee's Mazda for the trip to the lake shore.

We were going to camp, Lee and his young brother in one tent, Richard and I in another. Once camp was set up, Lee's parents headed off back to Lilongwe, they would return the following week to pick us up again. Our first pitch turned out to be on an ant's nest and we had to hastily move before we were bitten to death.

Richard was still sporting a black eye from an incident at the Portuguese Club which I never got to the bottom of; and he came in for a lot of stick about that the entire week. We spent the week scrambling around the hills behind Salima, messing about in the water and playing cards. It was a great week that went far too quickly but we were happy to see Lee's parents as his mother had come with food that she had prepared and we ate like kings for the first time in a week.

Back in Lilongwe, we played squash a few a few times and hung around the Capital Hotel and it was soon time for me to go back to Blantyre to contemplate my future.

The high plateau of Namwera, surrounded by mountains, was originally home to a famous Yao chief (presently known as Jalasi but formerly referred to as Zarafi). Jalasi, along with other Yao chiefs such as Mponda and Makanjila, were involved in the lucrative slave trade. They would raid villages of non-Yao and capture men and women, selling them to the Arab Slave Traders in Portuguese East Africa (Mozambique).

To maintain his income from slaves, Chief Jalasi fought off the British in 1891 but a stronger attack overwhelmed his people in 1895. The British Officer who led the attack was Major Edwards, who was allegedly the first white man to step into the village on the 28th of October 1895. On entering the village Edwards found it completely empty, the estimated 25,000 Yao had fled, along with their chief.

The area was called magoji, named after the Yao word for the type of tree that was common in the area and used as a local variety of rope for tying. This later became Mangochi.

Lieutenant E. G. Alston was then commissioned with building a permanent fortress on the site, the remains of which still stand today, although it is a trek to see it. A number of buildings feature sign posts indicating what purpose each structure served, including servants quarters, a flag post, Indian hospital, parade grounds, etc.

It is said that Chief Jalasi fled to Portuguese East Africa and died there in 1906 but many of his subjects returned home to Magoji.

The fort was used as a prison from 1907-1910 and as a training camp during World War I by the King's African Rifles.

Mangochi Mountain (seen in the photograph) dominates the tobacco farmland of Namwera. The mountain varies from 4,500ft (1,370m) to its peak at 5,713 ft (1714m) and is home to lions and elephants, both of which raid the farms below.

One of the most famous Yao was Jacob Wainwright. His real name was Yamuza and was born around 1859. In his teens, he was kidnapped by Arab slave traders, but was rescued by a British anti-slavery ship, baptised a Christian and given the name "Jacob Wainwright."

Wainwright was educated at a Church Missionary Society school in Bombay, British India. At the age of about 14, Wainwright was hired to accompany Dr. Livingstone as he explored East Africa. With his knowledge of both Chiyao and English he must have been a great asset to Livingstone.

As we know, Dr. Livingstone died at Ilala, near the edge of the Bangweulu Swamps (in modern Zambia) on 1 May 1873. Wainwright and two other Africans, Abdullah Susi and James Chuma, resolved to bring his body the 1,000 miles (1,600 km) to the British consulate at Bagamoyo in Zanzibar. Before the journey, Livingstone's heart and entrails were removed from his body and buried in an iron box. Wainwright recorded that a massive blood clot, possibly a cancerous tumour, was found in the lower bowel. At the burial ceremony Wainwright read from the Book of Common Prayer. He was also given the responsibility of making a full inventory of Livingstone's possessions.

Before the party left Ilala, Wainwright carved an inscription on the tree marking the grave of the metal box.

Jacob Wainwright accompanied David Livingstone's coffin on board the SS Malwa. As the most literate member of the party, Wainwright was also responsible for writing a letter to the relief expedition which included Livingstone's son, informing them that Dr Livingstone had died. When the coffin party reached Zanzibar, it seems that the British assumed that Wainwright was the leader, despite his youth, because he was the only African who could speak and write in English. He was dispatched with the body to England. Wainwright guarded Livingstone's coffin on its journey to Britain and was the only African among the eight pallbearers at the explorer's funeral in Westminster Abbey on 18 April 1874.

Wainwright died at the Urambo Mission in modern day Tanzania in April 1892, aged just 33.

CHAPTER 37

BEWARE OF GREEKS

I had just left school and since my birthday was July the 17th, I was just a few days past my seventeenth birthday.

Half of me just expected to continue the carefree life of catching snakes and not having any responsibilities. The other half of me realised that this was never going to be an option; I had to think about a job and a career. I had always wanted to work in the Game department or be in the army but the army was out for the time being anyway and there were no opportunities for non-Malawians in the Game Department.

I have a far distant memory that my choice to be a farmer had something to do with Mrs Betty Fitzsimmons although I am not sure what or how. Anyway, farming had seemed a good idea to me. I would be outside, in the bush, surrounded by snakes and I stood to make good money. I never saw myself in an office that's for sure.

Malawi's economy largely revolves around agriculture, predominately tobacco and tea, with a little coffee. So, the only real choice for me was did I want to work on a tobacco or tea estate?

My mother smoked and I detested the habit so I was not too

keen of working to grow the stuff, although I hated the taste of tea also but tea had more appeal for me. So that was it, I'd be a tea grower! My parents arranged for me to go down to Lujeri Tea Estates at the foot of Mulanje Mountain to have a look around their operation.

The tea estates of Malawi are very beautiful places, acres of rolling slopes covered by rows of tended evergreen tea bushes, dotted with ring-barked tall standing trees to prevent light aircraft from mistaking the green mat as grass and trying to put a plane down it. Most estates are scatted around the slopes of Mt. Mulanje, where the cold, clear mountain streams come straight off the mountain and flow through the surrounding estates, usually ending up in the Ruo River that then flows into the Shire at Chiromo and then down the Zambezi and out to the Indian Ocean.

In my naivety, the thought of working the week on a tea estate and spending week-ends climbing Mulanje, fishing for trout in its streams was of great appeal. I had spent many week-ends on the mountain when I was at school and loved the mountain.

I was due for a rude awakening.

A tea estate, or in fact any farm for that matter is not a five day a week job. There were very few free weekends here!

"But you have holidays, right?" I asked, I was beginning to think I was in the wrong place.

"Yes, you do get holidays." The manager said.

We then did the tour of the tea factory where the first part of the tea drying process is done before the tea is bought by the multinationals and blended for sale as the tea you and not I, drink!

Well, the smell in the factory turned my stomach. It certainly didn't smell like a tea caddy. This was awful, "You get used to it", the owner said.

I left Lujeri in the afternoon after lunch with a lot of boxes ticked but a large red cross on the box named SMELL.

The strange thing is that in September 2016 I returned to Malawi to spend two weeks with Gary Brown on a trip to Mulanje Mountain in search of reptiles. In a twist of fate, we stayed with Gary's friend at Lujeri Tea Estate. We were given a tour of the Tea Factory and bizarrely the smell was wonderful. I remember walking around the factory and estate thinking how different my life may have been if I had chosen tea. It's a strange world.

Mrs Fitzsimmons then paid the usual impromptu visit to discuss my future. My mother mentioned to her that I was now not too keen on the tea estates. Betty said that there weren't any estates that just did coffee but she could help with a tobacco estate, so my next option became tobacco. She said that if I was going to go to a tobacco farm to eventually learn the business then there were only two people in Malawi worth mentioning. The first was Mr Jerry Parker, an ex-Rhodesian, who farmed in Mchinji west of Lilongwe. I knew his kids from school, he had two sons, Jerry and Gary and a daughter Angela. Angela was a complete babe, possibly a year or two my junior, so my brain started to see endless possibilities of working on Mr Parker's farm!

The other, she said, was a Greek guy, that I'll call Jorge, who farmed in Namwera. The Greeks and Namwera were well known to me as a school boy and not for the best reasons, but I won't talk about that.

I spoke to Mrs Fitzsimmons and told her I would like to see Mr Parker with a plan to working for him so he could teach me the tobacco industry. I thought it best not to mention Angela at this early stage. She said she would speak to Mr Parker and get back to me. As the weeks went by, I heard nothing from Mrs Fitzsimmons, until one day she spoke to my mother over a cup of coffee and I was summoned into the lounge.

"Mrs Fitzsimmons has spoken to Mr Parker but he is unable to offer you a place on his farm…..blar, blar, blar."

My heart sank.

"………..but she has spoken to Jorge and he is happy to have you on his farm for a year, isn't that great?" My mother said waiting to see the look of joy on my face. I faked a look of enthusiasm but don't remember being able to say a single word.

My hopes of being Mr Parker's future son-in-law were gone and now I was just about to be thrown into hell where ALL the Greeks hated the "English Boys". I was going to die.

Over the next few days I tried to speak to my mother about it but I wasn't getting anywhere.

"Mrs Fitzsimmons says Jorge is different, he is more English than Greek and he is one of the best farmers in the country."

"Can I at least go and see the farm and meet him first?"

"No, the farm is in the middle of nowhere, so Betty has arranged for you to go straight up there."

What? I was being sold down the river! I pleaded and begged but it was no use. A date was agreed between Mrs Fitzsimmons and Jorge for me to be taken to the farm and there was not much I could do about it.

I spent the remaining weeks thinking about Mr Parker, Angela and how cruel life was. Waiting for the day of departure was like living on Death Row.

To ease the waiting, I decided to hitch-hike up to Cape Maclear for five days camping. The trip was uneventful but when I got up there, I found that half the school was there, but life had been cruel to me again. Mr Parker was up there with his family so I spent days seeing Angela from a distance, wondering how she might have saved my life at the hands of the Greeks and would she be sorry when I was dead and would she come to my funeral!

God had one more hand to play.

For some reason I found out that while I was at the lake I

had acquired the affections of a girl I knew from school called Jenny. She was an ex-Rhodesian girl, a year younger than me. She was extremely good looking but again sadly I didn't cotton on at first to what her intentions were. Her father also farmed in Mchinji and before the end of the week I was already starting to wonder what my chances were of getting her to speak to her father to see if I could work on his farm instead of going to Namwera but I just knew that mother and Betty would not agree to that. So, when my five days were up I hitched back to Blantyre to await my impending doom.

Interestingly years later I learnt that Tony Hawken had a hand to play in me going to Namwera, and that he had personally vouched for me, so thank you. I may not have known at the time, or appreciated it, but I do now.

I was saddened to hear that Betty Fitzsimmons passed away in 2015.

Jerry Parker sadly died of cancer in march 2020.

CHAPTER 38

I'VE JUST BLOWN IN FROM NAM…. VIETNAM

I t was a quiet Sunday morning in November when Jim pulled up outside Petroleum Services. I don't remember what time it was, probably around 6 am. Africans were shuffling along, some hurrying, some were dawdling. Not a lot was said in the car either on the way or while we waited outside for Jorge's lorry to arrive. There was probably the usual talk about everything and anything except the issue of the day, which was I had just left school, I was going away from home for the first time to a place I had only heard about, to a group of people, that if I was honest scared the hell out of me. I suppose there wasn't a lot Jim could say. Neither my mother, Amy nor Isabel, as I recall, had got up to say goodbye, which said just what an impact my departure was causing.

Finally, a large white Toyota lorry pulled up in front of us. The time had arrived. There were no hugs, no "good luck dear boy", no "don't let the side down", nothing. Most kids would have got a packed lunch, some sandwiches for the trip; I got nothing. Most kids leaving home for the first time would have got some money thrust into their hand, just for "well you never know, you might need it"; I got nothing. Jim grabbed my bags from the back seat of the car and handed them to me. I took the bags and walked across to the truck. The drivers' assistant opened the door and then shuffled across next to the driver and I climbed into the cab and slammed the door. The truck pulled away under the strain of its load and I looked across at Jim who had got out and was stood next to the open door of the car. There was no wave. I couldn't find what was needed to wave either. I turned forward again and we disappeared down the road and left onto the highway at Ginnery Corner. We were on our way.

Being aboard the lorry suddenly felt exciting and I started to forget about the hazards I was due to experience at the hands of the Greeks in a few hours' time. I'd never been in a lorry before and the commanding view of being so high up in the cab made one feel important, like the road was yours. As far as conversation went there was silence in the cab, but I was used to that at home. The silence here was due to the fact that the driver didn't speak English and my Chichewa was themed around snakes, and not idle chit-chat.

I kept looking across at the driver from the corner of my eye, watching him change gears, and turn the large steering wheel. He was a small man yet he seemed to me to have been doing this job a long time, there was that look on his face. He seemed to feel at ease behind the wheel. I notice he had a tattoo on his forearm that was too blurred to make out. I felt surprised at the tattoo, as Africans didn't generally have tattoos. I gave it no more thought and sat back to enjoy the moment of adventure and to imagine what lay ahead on the farm.

The road from Blantyre was familiar to me; I had travelled it many times with my family on trips to Zomba and the Lake. I knew the corners, the little African shops, places like the Chiperoni Blanket factory; I knew the individual trees on the sides of the road and the mountains and hills in the distance. We passed Njuli, where Mr Del Buffalo had a coffee estate on the left-hand side of the road and Chiradzulu Mountain on the right, we passed Namadzi and Thondwe. The miles seemed to fly by.

Just as Zomba Plateau came into view, around Chidothe, the driver suddenly eased off on the accelerator and began speaking to his assistant. I couldn't understand the technicalities but from the concerned look on both their faces I knew something was wrong and it looked serious. The driver looked up the road ahead as if looking for something and again gave a few words to his assistant who by saying nothing in reply, acknowledged that the driver knew best. On some level ground at the side of the road the driver pulled over and jumped out, as did his assistant. They both came around to my side of the lorry and began to investigate the front wheel. "Puncture" I thought, "these two chaps will have this fixed in a jiffy" and I hopped out of the cab to stretch my legs. The tyre didn't look flat, but I just thought "maybe this old-timer can feel the nail at the precise moment it goes through the tyre", it wouldn't have surprised me. Quick as a flash the assistant had the front jacked up and then stood back, allowing the master to examine the wheel. The driver got hold of the wheel at the top of the tyre and gave it a push and a pull and gave a knowing nod of the head and then stood back and gave the offending wheel a look of understanding disapproval. The assistant then stepped forward and gave the wheel the same push and pull as if to learn from his master the feel of the offending problem for future years. I looked at my watch and it was just coming up to 9am.

The two guys had the wheel off and then started to take the hub off the axel. I was no mechanic but this looked serious. Still, I had every confidence in this old chap; he could probably whittle a new part from a branch of a tree while we had a cup of tea.

As the parts started to be separated from the lorry and the driver became more and more covered in dirty old grease I stared to realise that this was getting very serious. Doubts started to creep in. "I hope this chap knows how all this goes back together?" my mind thought. "Of course he does! Relax" my heart told me.

The time rolled by. At about 10am that Sunday morning I found out that the wheel bearing had gone. I tried to find the Chichewa words for "well get the spare wheel bearing out of the box in the back of the truck that you obviously carry for situations like this, put it on and then let's be on our way", but those weren't the common phrases I had picked up while catching snakes with Richard.

At that point the driver had a small chat with the assistant and trundled off up the road, leaving assistant and me with the truck. After a short time, he returned with a loaf of bread, one bottle of coke and two Fantas. "Where is the new bearing? Oh I see, you went shopping while we have a disaster here, great! Then I realised the coke was for me and he was going to share the loaf and this was lunch!

We all climbed into the cab to eat. With my share of the dry loaf of bread and my coke, I thought about the packed lunch that I never got, hey ho! I also thought about the fact that my pockets were empty and I was only eating this meal because of the thoughtfulness of this old African. I felt sad and upset; the coke did little to help the bread down due to the lump in my throat. As it turned out the driver, while getting us "lunch" had also phoned the farm and told his boss about the sorry state of affairs we had and they were sending the cavalry. Yippee, we would be on our way soon.

The afternoon turned into evening, and evening into night. We weren't going anywhere, so after another coke and another shared loaf of bread, the three of us curled up in the cab and made ourselves comfortable. "We will be rescued tomorrow" I thought and I fell asleep.

At about 10 o'clock on Monday I heard a car horn and

judging by the rejoiced look on the faces of my two now "new and closest friends", I gathered that the cavalry had finally arrived.

A blue Toyota FJ45 Land Cruiser pick-up screamed past us from the direction of Blantyre and screeched to a halt in a cloud of dust and burning rubber in front of the lorry. A European man jumped out dressed head to toe in camouflage. (This is Malawi, where the wearing of camouflage is illegal by anyone other than the army.) He was so full of life that you would think he was either drunk or on drugs. He then jabbered a few words to the driver and the assistant; in seconds the two Africans are in fits of laughter. He handed the driver a new, boxed bearing and you'd think it was Christmas, the driver was ecstatic.

I then half expected for this camouflaged drunk/high European to then jump back in his cruiser and disappear once again in a cloud of dust. Instead he came towards me and introduces himself.

"Rupe, I'm Costa, we will take you up to Namwera with us, where's your stuff."

It's at this point that I realise that this is the guy that the Major banished from the school due to the lack of an exhaust.

After two days on dry bread and coke, I didn't wait for a second invitation, even though this guy was scaring me a little. I grabbed my bags from the lorry, said my goodbyes to my two friends and dashed for the cruiser. As I reached it I saw that in the front was sat no other than "John Travolta" (who I will from now on call JT), the other guy from the school incident. Seeing as the cruiser only had two real seats in the front I started to climb up onto the back of the cruiser.

"Where you going? No get in the front with us." Costa said, so timidly I obeyed and got into the front of the cruiser and squeezed up against JT with the gear stick between my legs.

JT had a huge "Ghetto Blaster" on his lap. I said hello and at that moment Costa got in beside me. I tried to make myself as small as possible in the middle of these two strange men. Nervous was not the word. JT hands the stereo to Costa and starts the engine.

"You ready Boss?" JT asks.

"Gun it!" Costa commanded, pointing down the road ahead with his hand and JT floored the Land Cruiser, causing a wheel-spin that sprayed dirt and stones high into the air, generating a huge applause and great cheers from the truck driver and his assistant. We tore off up the road at a hair-raising speed.

Costa then hit the play button of the stereo and blasted out *The Long Run* by the Eagles, while singing along to most tracks. I just sat quietly trying to merge into the back of the seat and trying to avoid being castrated by JT as he changed gear while they sang "*The Greeks don't want no freaks!*" at the top of their voices. I felt like the freak and wondered had I got just days to live. My life did actually flash before my eyes and it wasn't a pleasant sight. I was going to die!

Both windows were open, with the Eagles blasting out. The city of Zomba flew past in a blur with the speed we were doing. At Domasi there was a police check point consisting of two 44 gallon oil drums painted yellow and a red and white striped pole between the two barrels. Two policemen armed with old .303 rifles stood chatting. Costa leaned across me and started honking the horn again. JT made no attempt to stop him even though they were police. I sat there terrified, thinking that I would end up in Zomba Prison and never even make Namwera.

The policemen glanced up the road towards our speeding Land Cruiser; Costa continued honking the horn and then I saw the police waving us past, so JT swerved to the other side of the road and Costa leaned out of the window and shouted some-thing at the police as we flew past the road block that caused smiles, cheers and clapping from the two policemen and on we went.

The townships of Malosa and Likenu flew past in equal

speed. As we came through Kasupi the road snakes round with some almost vertical drops on one side as you leave the shire highlands and descend down towards the Shire River at Liwonde. Most people at least have their foot on the brakes to negotiate the steep descent but as I looked down into the driver foot-well I noticed that JT still had the accelerator pedal buried into the floor. A warning triangle came into view at the top of the decent but this flew by in another blur. Then came a speed sign, which equally made no difference to either one of my lunatic companions. I later realised that in Namwera a speed sign of 80 miles per hour was merely a challenge of the minimum speed you should be doing on that stretch of road, not the maximum!

Just before we got to the bridge that crosses the Shire River at Liwonde, just past the Shell filling station on the left, JT suddenly swerved the vehicle almost at right-angles across the road in a screech of tyre squeal and turns right onto the road that leads to Liwonde National Park. How we did not roll I will never know. We drove on past the turning for the park where shortly the tarmac ran out and we hit the dirt road. I expected our speed to decrease accordingly but not a chance, if anything it increased. At times we took corners side-ways and out of the corners we fish-tailed, I wanted to hold on but there was nothing in the cab to hold on to, plus I was literally wedged between these two mad-men so decided to just hope for the best.

Signs flashed past, Nsanama, Ntaja, Thomo, Nzinda, Somba. After some miles just past Jelamu, we turned off to the left and crossed a rickety old wooden bridge with banana trees on either side, again at the same hair-raising speed. Fields came into view and in the near distance I could see a small hill and a house surrounded by rubber plant trees. Costa leaned across me and started to press the car horn like a demented child. A yard came into view with tractors and machinery parked to one side of a

203

large house. Costa was still pressing the horn as JT swung round in front of the house and screeched to a sudden stop. I breathed for the first time since Zomba.

"Rupe…….Welcome to Nam!" Costa said to me in a movie style voice like someone in the Godfather film who was just announcing the arrival in hell. He then jumped out of the cruiser.

I eased myself across the seat and jumped onto the ground. I think I was actually shaking. I turned around to the back of the cruiser to get my bag but already an African had appeared and wrestled it from my hand.

"Come on Rupe" said Costa as he walked up the steps to the house, "I'll drop you off at Jorge's this afternoon."

Africans seemed to appear from everywhere, emptying the cruiser like ants. Some were taking boxes towards what looked like a workshop, others taking bags to the house.

As JT drove off at high speed with the now usual horn blasting, I followed Costa up the steps and onto the veranda of a large colonial type house with a green painted corrugated iron roof. I sat down on the veranda when Costa suddenly reappears with an elderly lady.

"Rupe-Rupe, this is my mother" Costa says. "You will have lunch with us then I will drop you off at Jorge's."

I was relieved to see that she was not wearing camouflage and looked a nice lady; I shook her hand emotionally, thinking that at least she would stop anything bad happening to me - I hoped anyway!

Coffee was then brought for us. As we sat there, a constant stream of Africans came up to the veranda to talk to Costa, updating him on the happenings at the farm while he was in town, and as a consequence not very much is said to me. He asked individuals about the progress on the farm while he had been away and received reports on different aspects. I just sat there and drank my coffee listening to this new life.

After the reports had been concluded and the coffee drunk, the cook arrived to say that lunch was ready.

I don't remember the conversation over lunch but there must have been one. What I do remember was how good the food was, it was really tasty; probably the best food I had tasted till that time. Many of you will say that was because I had just spent twenty-four hours on a lorry eating bread and I guess to a point you would be right but even so Costa's mother certainly did make a good lunch.

Once the meal was concluded Costa jumped up and said he would drop me off at Jorge's. I grabbed my bags.

"No, leave those, I'll get my boys to drop that to you later, we'll go on the bike."

So, I follow him out and across to a large red Honda 250 XL trail bike parked under a tree, it seemed bigger than I was. Costa jumped on and kicked the Honda into life. My first thought was "Was he not going to wear a helmet and where was mine?"

My second thought was "I hope they don't ride bikes like they drive cars!" and looked for somewhere to hold on to, there wasn't much hope of either!

"Ready!" Costa said, which wasn't a question; it was a warning since he gave me no time to answer and immediately let the clutch out and the bike leapt forward almost throwing me clean off the back. By the grace of God, I managed to keep my seat and we disappeared off up the road in a cloud of dust.

The nightmare had begun again! I looked back forlornly at the house hoping for Costa's mother to come to my aid but there was no sign of her, so I just turned forwards again and held on for my life.

I remember being aware of Costa's aftershave, something that I was not aware of in the cruiser on the way to Namwera; but now I was aware of it. Sure, I knew what it was but Jim never wore the stuff and I hadn't ever had a bottle. As we rode along, I thought how, in all this dirt, dust and heat the smell of the aftershave made everything seem clean.

As the fields gave way to bush on both sides the road started to go slightly downhill. At this point Costa looked back over his shoulder and spoke to me. He only said one word.

"Terrorists!"

"Terrorists?" I asked stupidly in a scared whimper thinking that maybe with us being so close to the Mozambique border that possibly there were cross-border raids.

Costa then looked front again and let go of the handle bars completely and pretended to be holding a machine gun with both hands. He then made machine-gun noises as he spayed both sides of the surrounding bush in a hail of imaginary bullets. Because of the slight decline our speed did not really slow down.

"Oh my god, we are going to die" I thought as Costa leaned the bike over to enable us to take a slight bend in the road, while still spraying the bush with imaginary bullets from his imaginary machine gun, at the imaginary terrorists.

I am sure at this point I must have just closed my eyes and just held on tighter and tried not to move. This went on for a few seconds, and then he grabbed the handlebars again and turned back to me.

"That was close Rupe-Rupe but I think I got 'em all!"

I didn't know whether to laugh or burst into tears. As we rode on more fields came into view and in the distance I could see a collection of red brick buildings.

"Jorge's place" Costa informed me and I started to breath normally again thinking that the hell ride would soon be over. My hope was short lived.

The road came to a ford where a small stream crossed over a large slab of concrete in the road. Two African women were just about to wade through the ford with heavy loads on their heads but they hesitated as we approached on the bike. As Costa slowed down a little, but not much, a sheet of water was thrown up where the women would have been if they had not stopped. They laughed and clapped as we tore past them.

At this point I realised that we had turned left and not right and were now going away from the direction of the buildings. My ride from hell was obviously not over yet and so on we went.

A village came into view and the sides of the road appeared to be lined with kids waving and shouting "Costa, Costa, Costa". As we rode past Costa pulled the clutch in and revved the engine several times and sounded the horn to some tune or other, the kids cheered and tried to run alongside but Costa then accelerated off up the road leaving the cheering kids in his dust and again my knuckles went white as I tried to prevent myself from falling off the back.

Very soon after the village the road dipped down to a small wooden bridge that crossed a river. I glanced at the bridge and was relieved that its condition was slightly better than the one we had crossed at Costas's farm. Stupidly I hoped that our speed would decrease as we came down to the bridge but again this was Costa, and this was Namwera and we did not.

On we went when finally some buildings came into view. Just before we reached the buildings there was a small hump in the road with white painted concrete blocks each side where presumably a drain went under the road and Costa accelerated towards the hump and we became airborne for what felt like minutes. Finally, we hit the ground again and a thud went through my spine.

As we approached the buildings Costa sounded the bike's horn again like some demented child. We skidded to a halt outside a large brick open-sided building that had rows of tractors lined up in it. I staggered off the bike and wobbled about like a sailor who had been at sea too long and had just stepped on land.

To our left, set amongst the trees was a large colonial type house, very similar to the one Costa had and emerging from it was a man who looked like Henry Stanley. He was so sun-tanned that I almost mistook him for an Asian man. He had a receding hairline and large black beard. He was dressed in khaki drill shirt and shorts. All he needed was a pith helmet. At his side walked an Alsatian dog.

"That's Chililie, and his girlfriend." Costa joked at me in a whisper. "Howzit Chi Lilly" he shouted across to Chililie.

"Howzit Boss!" Chililie said with large smile through his beard. "Is this Rupe?" he asked and stuck out his hand to me.

I had arrived and I was now "home", or what would be home for the next twelve months. I don't remember much of that first afternoon and night. I think I must have just been waiting for father time to collect me.

When I woke up at six the next morning the truck had arrived during the night. I went to greet the driver and felt a little guilty at having abandoned them, but I think this feeling was only my thought. The driver was Gerald, and as it turned out had learnt his driving with the Kings African Rifles. He was one of the best and most respected drivers in Namwera. I would travel with him many times after that, thankfully not requiring a loaf of bread and coke!

Costa, or "The Boss" as he was known locally would turn out to be a great guy and a good friend. There was no side to him, what you saw was what you got. Yes, he was totally mad, lived in his own world, but there was nothing wrong with that. Namwera created eccentrics and the "The Boss" was the funni-est. He had a heart of gold and would do anything for you. He always put a smile on my face and the Africans loved him too, which said a lot in my opinion.

~

The Boss sadly passed away in December 2012 after a long illness.

The old Toyota truck that brought me to Namwera - well almost!

The house where the Boss lived in Namwera

Costa "Boss" Yiannakis

CHAPTER 39

MALAWI'S "WILD WEST"

A t this point in the story I would like to just explain a bit about Nam and the Greeks and I take my description from a young Greek guy who grew up in Namwera, but shall remain anonymous!

"The Greek Malawians (Aka – the Animals) - tend to keep to themselves, calling anyone non-Greek "Xeni" meaning foreigner or stranger – essentially this breed of animal left Greece in the 1940s have kept the culture but at the same time modernised in the area of technology. Very much like a hybrid episode out of My Big Fat Greek Wedding and the Sopranos - are all in some way related, have the same names and for some reason keep marrying each other! On top of that the Greek guys will move around in packs or herds (bit like gorillas), smoking crazy amounts of cigarettes, wearing sunglasses in the dark and saying "hey boys, hey boys, let's get some Greens" (This means that they are out to get totally smashed on Carlsberg Green Label Beer) and acting somewhat inappropriately in the presence of women. A good analogy would be Joe Pesci and Robert DeNiro wanna be's (based on the films Good Fellas and Casino). They all have 'Godfather' type nicknames:

Little Tony Tselingas, Yianni Psile, Costa Thuthu, Costa MaGlass, Costa Kichasu, The Boss, Nick the disco king, Nick what ya gonna do, Pete on the Beat, Jimmy the Kid, Tony Kalemba, Pano the baker, Chris Sharp-Shoot, Kacherri, Bazooki, Saki or Sach, Miklo Mick, Magnet, Kwech, Pancake aka D9, Jimmy six guns, the Sundance Kid Bad Intentions, The Kandodo Kid, Big John, Fat John, Taki Arafat and Tony Polony, the list goes on."

These names were handed out like badges of honour after a gangster shoot-out, you earned your name, it wasn't just given to you. For example, Kacherri used to spend all day asleep under a tree on the farm when he should have been working and the tree just happened to be the Kacherri Tree, hence he got the name Kacherri. The thing was that most people didn't know what the real name of many of these people had been before their Soprano name was given to them.

Namwera was the Wild West, rules did not mean a lot to the Greek farmers. Trips to town were always a race to get there faster than anyone else had done previously. Dress code was non-existent, if like the Boss you wanted to wear full camouflage that day, then you wore full camouflage, whether it was illegal or not. It was not uncommon for you to find a farmer walking round his farm in his underpants. If someone's domestic animals strayed onto your farm you simply reached for your nearest gun and shot the offending animal. You would fit bull-bars to the front of your vehicle so that you could still drive foot to the floor and if you did hit a herd of goats without writing your vehicle off. If three or four goats were killed in the process then that was great because your score card looked more impressive.

If you came up to a roundabout and your passenger said "Hey Boss, bet you can't go round the wrong way?" then you would simply swing the wheel right instead of left and if you "totalled" your Mercedes in the process, then so what, the funnier the driver and passenger would find it. The Boss did this once in his Mercedes.

There were "family" feuds but these were quickly sorted out by the Godfather who would call each member and talk to them about how this problem was going to get resolved. Weddings were orchestrated to link a weaker family with a stronger family and alliances were formed through the children. It was like the bloody Mafia.

There was nowhere like Namwera anywhere else in the country. Nothing would ever surprise you. You would just simply shrug your shoulders and say "Namwera" or you wouldn't even notice that it was strange in the first place. After a few years in Namwera my mother gave me one of those small bottles of wine, the type you get given on a plane. She was horrified when I thanked her for the bottle, took the lid off and downed the entire bottle in one go and gave the empty bottle back to her. I had obviously been Namerized! I did say thank you, I still had manners after all. Finally let me just share a little story that really sets the tone for the stories that will follow and give you a flavour of the Nam Mentality.

A few Greeks, including the Boss had gone to the Hong Kong Restaurant in Blantyre for a meal and as usual the beers and whiskey had started to flow. After numerous requests by the restaurant's owners for the Greeks to stop abusing the waiters they had no option but to ask for the Greeks to leave, which they duly did and the restaurant heaved a sigh of relief and normal service resumed for the other remaining guests. However, the relief was short lived as a few minutes later the restaurant was illuminated by the headlights of a Land Cruiser approaching the entrance at some considerable speed. Seconds later the vehicle screamed up the steps and crashed through the doors of the restaurant much to the amusement of the Boss and his drunk friends.

It is the kind of thing you would see in a movie but here it happens for real. What I will say is that knowing the Greeks as I do, and the Boss who was driving in this particular incident, I know that when he had sobered up the next day he went back to the restaurant and paid for the damage – in cash! It doesn't make it right, but it shows that the Boss at least had some remorse for his actions. So this was Namwera and the Greeks, and now I have painted the picture I will continue my story.

CHAPTER 40

LESSONS IN FARM MANAGEMENT

Jorge arrived a few days after my arrival at the farm. I had heard a lot about Jorge from Mrs Fitzsimons, and gathered that he was one of the more open, broad-minded and forward thinking of all the Greeks in Malawi. I liked him, he was not afraid to stand up and speak his mind, no matter how many it was against. This caused a few of the Greeks to speak badly of him behind his back, but Jorge then gave me the first lesson from "Jorge's School of Farm Management".

"When they talk about you behind your back, it really means they hate you because you're doing better than they are. When they come visiting and are full of smiles it's because you're a crap farmer and they want to laugh at you." He said wisely, like he knew this from first-hand experience.

The Greeks would certainly talk about me behind my back many times but I always remembered Jorge's wisdom. Jorge and I seemed to hit it off straight away, I guess he liked having a young "English" boy to pass on his knowledge of farming and I looked up to Jorge because I admired him for what he stood for and how he ran the farm, and run it he did.

Chililie, it seemed, was in charge of all mechanical issues and I have to say he knew his way around a workshop. Although we didn't really see eye to eye, he taught me to weld, ride a motorbike, and drive a car. I've never seen anyone strip a Mercedes car to the body shell, re-spray it and assemble it again so fast and have it look like it just came out of the factory. He certainly had a gift.

I wasn't quite sure what I expected the day-to-day life on the farm to be. All I knew of the Namwera farmers was when I had seen them in town, driving their muddy 4x4's and throwing money around and behaving wildly. I certainly didn't have the misconception that life on the farm was going to be just sitting on the veranda watching the work being done, however nothing could prepare me for what happened over the coming week.

The first thing that Jorge said to me was "get a note-book and write down everything I tell you". Later that day, with a new note-book in my pocket, Jorge sat down with me to give a crash course on the workings of the farm. His face was serious and I knew that the teaching had begun.

"Rupe, get your notebook out, write this down. Let me tell you about the workers on the farm. They are not like us, if they find something or you give them something, they will do one of five things. First, they'll try to eat it, if they can't eat it they'll fuck it, if they can't fuck it, they'll sell it. If they can't sell it, then they'll break it. And if they can't break it, they will lose it!" He then got up and said "Follow me".

There endeth the second lesson of Jorge's School of Farm Management

I had actually written everything down as Jorge spoke.

During the first week Jorge told me about the farm and a bit of its history. It had belonged to his father and had been handed down to Jorge and his brothers when his father had retired back to Greece. Sadly Jorge's old man had passed away very soon after returning to Greece. The farm covered around four thousand acres, being split into two parts, Estate 1 and Estate 2. I was never sure how many staff the farm employed but what I do know is that it took two days to pay them all. All the staff lived on villages either within the farm or bordering it. This meant that we also took care of each man's wife and any kids that they had. Altogether it must have run into thousands. Jorge was often the police, the judge, the lawyer, the marriage counsellor, the midwife and the doctor.

After a week of shadowing Jorge he sat me down on the veranda to give me my third lesson from "Jorge's School of Farm Management".

"Rupe, how can you give out tasks in a morning without having an understanding of what you are really asking of your staff? If you give each man a thousand yards of tobacco rows to cultivate a day, how do you know that a man can actually cultivate that amount?" He looked at me seeing if it had actually sunk in. "You need to know what you are asking of your workers and the only way to do that is by doing the task yourself, so you know what it's like to cultivate a thousand yards." Again, he looked at me for a sign of understanding. I nodded in agreement; I could see his point.

"If I am away from the farm then you are in charge, these are your staff, your workers. They will work for you but only if you are fair to them. I want you to do one farm task for a week, just as the Africans do. If it's cultivating, then for a week you will cultivate with them, you'll start when they do, eat what they do and finish when they do. Is that okay with you?"

"Yes, that's fine, No problems." I answered without much thought to what I had actually agreed to.

"Good, you start tomorrow, milking the cows and cleaning the cattle Boma. Now let's get some supper."

So, the next morning I reported to the cattle Boma. Jorge had given the Africans at the Boma strict instructions that I was not to be treated like a Mzungu but made to work. I sat down and was taught how to milk a cow by hand. After a few minutes my hands cramped up, and this was just the first cow! Finally all the cows were milked but before I could rest my tired hands I was given a shovel. Let me tell you, shovelling cow crap with temperatures hitting mid-thirties was heavy work but together with the flies and the stench it was pretty off-putting work to say the least. The more I shovelled, the more shit the cows produced, it was like painting the Forth Bridge.

On about the fourth day of shovelling shit, the Boss arrived at the fence of the cattle Boma.

"Shit Rupe-Rupe, what the hell are you doing?"

"Shovelling cow shit, what does it look like!" I was getting pretty hacked off by now with the task, so the Boss got no change from me. I didn't even break the swing of the shovel, just in case Jorge saw I had stopped to talk to the Boss.

"I'm goin' to have a word with Jorge, this is nuts." and off he disappeared. Sadly, neither him nor Jorge returned by the end of the day so at 5pm I knocked off and headed to the house to get a bath and something to eat. When I got to the house, Jorge didn't mention anything about the Boss and the next day it was back to the Boma. Weeks later I found out that the Boss had gone to the house and spoken to Jorge about him making me work like an African. Jorge's reply had been something along the lines of "he's working for me on my farm and I'll treat him how I see fit and I'd ask you not to interfere."

The end of the week could not come quick enough, what-ever Jorge had in mind for the second; nothing could be as bad as the cattle Boma.

Monday morning and guess what? Yeah you guessed it, back to the cattle Boma! You must be bloody joking I thought, I was told this was only for a week. The thought of throwing the shovel and walking back to Blantyre entered my mind for a split second but was soon gone. I started shovelling. Within an hour

Jorge arrived on his motorbike. "Put the shovel down and come with me."

What? I wasn't slacking honest. I followed Jorge to his bike and jumped on the back. Moments like this I dreaded if I'm honest, I always expected that my time was up and I was being given my marching orders.

We drove out to one of the fields where Jorge had a few words with the Kapital and was handed a hoe, which he handed to me.

"That's your row there, where that stick is in the distance marks your task for the day, you'd better get cracking, you are an hour behind everyone else!" and he jumped on his bike and was gone. An hour behind everyone else, you bastard I thought as I started hoeing. The anger fed my muscles as I swung the hoe into the row; I wanted to kill him or someone, anyone.

Cultivating is back-breaking stuff. The young tobacco plants are planted in ridges and weeds grow on these ridges, feeding on the fertiliser that is meant for the tobacco. They have to be removed by the action of the hoe. At the same time soil washed down from the ridge by rain needs to be brought up from the furrow back up onto the ridge. You are always bent over and it's only your arms that really get to move, your back just gets stiff and painful. You can't rest because if you do, the rest of your section would just get away from you. Jorge paid his staff per yardage that they cultivated, rather than an effective daily rate. If you were quick you could do the yardage and be finished by halfway through the afternoon. If you were slow then you'd be there till 5pm, the choice was yours.

Any stragglers would continue cultivating long after the tractor had taken his mates back to the farm, walking home when he had finished. This was not a fate I wished for myself, and knew I would have to walk; there would be no favours with Jorge.

The movement of the hoe handle in my hands started to give

me blisters. Shit, this was only the first day. I straighten up and looked for the yard marker stick. The sweat in my eyes blurred my vision, it was at that point that I realised that I wasn't wearing a hat, most of the boys were. I also realised that standing up caused a pain to shoot up my back. I immediately bent over again to ease the pain and continued hoeing.

Midday finally came with the arrival of the lunch trailer. Jorge had lunch delivered to his staff in the fields, this solved two issues; firstly, it was a free meal and second it didn't waste time transporting the staff back to the farm for lunch and then back to the field afterwards. Lunch was pretty much always the same; boiled maize flour or Nsema and either boiled brown beans or dried fish, served on tin plates. Fresh drinking water was also supplied and I collected an old tin can that the cook was handing out. I drank probably three or four cans of water before picking up my chipped enamel plate and joining the food line. I did not push in but joined the back of the queue, I thought it only right, I was one of them, an equal, not a Mzungu! I do remember looking down the line hoping that the food would not run out before I got there.

The food didn't bother me, I was used to this kind of food. I think I cleaned my plate quicker that most of the other guys ahead of me in the queue. I drank several more cups of water and went back to my row. None of the Africans had gone back to work yet but seeing as I had an hour to make up, I couldn't afford to let my food digest. Also, I was seriously worried that if I sat for too long that I wouldn't be able to stand up again!

With just a few minutes to spare before 5pm I reached my stick. My hands were shot to pieces, the blisters had burst and some had even started to bleed. I sat quietly on the edge of the road in a daze; I was covered in dust that was caked on with sweet. As the tractor arrived, we all piled onto the trailer and headed for the farm buildings. The mood was jovial on the trailer, the guys were all chatting, about what I didn't know; some were even singing.

I handed my hoe in to the store man and watched while he crossed off my name next to number in the page of his dirty exercise book. I notice my name that was written down, "Bwana Rupatee". I hadn't the energy to explain the correct spelling and went to the house in a daze.

We had supper and again Jorge didn't ask how my day was, or if I had completed my task or anything. But he did tell me an amusing story which kind of related to my day and I will recall it for you now.

A European farmer had given a cultivating task to his workforce but after a few days the field was far from finished. Every time he arrived at the field his workers were hard at work but by the end of the day very little area had been cultivated. The farmer decided to leave the field and when he got back to his house he collected his binoculars and set out on foot to climb a small hill where he would have a good view of the field and the workers. When he got to the hill, he saw the workers sat in the shade of the trees asleep. Fuming he drove out to the field and on arrival the workers were hard at work. They swore blind that they had not been sat under the trees. The farmer happened to have lost an eye in an accident and removed his glass eye and placed it on a fence post facing the field, in full view of his workers. "I'm leaving my eye here to watch you" he said as he left the field. He went back to the hill and using his binoculars looked across at the field and the workers were hard at work. His plan was a success. The next day he went to his hill and again the workers were cultivating. On the third day when he looked across at the field, to his dismay, the workers were again under the trees. He drove out to the field to see why the glass eye trick was not working. When he got there, he found that one of the workers had placed a hat over the eye so it couldn't watch them!

While it was an amusing story, I understood the point. Expecting 100% out of your staff would require more than trickery, Lesson number five. After I finished supper, I retired to bed exhausted.

At 5.15am I was woken from my sleep with a cup of coffee. "God not that time already!" I thought as I dragged myself from the bed, I was absolutely shattered. I headed into the bathroom to wash and try and wake up. My hands were now more painful than yesterday. What was I going to do? I couldn't call in sick, I'd look like a wimp in front of Jorge and the guys in the field. I'd let him and them down, what would the other workers think of me? Jorge would probably kick me off the farm and I'd have to go back to mother and Jim. I'd look like a failure; oh, they'd love that. I got dressed, grabbing my hat this time, I was learning. I ran to the stores, drew my hoe and jumped on the waiting trailer.

The day was agony, the sun was beating down and the stick looked miles away but I kept thinking that there was at least an end. I also kept thinking that I was never going to go back home with my tail between my legs and face my parents.

Friday finally came.

The weeks continued and gradually I began to make a bond with the workers on the farm. I felt a change in them and started to feel some kind of respect from them, not just because I was a Mzungu but because I could step up to the bar and match them yard for yard.

One afternoon I was passing the village where months before the kids had cheered the Boss as he took me to Jorge's on that first day. As I came up to the village on my bike the kids ran out onto the side of the road. As I rode past, they shouted "*Chikwandala, Chikwandala!*" and waved with huge smiles on their faces. When I got to the farm, I told Jorge about the kids and asked him what "Chikwandala" meant.

"Well you know on the African mud huts there is a thin strip of metal cut from an oil drum that goes over the main roof poles and is nailed into the wall; it keeps the roof on the house. Well that thin metal strip is called a Chikwandala. It's the name the Africans have given you because you are thin but strong." He smiled. "You should take it as a compliment".

"Wow" was about all I could say. I felt that all the days alongside them, all the endless yards in the fields had been rewarded the only way the Africans knew how. The Africans usually gave names to people, sometimes they were derogatory or as in my case a compliment. When the Africans gave you a name it was like a medal or badge, they had an uncanny way of sussing you out to a "T". I felt proud. I now had my Namwera name.

A few days later Jorge said that Gerald was going to town the coming Friday for supplies and I'd be going with him. I'd earned a weekend off. Gerald would drop me at my parents' house Friday night and pick me up on Monday morning to come back to the farm. I hadn't left the farm since arriving, the only people I saw were Jorge and his wife and the occasional visitors to the farm. I felt I'd earned my weekend too.

The Friday came and it was like the departing of an ocean liner, the farm was a hive of activity, people bringing lists of stock to be purchased, others giving all the reasons in the world why they needed to go to town. I packed my bag and headed out to the truck.

"Hope you checked the wheel bearings?" I said to Gerald with a smile as I loaded my bag up into the cab. Jorge came to see the truck off and thrust some money into my hand.

"For the weekend, have a good time."

When Gerald pulled the truck out of the farm road on to the main road, I opened my hand and I checked the money that Jorge had given me, it was 30 Kwacha, a huge amount to me at the time, and my first wages!

The trip to town was very uneventful; I think I slept most of the way. I remember waking up as we went under Independence Arch and down Kamuzu Highway. I saw the streetlights illuminating the road ahead. I was hypnotised, I hadn't seen streetlights or a tarmac road since I had left Blantyre all that time ago. Then it hit me, I'd been on the farm for 3 months!

I did not get the reception I had hoped for at the house from Mother or Jim. It was as if I had just popped out for a pint of milk, no big deal. But it was a big deal to me; I hadn't been away this long ever in my life. I hadn't been kicked off the farm, or jacked it all in and run back to "mummy". If they were impressed, they didn't show it. On Saturday morning I walked into town, with the money Jorge had given me safely in my pocket. I spent almost all of it on toys and books for Isabel, apart from treating myself to a coke-float and a burger at the Ice-Cream Parlour.

The weekend went by fast and the truck was soon pulling up outside the gate ready to take me back to the farm. I wasn't sad to get into the cab. I had left home, and I guess there was no room for me anymore.

As we pulled out on to the road, I passed Gerald some change from my thirty kwacha to reimburse him for his generosity on my first trip to the farm when the truck broke down. I had been grateful for the bread and coke then.

CHAPTER 41

TIME TO SHOOT A LION

I continued to learn all aspects of the farming year. I learnt what it was like to remove caterpillars from the tobacco plants, to remove the "sucker" leaf that grows as a secondary leaf and if not removed decreases the size of the primary leaf. I learnt the removal of the flower stalk, or "topping", I harvested the tobacco leaves, and hung the leaves in the barns ready for curing. I even did the night shift at the barns stoking the furnaces from 6pm till 6am. I ploughed acre after acre with a tractor in the beating sun and in the end could almost fill anyone's "boots" on the farm.

Life wasn't all manual labour; the monotony was broken by the excitement of lions! During the day you wouldn't know they were there but at night, in search of an easy meal, they would break through the cattle Boma fence and attack a cow. The cattle watchman or Londa would usually raise the alarm and send someone running up to the house to get Jorge.

One night, Jorge woke me at around 1am. "Lions, get dressed and come with me!" he whispered.

My first thought was "No, let's just lock all the doors and

windows and stay here in the house till the lion has gone; now how would that be?"

The thought of actually stepping off the veranda into the dark night knowing that there was actually a lion out there, which was hungry enough to come and kill a cow, just seemed like total suicide to me. But when Jorge said "Come with me" you went with him, simple as that! You knew that if he said it was alright then it was and I would have followed him anywhere.

By the time I got to the veranda Jorge was loading his Holland & Holland .375 magnum rifle. "Grab the torch over there, let's go" he said and we stepped off the veranda.

When we arrived at the cattle boma the Londa had, by all accounts, chased the lion away from the now dead cow, meaning that the lion was now on the outside of the Boma fence. Hey, hang on a minute, that's where we are isn't it? I suddenly had the urge to jump the fence and seek the safety of the Boma, but by this time Jorge had already asked the Londa where the lion was, and was being told that the lion had gone off about fifty yards from the Boma to a patch of long grass. Thankfully Jorge thought it unwise to follow the lion and ordered that the dead cow be roped to the fence to prevent the lion coming back into the Boma to try and drag the carcass through the fence into the bush. A rope was soon found and the carcass secured. Jorge looked at the fast approaching dawn, "soon be light, the lion won't come back now, she'll wait till it goes dark again, let's get some sleep."

I was too excited to sleep and spent the next hour laid on my bed imagining the lion, how big was it? How many were there? Would Jorge actually shoot it?

The morning soon arrived and it was work as usual. I must admit, I spent a lot of time looking at all the long grass on the roadsides and edges of fields now more intently, knowing that in it could be lurking a lion, eyeing me up for its next meal.

Jorge had shot a lion on the farm the previous year and the Game Department had gone nuts at him, "We'll throw the book at you" was the only phrase Jorge remembered from their brief but heated meeting. Things had only calmed down when Jorge said that he promised not to kill lions on his farm anymore. So later Jorge contacted the powers that be, and that afternoon the Government hunter arrived to "deal with the lion".

The Africans on the farm swarmed round the hunter like flies, you would have thought a Hollywood superstar had just arrived and boy did he love the hero status that was being showered on him. Jorge asked me to take the hunter down to the Boma and show him the dead cow and explain to him the events of the previous night. As I walked down to the Boma with him I noticed that he carried a 450 rifle. As we neared the Boma the hunter stopped to load his rifle. The bullets were massive and looked like they would have stopped a train. As he tried to load them into the internal magazine the bullets just weren't going in, then I noticed that the reason why he was having so much trouble loading them was that his hands were shaking like a leaf. Shit I thought, if he's worried about this lion in broad day light then maybe I should be worried too. I reassured myself that I was in safe hands and that he knew what he was doing so I asked him,

"Have you shot many lions?" I asked him.

"No" he replied.

"No?" what an odd answer, "You mean no, not many?" I waited for the reassurance.

"No, I've never shot a lion" he said sheepishly.

"Are you scared?" I asked, thinking how I would be if it was my task to shoot this lion.

"Yes Bwana, very much!" he said, his voice faltering as he spoke.

I showed him where the lion had entered the boma fence; the paw prints were still visible in the dusty earth. After much pondering and soul-searching, the hunter made his plan. The carcass would be dragged out of the boma and tied to a tree very close to the patch of grass where the lion had sought refuge the night before. Jorge and I would then park the open backed Land Cruiser within thirty feet of the tree and facing the carcass so we could flick the lights of the vehicle on if need be to illuminate the dead cow and feeding lion. The hunter would be standing up in the back of the Land Cruiser, ALONE, using the cab roof as a rest for the rifle and he would shoot the lion. Then we would all have tea and cakes and pose for photos, simple.

To say that this guy was the government hunter, he had not come very well prepared. Jorge ended up lending him his Winchester head torch.

"Do you know he's never shot a lion before. This is his first time?" I warned Jorge.

"Oh, there's a bloody surprise! It's going to be a circus!"

As it began to get dark the hunter mounted the back of the Land Cruiser, like some Victorian general heading off to battle in a chariot. We parked in front of the tree at the spot marked by the hunter as thirty yards, I guess his rifle was zeroed for that distance, but what did I know about hunting, I was just a kid!

The hours went by; in whispers Jorge told me about the lion he had shot the previous year. How he had wounded it and eventually had to follow it into some long grass at the edge of a Dambo. The wounded lion came out of the grass at full tilt, not as wounded as Jorge had hoped. He shot it in the chest and it tumbled almost at his feet. "I nearly shat my pants" was how Jorge put the event.

I think the hunter was being trouble by mosquitoes because there was quite a bit of movement from the back of the Land Cruiser. I'm not sure how long we waited but slowly out of the grass appeared a lioness, not big, well not as big as I was expecting. She froze momentarily investigating the vehicle deciding whether there was a danger. She then looked at the carcass of the cow she had killed the previous night. I guess her hunger got the better of her and she stepped out of the grass.

Jorge slowly leant his head out of the driver's side window and up towards the back of the Land Cruiser. "Mkango" he whispered.

The hunter then switched on his head torch and for the first time the lioness was bathed in a yellow light. She stopped eating and looked up towards the source of the light. At that moment there was an almighty crash from the back of the Land Cruiser and the light went out, followed by the sound of six D-cell batteries rolling around in the back of the Cruiser.

"What the hell's he doing!" exclaimed Jorge. This was more of a statement rather than a question and I was not required to answer.

The hunter scrambled around the floor collecting the batteries and rammed them back into the torch. The lioness remained fixed on the vehicle but did not run. The light of the torch went back on and still the lioness stood there. I suddenly felt quite sorry for her, she had no idea of the danger that was ahead of her. She was not the ferocious lion I imagined; she was just a hungry animal that had seen the cow as an easy meal. As I was thinking of her fate, she lowered her head and began to feed on the dead cow.

"What's he waiting for?" Jorge whispered to me. He then slowly leaned out of the window and whispered "Shoot" to the hunter and brought his head back inside.

A good thirty seconds passed in total silence, then there was the loudest bang I'd ever heard and a flame shot out over the top of the windscreen and over the full length of the bonnet. He had fired.

After a few seconds our eyes had adjusted to the near apocalyptic blinding light of the flame and Jorge turned on the headlamps of the vehicle. I expected to see the lioness lying next to the dead cow, but I couldn't see her, only the cow.

The hunter leaned into Jorge's open window and asked, "Did I hit her Bwana?"

Jorge didn't answer. He started the engine and inched forward towards the carcass. There was no sign of the lioness.

"The Bastard's missed! Bloody great!" was all he said and reversed back to the thirty-yard mark.

"Now what?" I whispered to Jorge, but then realised that there was no point in whispering after that bang.

"Now we wait, see what happens, if he missed she may come back, she's hungry. If she is wounded then we have real trouble."

So, we waited. Sure enough, after about forty-five minutes the lioness reappeared from the grass with a look as if to say "What the hell was that?"

The Winchester torch went on and the lioness was lit up. I sank my head into my neck and my neck into my shoulders in anticipation of the bang and waited. And waited and waited. Then it came.

The lioness tensed and lowered her body, like she was going to leap away but didn't, she held the position for a few seconds then resumed feeding.

Jorge couldn't contain himself anymore. "Oh this is a fucking joke! Rupe get up on the back with the hunter, SLOWLY, and see what's going on."

I looked across at the feeding lioness and fixing my gaze on her and slowly pulled the door handle. She didn't flinch, so as quickly and as quietly as I could I climbed out of the cab and swung myself onto the back of the Land Cruiser.

The hunter reloaded the 450. He rested the rifle on his folded jacket that he had placed on the cab roof. He lined up the open sights and aimed the rifle at the bewildered lioness. I watched his finger curl around the trigger. Any second now, get ready for the bang, then just before he pulled the trigger, he took his eye off the sights and curled his head down and backwards cowering from the expectant noise and the flash, and pulled the trigger.

BANG!

I looked over the cab roof towards the lioness, this time she hadn't even stopped feeding. I leant over and stuck my head into Jorge's open window and explained the situation we had with the hunter turning his head away as he pulled the trigger. I don't think I had got to the end of my sentence before Jorge was out of the cab, and stood beside the open door of the Land Cruiser. He had the rifle out of the hunters' hands and fired, all in about three seconds. I looked towards the lioness; she lay dead next to the cow. Jorge then handed the rifle back to the hunter with such force that it nearly knocked the bloke off his feet.

"There! And if anyone asks, you shot it, UNDERSTAND!"

"Yes Bwana, thanks Bwana" and we then retired to bed.

The next morning, we examined the dead lioness, Jorge had shot her through the neck. The hunter got paraded round the farm like a bloody hero and soaked up all the admiration like a sponge. The hunter later admitted to me that when he had switched on the Winchester head torch and saw the lioness clearly for the first time, he got the shock of his life. It was the first lion he'd ever seen. When she turned and looked at him, he thought she was going to attack and was shaking so much that the back came off the battery compartment and the batteries fell out. This then obviously caused his view of the lioness to be plunged into darkness, now he didn't know where the hell the lion was.

"Bwana, this has been the worst day of my life, I don't want to be a hunter anymore" were his last words to me. A few days later he quit his post for an office job, away from lions!

A lion is difficult to see in grass

From this position, a lion can be on you in seconds

CHAPTER 42

LESSONS IN BABOON MATHS

With all the maize we grew on the farm, some forty acres, raids by baboons was a real problem. We employed watchman that were stationed on the edge of each field to discourage the baboons but one man against a troop of baboons just isn't going to discourage them for long. As the days go by and the baboons get more and more hungry their fear soon subsides and testers are sent in to judge the resolve of the watchman. The rest of the troop sit either in nearby trees or on the nearest Kopie or large boulder covered hill and monitor the watchman's strength against these first tentative raids.

They watch the watchman leap from his small wooden tower that has been erected to enable him to have a bird's-eye view of the field and run off the first attack with yells and stone throwing. After a while the testers return in a second wave. Again, the watchman retaliated with more yells and wielding of his stick and the odd thrown stone.

The baboons can go on all day like this, the watchman however soon losses the fight as the baboons launch multiple strikes to all corners of the field. More than often the watchman usually retires to his watchtower and rolls a joint of cannabis and sits back to fall into a calm stupor of not-interested observation as the baboons help themselves to as many cobs as they can carry.

I once spent the day in a watchtower to wait for the baboons. It becomes a real cat and mouse game that you have no hope in winning. As the watchman rolled his joint and said calmly "it's enough fighting for today" we sat and watched them leave the field with their spoils. Their cheeks were bulging with cobs, and each hand held a few cobs as they ran upright on their back legs out of the field. Amusingly some baboons had even stuffed a maize cob under each armpit, which amused the now stoned watchman.

I mentioned the problem to Jorge who gave me another lesson from the "Jorge's School of Farm Management".

"Time for a maths lesson I think." He said.

Maths lesson, what the hell was he talking about? But Jorge didn't elaborate.

The next morning, we drove off to a maize field close the forest reserve. We waited in the car for about an hour or so till the baboons started to appear out of the forest reserve. Armed with a double barrelled shotgun Jorge, the watchman and I then entered the maize field in full view of the baboons.

"It's important you wait till they can see you. This won't work if you enter the field unseen."

We waited in the middle of the field for a while then Jorge told the watchman and I to go back to the car and wait. So we left Jorge behind in the field, and waited in the car. Within fifteen minutes of our exit the baboons left the trees and ran into the maize field. Within seconds there was the repeated blast from the shot-gun and baboons fled in all directions. After a short while the gun fire stopped and Jorge re-emerged from the field dragging two dead baboons.

He told the watchman to go in and collect the remaining dead baboons and finished off his lesson.

"Baboons can't count so when three people go into a field and only two come out the baboons don't remember how many went in. They won't be back here for a while!"

"There is another way to get rid of a troop you know? You make a small hole in the side of a termite mound in view of a troop of baboons. You then pour loose maize into the hole and a couple of maize cobs. Then scatter some loose maize around the mound and then retire a safe distance to wait and watch. The baboons then come down to pick up the loose maize. One observant baboon remembers you putting the maize in the hole and so pushes his hand through the hole and feels around inside for the maize. Sure, at first, he might just find the odd bit of loose corn and eat that, but after a while he finds the cob and grips it in his hand and pulls his arm out of the hole but the cob prevents his hand from passing out through the hole. So greedy is the baboon that he will not let go of the cob. The more he pulls the angrier and more stubborn he becomes. Even as you walk up to the termite mound he won't let go of his prize, even when all his mates have legged it! With the help of a few boys you can tie the baboon up, securing his jaws shut and his hands and feet together. You then shave the baboon completely and then paint him with whitewash. Once you've done this you then tie him to a tree and cut his mouth and limb bindings. You then keep him tied to the tree for several days just feeding him salty maize. After 3 days you cut him loose!"

I sat intrigued, listening to this lesson and making frantic notes in my note book.

Jorge continued..... "The baboon is so thirsty from the salt and so eager to get back to his troop that he takes off like a bullet in the direction of his troop. Except when his troop see this four-legged creature without hair and white they turn and run also. The faster they run to get away the faster the white baboon runs to catch up. They can cover 50 miles a day and as they disappear over the hills and into the sunset it's the last you see of that troop. By the time the whitewash wears off and his hair grows back both him and the troop can be 300 miles away!" and he smirked a small grin, but by now we are back at the farm house for lunch. Before I can ask a question, Jorge said "Let's eat!"

That mealtime we sat down as usual but the table was laid out differently. There was an air of silence around the table, which felt a little strange. Jorge then spoke.

"Rupe, today is the anniversary of my father passing away in Greece. To pay our respects and to honour him, we always have a special meal for him." he said and picked up a plate of what I took to be battered fish fillets.

"This is cows brain. You don't have to eat it but ....."

I cut Jorge off "no, I'd like to try it." and I took the plate from Jorge and took a slice of cow brain and put it one my plate. There were also dried fish, the ones that you find drying on the roadside on the lake shore road. Jorge said a small blessing of thanks to his late father and we ate. I felt honoured to be part of this meal.

That evening as I lay in bed a thoughts cross my mind. I thought of the meal, had I really eaten a cows brain? I also thought of the baboon hunt, and had I actually eaten baboon brain and not cow? I thought about how the baboons cant count and wondered if we could use the same trick to hunt a lion. Maybe I would ask Jorge in the morning and I fell asleep.

CHAPTER 43

ELEPHANTS & HONEY

The farm used wood to fuel the furnaces to cure the tobacco, hence the name Flue-cured tobacco. The farm did grow some blue gum trees for its own firewood but we were still in the process of tree planting and it certainly wasn't enough for the annual consumption. A licence was purchased from the Forestry Commission to enable us to cut indigenous trees from forest reserves. Looking back now I can't see how the Forestry Commission allowed this as the trees in the forest reserve would take decades to grow and were not replaced. Seeing Malawi recently I see that this practice was certainly the thin edge of the wedge. Sure, it provided a source of revenue but as with all things in Malawi, whether the money actually went back into the Government Department was another question.

One morning Jorge asked me to take the motorbike and go up into the mountains to check on the firewood cutters. Since I did not know the route into the mountains Jorge provided a boy who would guide me along the maze of small tracks to where the woodcutters were. So, with the boy on the back of the motorbike I set off.

I was excited to be heading off into the mountains as I had only seen them from a distance while on the farm. The lions that had come and taken the cattle had come down from the mountains and the woodcutters were always being harassed by elephants. It was "Real Africa" up there and there were real dangers.

As we came to a bend in the track, I would slow down in case a herd of elephants were crossing the track ahead or a pride of lions were resting across the track. Luckily for us we didn't encounter either and after an hour we came upon the wood-cutters.

The woodcutters would cut down a tree then cut the trunk and large branches into lengths of one yard. They would then stack these lengths a yard high and a yard deep. This was known as a Mendal. The woodcutter would then be paid on how many of these mendals he had cut. All I had to do was check and count the number that each woodcutter had cut then compare that with the amount he had declared to the Kaipitao, simple.

I spent the morning walking from one mendal to another and marking them with a chalk cross so they were not counted twice. Soon it was time to stop for lunch so I sat down on the ground with the wood-cutters and we ate dried fish, cooked beans and nsima (maize porridge). A small enamel cup of water was passed around for us to drink from.

One of the wood-cutters then stood up and removed a small burning piece of wood from the fire and headed into the forest. The rest of the men followed him so I joined them. Soon the men stopped at a tree and pointed to the swarm of bees flying around a hole in the tree. Then the man with the burning stick grabbed some dry grass and started to climb the tree. At the hole he lit the grass and blew the thick smoke into the hole. The bees swarmed around the tree and those of us on the ground dashed for cover. After a few minutes the wood-cutter pushed his bare hand into the hole and removed the honeycombs he could reach. and dropped it down to waiting hands. After a few combs had been removed he descended the tree. One of the woodcutters then broke off a piece of honeycomb and handed it to me. It was a little black with ash from the charcoal embers that were carried in the can before, or at least that is what I hoped the black stuff in the can was.

In amongst the honeycomb were dead bees and I looked gingerly at the other woodcutters to see how they were tackling the dead bees? I didn't want this young mzungu to embarrass himself. As I gave a sideways glance, I could see that they were just shoving the honeycomb into their mouths, dead bees and all, so I did the same. The trick was to just keep chewing the comb until you had extracted all the honey from it, which you then swallowed. You would then be left with a ball of bees wax which you simply spat out, oh and you either ate or spat out the dead bees. I was really enjoying the honey, the flavour was amazing, I must have eaten two large junks and was going for my third when one of the woodcutters stopped me.

"You cannot eat too much because the sugar in the honey will give you a really bad headache" he said in Chichewa.

So meal time was over, once the old enamel cup had been passed round for another drink of water. Once we had washed our faces and hands, we were ready to start work again. Throughout the afternoon I trekked through the open forest counting and marking mendal after mendal until counting suddenly ended - abruptly. Further up the slope in the thicker forest came a deep rumbling noise, like the gurgling of some large giants' stomach after he had consumed at large meal. The woodcutter and I stood in silence and as I glanced at him and understanding my unasked question he answered "Njovu".

I strained my eyes through the trees I couldn't see elephants but the rumblings sounded like they were really close. In a whisper I asked how far away they were.

"Pafupi" he whispered, saying that they were close, never taking his eyes away from the direction of the sounds.

Up the slope and to our left were a small outcrop of boulders and quietly, almost tip-toeing I followed the woodcutter to these boulders. As we gently scrambled up to the top of the largest rock I again strained to see the elephants. They were still rumbling but we couldn't see them. I knew that trying to get any closer would have be madness as we would not have stood a chance if they had run in our direction and the woodcutter knew this better than me, so we quietly returned to counting the remaining few mendals and went back to another cup of water. I spent the rest of the afternoon walking through the open forest lower down the mountainside from where we had heard the elephants counting the last few mendals till each woodcutter's weeks work had been accounted for. I then thanked them for the lunch and the honey, said my goodbyes and then the guide and I rode off back to the farm.

Back at the farm I compared the mendals the woodcutters had said they had cut and what I had actually counted that day and my count was short, not by a lot, but it was short. I presented my findings to Jorge, who shrugged knowingly.

"But Jorge, they're pinching from you!" I repeated.

"Rupe, don't worry. We'll have riot on our hands if we are not careful, it's not that important. I just wanted you to learn that you need to check everything they tell you because they may not be as honest as you or me."

I learnt another valuable lesson: Check everything, don't cause a riot, don't go too close to elephants and don't eat too much honey or you will get a headache.

CHAPTER 44

FLIED DAYS

I soon realised that there was a lot to learn about growing tobacco and I remember once envying an old Greek farmer who had been farming tobacco in Namwera for 31 years.

"Sure, thirty-one years is a long time," he told me, "but seeing as the tobacco plant has a life cycle of one year that is only really thirty-one experiences of growing the crop. Not a lot really." He probably knew more about tobacco than most farmers and I respected his modesty.

"Field Days" were good ways to pick other farmers brains and pick up some tricks from them. These Field Days were organised by the local Agricultural Liaison Officer or ALO. An ALO was usually an experienced ex-farmer who was employed by the banks to lend advice to their customer/farmers who had borrowed large sums of money to enable them to grow the crop for that year. The ALO would periodically visit the farmer and make sure that he was not making any fatal errors and to make sure that he grew as high quality of tobacco as possible thus getting the best sale at the auctions at the end of the year so he could pay the bank back. They were safeguarding the banks interests really. In Namwera the National Bank ALO was David Ball.

Dave and his wife Doreen lived in a house on Estate 2 that the bank leased from SC. Dave was a lovely guy approaching his sixties, I guess. He was English by birth but you'd never have thought it. If you got to know him, he was a really interesting guy. He had hitch-hiked from London to Cape Town at the age of nineteen. If you keep in mind that this was at a time before the overland lorries we have now, he had done it the hard way.

Anyway, back to Field Days. These were when a designated farmer would open his farm for the day to allow other farmers in the region to see how he farmed, for the farmer to seek advice from the ALO or the other visiting farmers if he so wished. It was a good place, if you kept your eyes open to pick up some little tricks that most other farmers didn't do. The problem with Field Days was deciding which areas of the farm to show, which fields to allow the competition to see. If you showed them your worst field, a real problem area, then they would all laugh at you. If you let them see what you thought was your best field and the ALO tore it apart then they would laugh at you. It was a tricky situation. If you didn't allow Field Days on your farm, then everyone thought you had something to hide, a real secret weapon that you wouldn't let them see.

Before Jorge hosted his Field Day, we spent weeks deciding where to take the farmers and where not to take them. I remember Jorge moving cured tobacco so the good stuff was hidden and "the shitty stuff" was put on view. It was all very cloak and dagger, like a game of poker, bluff and double bluff. I couldn't see the sense in it to be honest. If you had shit show it, if you had good stuff show it, you would all meet at the auction floors. I think to Jorge it was a bit of a game, fooling the farmers that he had a rotten crop that year, so they would laugh behind his back; only to be shocked when he got to the auction floor and presented bale after bale of grade one tobacco.

Before the Field Day Jorge had asked me to mingle with the other farmers to see if I could catch any comments they made about his farm. The farmers and visitors usually all arrived at the farmhouse then we would all drive off to the designated first field, three or four farmers to a vehicle. One farmer named Taki asked if I was going with him so I agreed and jumped into the front with him and his son Thanasi. Doreen, who never missed a Field Day climbed on the back with two other farmers and off we went to the first field. We hadn't travelled more than half a mile when we started weaving and drifting all over the road.

"Dad, you ok?" Thanasi asked.

"Yeah, fine" came the unconvincing reply. We then narrowly avoided going straight at a corner, which was thanks to Thanasi grabbing the steering wheel at the last minute and shouting at his dad.

"What the hell's wrong with you!" he demanded.

I just thought it was just Taki having a bit of fun.

"Take a look in the back" said Taki. So Thanasi and I both turned around to look over our shoulders and through the back of the cab window. It took us both a few seconds to see what Taki was on about but finally we saw. There was Doreen sitting there in the middle of the bench seat with her skirt pulled up to her knee, her legs apart and no knickers! Thanasi and I spun our heads back to the front.

"Oh shit Dad!" Thanasi yelled, "It's a bit early in the day for me to see Granny Fanny". He adjusted Taki's rear view mirror down. "There, now you can't see either! Maybe now you might just get us to the field without having an accident!"

We all laughed.

On arrival at the field Thanasi and I decided we had seen enough of Doreen for one day, so elected to find another driver. Taki certainly had no trouble finding our replacements; at last count I think he had six in the front of the cab. Thanasi and I had a light lunch that day. I think Doreen knew what she was doing, and probably quite fancied Taki.

I got on really well with Dave Ball; he was always there to give sound advice on all things Namwerarean, farming or otherwise. One day shortly after the Field Day I paid him a visit, checking with him beforehand to make sure it would be ok, I told him I was starting to have second thoughts about going to agricultural college in England and thought South Africa might be a better option since they would teach me subjects relating to African farming. I told him I was also having doubts about going to college at all. The farmers in Malawi hadn't been to college and they were doing very well thank you!

"Now you listen here Rupert," Dave began as we shared a cold one, "firstly you must get qualified. You may not always want to be a farmer but that bit of paper will show anyone that you are not stupid. You may want to get into engineering or whatever and that paper will show you have a mental capacity to be taught something, retain it and recall it when required. A qualification is everything." He paused and raised his eyebrows as if to say, are you following me?" Before I could reply he continued.

"England or South Africa?" again he paused, "England and I'll tell you why. Sure, right now you want to farm in Malawi but you may decide to move, you may get offered a job in the States or Australia. Neither of them will accept a qualification from South Africa, not with the present climate. A British quali-fication will be recognised and accepted anywhere in the world." He stopped.

The message had been received and understood. Dave had a way of making the answer so easy that you were always ashamed that you had gone to him with the question in the first place. Sadly, Dave and his wife moved on to another posting and I wouldn't see them again.

CHAPTER 45

I t was now the 8th of June 1981 and I'd been on the farm for eight months, but in that time, I'd grown from a schoolboy into a young man. I'd done my groundwork, it was now time to go off to Agricultural College in England, get qualified, get my "bit of paper", as Dave Ball had put it. Then get back to Malawi, and hopefully back to Namwera as fast as I could.

Before I left, Jorge got the farm workers together and told them that I was leaving the farm to go to college in England but that I would be back. He explained that I was going to a college, similar to Bunda College, Malawi's Agricultural College, and that I would remember all that the farm staff had taught me. I looked out at the sea of faces. There was Gerald the truck driver, Juwao who had taught me to weld, Majidu who had taught me to driver a tractor and the one-eyed cattle boy Smosh who had taught me how to milk by hand.

Jorge asked them not be sad that their friend was leaving because he knew I would be back. I then said thank you to them all and said goodbye. Jorge then took me back to the house and made me go out of the back door of the house three times, locking the door each time. "This way it will make sure you come back, its a Greek thing." He said and then we headed for the car.

When Jorge dropped me at my parents' house in Blantyre he handed me two envelopes. The one which was not sealed Jorge asked me to open there and then. It contained a personal letter from him and attached to the letter was a cheque, a thank you for all my hard work. I was very emotional.

"You've earned it and more!" Jorge said.

I opened the second envelope after Jorge had left. It contained a letter of reference for me to hand to the College in England. As I read the letter, I felt proud of what Jorge had written.

"All the time he was here he proved to be very hard working, obedient, keen and honest....his mind is set on following agriculture as his career and I am also certain he will succeed...I therefore do not hesitate to recommend him to any institution."

My pride in the letter was not shared by the family. Not because it hadn't said enough or was worded wrong, which it wasn't. It was just if they were proud, they couldn't tell me or show it.

I think mother said something along the lines of me being used as cheap labour! I blocked her words out and sat in my room to read and re-read the letter.

A few days later I met some friends in Blantyre and they asked me what it was like working in Namwera for Jorge. At the time my answer was short, and non-informative.

"I didn't work for him, I worked with him" was my answer.

This was in fact true; I had gone there to learn and by working alongside Jorge I was able to learn from the best. If I had worked for him, he would not have been able to share his knowledge and insight with me. The relationship would have been completely different, and Jorge again knew that. I had always maintained a code of conduct while at Jorge's. I never

246

spoke about my time there, or what Jorge did, how he farmed or his pearls of wisdom. I would always get interrogated by the other Greeks on how Jorge farmed, what he did, fertiliser mixes, how he grew his tobacco seedlings etc, but I never spoke. He protected me and in my small way I protected him. My answer to questioning Greeks was always the same.

"I don't know, he never tells me shit!"

Following Jorge with my little note book not only did I learn how to grow tobacco and run a farm, but the lessons I learnt from Jorge would and have stayed with me all my life and have made me the person, some would say successful person, I am today.

There are some that will have read about my time on the farm, or have been witness to it who will condemn Jorge for his treatment of me. To them I would just like to say the following:

Jorge and his wife took me onto their farm and into their home purely on the recommendation of a friend. They treated me like family, like one of their own sons. I was never hungry, I never got sick, I had a bath every day, and my clothes were always clean and ironed. Whenever I went to town Jorge always made sure that I had some money in my pocket. I am embarrassed by my mothers' attitude for the way she saw my time with Jorge. My family never thanked Jorge for what he and his family had done for me. They never sent even a penny for my upkeep in the whole eight months and that horrifies me even today. I am so sorry. I owe Jorge and his family a huge debt of thanks for what they did for me. The lessons, their kindness and their protection in those eight months have always stayed with me and not a day goes by when I do not think of that time and draw on the knowledge and wisdom that Jorge passed on to me. It was some of the happiest eight months of my life. I would do it all again if I had the chance, only this time I would ask more questions and try to learn even more. I am eternally grateful to Jorge and his wife for what they did and always will be.

ASKHAM BRYAN COLLEGE OF AGRICULTURE & HORTICULTURE

YORKSHIRE, ENGLAND

Askham Bryan College is a specialist land-based college based in Askham Bryan, York, England. It was built in 1936, but not opened until after World War II as the Yorkshire Agricultural Institute.

The college runs courses in Agriculture, Animal Management, Veterinary Nursing, Equine Management, Engineering, Motor Sport, Horticulture, Arboriculture, Floristry, Countryside Management, Outdoor Adventure Sport, Sports Development, Coaching and Fitness, Uniformed Public Services and Foundation Vocational Programmes.

The college farm covers 1,022 acres (414 ha) and supports three farms:

- Westfield Farm which accommodates a 250 Holstein Friesian dairy herd and the National Beef Training Centre.

- East Barrow Farm which houses the college Equine Department with 53 horses and Animal Management Department.

- Headley Hall Farm which is the arable farm formerly of the University of Leeds.

Newton Rigg College, based in Penrith, Cumbria, is also part of Askham Bryan College. It also has centres in Leeds, Newcastle, Middlesbrough, Guisborough, Bradford, Wakefield, Scarborough and Penrith.

Alumni include Geoffrey Smith, horticulturalist, writer, broadcaster and TV presenter on Gardeners World (1980 to 1982).

CHAPTER 46

I t was decided by mother and Jim, well probably mother since she did most of the family organisation, that I would go to a Yorkshire based college and that she would apply for a grant for me from the County Council. She had heard that grants were available for students within the county and mother set about proving to them that although I only lived in Yorkshire for ten days after my birth, I was indeed a Yorkshire man. After much correspondence she somehow managed it but the County Council said they would only pay my tuition fees, accommodation and extras like clothing and equipment would have to be funded by us. She accepted this arrangement and set about finding a college who would give me a place. There were a number of agricultural colleges in Yorkshire and finally Askham Bryan wrote back saying that they would except me, which I suppose was handy as it was close to my Grandfather "if anything went wrong", my mother's words, not mine.

So, the family and I made the trip to the UK and to Greetland. We had received a list of clothing that I would need for college and it was endless, white lab coat for science, white lab coat for dairy, white peaked hat for dairy, blue boiler suit for pigs and sheep, steel toe cap boots, Wellington boots, even a folding magnifying glass. The list just went on and on.

At the beginning of September my grandfather drove mother and I out to Askham Bryan. The day was a bit of a blur, but I remember just getting the key for my room and being left on my own as quickly as possible. As mother and my grandfather left there were no real goodbyes, of course I got the firm handshake from Tom Moore. The firm squeeze of his hand felt reassuring to me, like a confidence which flowed into me through his hand; as did his secretly transferred ten-pound note that was concealed in his hand. After they had gone, I slowly walked back to my accommodation block which was called Iburndale. I was alone again.

I sat on my bed looking around the small 5-foot by 8-foot room. Everything was built in, the desk, wardrobe, the cupboards, even the bed. I was used to free standing furniture and it felt like an institution, which I guess it was. In one corner was a sink with a mirror above it. I got up and turned on the water from both taps, I don't really know why or what I expected to see, maybe I expected to see brown water come out like in Africa.

I felt suddenly very alone. I opened my door and went back out into the corridor and had a look at the kitchen that was for use by all eight rooms in the block. Although the college had a huge dining room in the main building where we take all our meals, I guess the kitchen was more of a social meeting point for the eight students, where we could meet for coffee and pass the time of day. Downstairs were a few more rooms but the area was taken up mainly by the shower facilities, I'd never used a shower before and they impressed me. To one side of the shower room were tall metal lockers, labelled with the same numbers as the rooms and my number eight-room key also opened my locker.

After some days I realised that each accommodation block

was made up of agricultural as well as horticultural students, Agrics and Hortics as we were known. I also realised that my block was a recent addition to the campus; some students were housed upstairs in the main building, which was dark and reminded me of saints, with old worn dark doors and furniture that showed the years of use and the abuse inflicted on it by ages of previous students. There was another accommodation block that was probably ten years old; it had that 1970's look to it. I was happy to have my room in the new block.

The first real day at college, one that we sat down in a lecture room was to sit an exam, "to teach you how much you don't know," the vice-principle had said. I got 2%! The next lowest was about 35% I think. Well it was on potatoes, sheep and wheat to name but a few, things I knew nothing about. The VP was horrified with me. He asked me to stay behind afterwards.

"Mr Prickett, if you think you are here to waste my time and take the place of an Englishman who genuinely deserves the place you are mistaken." I opened my mouth to tell him I was born in Sheffield but he held up his hand to stop me and continued. "I'm going to overlook this mark today, but at the end of each week for the rest of the year I am going to give you a test. To stay here you must pass the test every Friday, fail it once at any time and you're out!"

There was no point in trying to tell him I knew about things like tobacco, maize, and coffee; and avoiding elephants and shooting lions. I knew that wasn't his problem, it was mine. So, I agreed. I realised that I would only have a week to catch up with the other students so I spent the next seven days and most nights in the college library studying "English" crops and farming practices. When the next Friday test came for me, I passed and the look of disappointment on his face was obvious. Suffice to say I passed every Friday test and kept my place at Askham Bryan.

The other thing that he took great pleasure in informing me about was the way the exams worked at the end of the year. I would sit the National Certificate in Agriculture and if I passed, I'd be awarded an NCA. There was also a second exam set by the college. To pass this you had to pass each subject within the course, arable, mechanics, driving and accountancy. Livestock would then be split into Cattle, sheep and pigs and you would have to pass each. Fail a single subject, and you failed the college exam. Slightly unfair to say the least but that's how it was. We had the same lecturer for Accountancy and Sheep, a blond-haired witch. I can't remember her name either but I saw no point in accountancy, hey get an accountant; and sheep, well they would never survive lion attacks so I had crossed them off my list of must haves in the livestock wish-list. I really struggled to get my head round both subjects, plus I was terrible at maths anyway.

I muddled through.

The main building at Askham Bryan College

CHAPTER 47

A WARM DRINK

Although I hated the sheep lecturer, I got on well with the old shepherd who looked after the colleges' flock of sheep. I can't remember his real name as we always called him "Shep". He and his wife lived in an old stone cottage on the college estate. He was in his late sixties I guess, so he had seen a good many students come and go and wasn't easily fooled by students thinking that they were wiser and smarter than him; he'd seen it all before. He walked with a stiff leg that caused him to limp as he walked. The students would mimic him as they followed him to the fields but he would tell me later, "They think that I don't see them, but I see the buggers."

I liked Shep, he had done his time and I was about the only one of my group to show him any respect. In the late summer of our first couple of weeks at the college, we had to repair a few areas of the sheep fields where there were breaks in the electric fence. Shep took three or four of us round the field to find the breaks. We found one area where the nettles hand grown so large that they were brushing against the fence and shorting it out.

"We'll have to get those nettles shifted." Shep said and nominated Jason to run back to the farm and bring a couple of sickles so that we could cut the nettles down.

I already had Jason summed up and knew that he would see the task of getting the sickles as an excuse for a holiday. He would probably get back to farm; have a cup of tea, a sit down and possibly even a bloody nap knowing him!

The time slipped slowly by and Jason didn't appear with the sickles. Shep was beginning to realise that he had some "dead wood" in his charge. I was also getting pretty fed up by this stage too. At the end I lost my cool before Shep did.

"Oh for Christ sake, get out of the way, I'll do it!" I cursed as I waded into the nettle patch and began ripping them up with my bare hands.

Within minutes the nettles were in a pile behind me and the fence was free. I turned around to see the two other students just standing there in disbelief and Shep was just staring at me.

"What?" I asked.

"Nothing," said Shep but turned to the students and said "There you are boys, that's how they do it in Africa."

"Oh very funny" I said smiling at Shep.

I was so angry that I didn't feel the nettle stings but as soon as I calmed down my hands and arms were burning and full of red blotches. We met Jason on the road as we walked back and boy did he get a revving from Shep.

The nettle incident had sealed my fate with Shep. Any job in the future that he needed doing I was his man, he would lean against me and say out of the corner of his mouth, "I know these fuckers will be sat on their arses as soon as my back is turned." He was right, half the time they were. Being Shep's only really dependable worker had its advantages. Shep would call me aside as the other students walked back to the accommodation block to get cleaned up, "My wife made you this, its apple." And under the tea towel would be an apple pie. I would get a fruit pie most weeks.

His wife worked in the college kitchens and would be dishing food out in the dining room. As I queued up three times a day, she would look at me and without a word she'd give me an extra spoon of this or that. Sometimes certain departments within the farm would keep us working longer than planned, especially the dairy and by the time we got to the dining room for breakfast the sausage tray would be empty and scraps of what was breakfast remaining in the other trays. Mrs Shep would see me and disappear into the back and return with a plate piled high with a full English breakfast. "I've saved you this," she'd say.

Sure, I used to get stick from my fellow students but I used to tell them it was their choice, they could have food saved if they knuckled down and gave 100% to the work that was asked of them. I wasn't licking Shep's arse, I was just doing 100% of what was asked of me.

I'd worked in Nam, where you gave 100% or walked home from the field, where you had to work hard to keep up with the Africans. The work on the college farm was kindergarten in comparison. Most of the other guys hadn't done a real day's work in their lives.

Sheps' favourite comment was, "Thank fuck there isn't a bloody war on, hey Rupe. God help us if these blokes were on the front line," he'd say. "Ooooh my boots are too tight, I'm hungry, my gun's too heavy, I miss my mummy. We would all be speaking German now if you'd all been fighting for us." He'd continue. Whether he was in the Second World War I don't know but he didn't fancy my fellow students' chances if there was a war.

He had a wicked sense of humour too and I recall one freezing December morning, I think the night temperature had dropped to -18 degrees. We had been shovelling a path in the snow that had drifted on the farm road to about 3 feet deep. We worked so hard that day that I had already stripped down to my t-shirt and working kept the cold away; it was bitingly cold when you stopped shovelling. Not all the students were so determined at getting the work done as fast as possible and they were set on moaning and whinging the morning away rather than working. Shep was soon tired of the complaints and "marked their cards". Later in the day as we walked back to the farm buildings Shep was lagging behind a bit and I looked back to see what was holding him up. He was stood facing a wall of one of the farm buildings. He caught my eye and realised he had been seen, quick as a flash he yelled out to one of the whingers,

"Hey Keith, you still cold, do you want a warm drink?"

Keith was almost blue with cold and expecting the offer of a mug of tea was quick to take Shep up on his offer.

"Here you are then Keith, get your mug." He replied and with that Shep turned to face Keith, continuing to pee as he walked towards Keith. We were in stitches, but Keith didn't see the funny side.

My accommodation at College. My room is top right window that's open.

CHAPTER 48

IS GRASS A CROP?

After a few weeks at college a guy came up to me as I sat quietly eating my supper one evening.

"I went to that school." He said pointing at my t-shirt. I was wearing my St Andrews T-shirt.

"Yeah right, leave me alone." I just wanted to eat in peace.

"No, really I did!" he insisted.

I again looked up from my plate, "I've had a long day and I'm not in the mood, go and disturb someone else. I'm eating."

Then he asked the question, "Do you know Gray Bowden?" My jaw dropped.

"Yes" I said, knowing that this question changed the intrusion.

The guy turned out to be Mike Ashman, he had been a good friend of Gray's at Saints and because of that Mike was also a fellow snake man. He had lived in Limbe for years as a kid but now his parents lived in Zambia. It was good to meet a fellow African, and a Malawian at that. We ended up talking to each other in Chichewa whenever we would meet. He was in his final year of a three-year Ordinary National Diploma in Agriculture.

We drank a few beers in the college bar in our year together, talking about Malawi. Great times.

Early on in the course I had a few confrontations with authority, not that I was fighting against it, it was just that I believed the authority to be wrong on a number of occasions. I had already upset the VP with my low exam mark but had cleared the bar set by him, which pissed him off. I just can't remember the idiots name for the life of me, but it's not important, I bet he still remembers mine. He was our arable lecturer. He was a little man and there, I guess, laid his problem! In one of his first lectures he asked us to name some crops, sort of to get the ball rolling on the subject he was going to spend the rest of the year lecturing us on. Various crops were suggested until one guy said grass.

"Grass is not a crop" bellowed the VP.

I thought for a moment and then stuck my hand up, "Yes it is." I said.

"Grass is NOT a crop!" he repeated.

I should have let it go here but you learn, "Silage" I said. "You prepare the soil, sow the seed, add fertiliser, harvest it, and then feed it to cattle. It therefore must be a crop." I stopped.

There was much agreement within the room but he was having none of it. As a near riot erupted, I sank down into my seat and watched him get into a slanging match with some of my fellow students who had picked up my baton and run with it. He never backed down over the grass thing and the class continually raised the subject at every available opportunity. The VP blamed me for starting it all off, which I guess I did but it was his pig-headed stubbornness that kept it going. The subject got to the hearts of my class to such a level that several months later the VP woke up one morning to find the words GRASS IS A CROP in four-foot-high letters burnt into his manicured front lawn with weed killer. Of course, he accused me, although I had nothing to do with that prank.

He also blamed me for the four-foot high letters painted in white on the roof of the main building saying "SID'S CAFE". Since the lettering faced the road and the road just happened to be the A64 from Scarborough to Leeds, a large number of heavy goods lorries soon started to pull up in the college car park with burly truck drivers demanding a full English breakfast.

He also blamed me for the 18-foot-long straw bailer that was taken to bits part by part and re-assembled in the middle of the dining room overnight. What a sight, the bright red bailer sat there in the middle of this vast sea of tables, full of students eating their breakfast and the Principle and VP sitting at their tables on the stage looking down at this sight. I still believe that grass IS a crop, and that I was right and he is still wrong.

Years later I caught the British TV programme Country File where they happened to mention that grass was a crop – the college VP would be turning in his grave.

CHAPTER 49

A JOKE TOO FAR

Most pranks were not just restricted towards the staff. Students were not safe from attacks by other students. For some it was just a holiday camp for the year.

I was out for a Sunday morning run with a friend when a Land Rover screamed past us and disappeared over the crest in the road.

"Shit! Run!" yelled my mate and jumped the hedge at the side of the road and ran for his life through the field.

I just stopped running and stood there, thinking what the hell was going on. Just then the Land Rover reappeared back over the crest, and reversed at high speed. It stopped feet from me and about five blokes I had never seen before grabbed me and threw me into the back of the vehicle. I fought and struggled but I was going nowhere. The Land Rover then drove off with me captive.

After a few minutes the Land Rover skidded to a halt and I was dragged kicking from the back. We had parked on the grass bank of a village pond. On the far bank was the quintessential English pub, wooden benches outside, with people enjoying their pints of beer. Before I had time to work things out or shout for help I had two blokes holding my arms and two holding my feet and after much swinging I was tossed into the pond, to the cheers and claps of the drinking pub-goers.

The pond was about five feet deep, one foot of it being green water and the bottom four foot being a mixture of mud and decomposing duck crap.

After much coughing and spluttering I emerged from the muddy slime onto the grass bank. Before I got to my feet the guys piled into the Land Rover and drove off, leaving me to endure the cheers, applause and whistles coming from the pub. There was nothing to do but for me to run back to the college. I ran as much as I could through fields since I was brown with mud. I arrived back at my hall of residence and bolted for the shower. As I cleaned off the mud and slime my fingers caught something sharp on my lower back and I pulled a piece of glass from my lower back and another piece from my upper buttocks. The shower water turned red around my feet. Judging by the glass I must have landed on a broken bottle; I was now mad. I got cleaned up and dressed the deep cuts as best I could. Hours later I found my mate who had abandoned me. It seemed he was familiar with this North Yorkshire prank of kidnapping joggers and throwing them into village ponds, I it seemed wasn't.

Most pranks were not as injuring as "being thrown in a pond". There were about three hundred rooms in the residence but only a hundred and fifty different locks, which meant the key for your room also gave you access to someone else's room, it was just a matter of time till you or someone else figured out which room.

They would often switch your room with your opposite key holder so when you opened the door it was not "your" room; they had switched everything down to the contents of the rubbish bin.

The other trick was to wait till you went away for mid-term

or Christmas and sprinkle grass seed onto the carpet of your room, then lovingly water it and feed it for the whole of the mid-term break. When you came back you had a foot high grass growing out of the floor of your room. It's funny now, but at the time it wasn't.

They would also empty the contents of your shampoo bottle and replace it with hair dye. They even entered one room while the guy was sleeping and sprayed a bronze stripe across the sleeping guys pillow and head so he had to sport the bronze stripe for days till he could get to the barbers to have it cut out.

Guys would go out to the car park to go home for the weekend and their car would be missing. They would finally track it down to a field on the college farm where it had been placed length-ways between two trees with the farm's forklift, which had now also mysteriously disappeared.

A guy reversed his car out of the parking space and a chain that had been attached to his bumper and fixed to a fence post, ripped his bumper clean off.

One bloke had been having an evening of passion with his girlfriend who had come to visit him for the weekend. Exhausted the two of them had fallen asleep in each other's arms. Suddenly, the boyfriend is woken by a hand around his throat. As he struggles and fights to loosen the grip around his throat his girlfriend just lays there screaming her head off. Eventually the boyfriend wins the struggle and pulls a fellow student out from under his bed! The bugger had been laid under it all the time and had heard the two lovers most intimate moments. The boyfriend throws the student out of the room and eventually calms his hysterical girlfriend. They fall asleep again. Some time goes by when a hand gripping his throat again wakes the boyfriend, yes you guessed it, there was a second bloke under the bed. Needless to say, the girlfriend never stayed again.

They tied one bloke to one of the calf pens and dropped his

trousers and pants; then they brought a bucket of milk and dipped his "John Thomas" in the milk. Then a new-born calf was brought in and encouraged to suck on this screaming bloke's milk tasting penis. The calf sucked away for some considerable time, trying to get milk till the blokes' screams were blood curdling and he was set free.

Most of the students' energies, when not being taken out on fellow students or the staff, were vented at Harper Adams, the rival college. They would raid our college in the night and steal a plough from us. We would then go to the local MacDonald in the night and steal the children's slide in the shape of a giraffe and leave in on the Harper Adams Lawn. They would then retaliate by stealing an eight-foot high Michelin man stolen from the local tyre outlet and suspend it from the flagpole. And so on. It was all kind of funny at first, but wore thin as the months progressed.

By the time I was thrown in the duck pond I had just about had enough of the childish games. These blokes had come from their dad's farm, and the highlight of these idiots' days was to grab a few beers and walk the wall, totally pointless so I would always excuse myself and get back to my books.

Whether they passed the course or not they would be still going back to their dad's farm. I didn't have that luxury; this course was important. I decided that I would pay a visit to the Vice Principle and see if there was anything he could do to get the childish pranks to stop.

"Look Mr Prickett, you are not a child anymore, I am not here to sort your problems out. It is really your own problem, not mine, you will have to fight your own battles and sort it out." He said and gestured me out of his office.

I didn't have to wait long before I was "disturbed" again. I was laid face down on the grass outside my hall of residence. I was on my tummy reading a textbook and didn't hear the approach of another student armed with a waste paper bucket full of steaming water. Needless to say I took all the VP had told me and "fought my own battle". Within hours I was summoned to the VP's office.

"What the hell do you think you are doing?" he exploded. "You can't just go around punching people, this is not the Bronx!"

"Sir, I came in to see you, asking for you to deal with this and you said I should deal with it myself, fight my own battles. Well I have, it's dealt with."

He was fuming, "If this happens again, I'll throw the book at you, you'll be out of this college so fast your feet won't touch the ground, do I make myself clear?"

"Yes Sir." I said trying to sound like I meant it.

Suffice to say it didn't happen again, mainly due to the fact that after my show of force people then left me alone.

Duck pond at Askham Richard

CHAPTER 50

I SEE RICHARD FOR THE LAST TIME

At half-term everyone went home for the holiday except the four "Africans", a guy from the Seychelles who was studying horticulture and the three "Agrics", me from Malawi, Barry from South Africa, Mike Ashman, whose family now lived in Zambia. We stayed and worked in the college farm for a bit of extra cash. Christmas was the only time we all went home, well they all went back to Africa, I went to Sunny Greetland! It was a chance for me to spend time with my Grandfather and I enjoyed that. We had gotten closer since I had been at college.

One cold, snowy December evening, while I sat watching TV with Grandad Tom, there was a knock at the door.

"Who the dickens is that at this time of night?" Tom asked, even though it was barely 7pm. He got up to answer the door expecting to see carol singers.

"Blazers!" he gasped, "come inside, you must be fair frozen." He said as he stepped backward into the lounge. "It's Richard!"

I was shocked; he had not told me he was coming up from Sussex, not that he needed to. Richard stepped into the house wearing just a black cotton zipped jacket and was as white as a sheet.

"Sit yourself down in front of the fire, have you eaten? My grandfather asked him, then not waiting for Richard to reply he said, "I'll fix you some grub." A few minutes later Richard was tucking into a plate of fried corn beef and onions, gravy, boiled potatoes, two slices of buttered bread and a large mug of tea. Mother would always claim that her father didn't like Richard but it was rubbish. Tom Moore didn't mince his words and boy did you know if he didn't like you and I can say that he was always happy to see Richard. Tom reminded us of when he had come out to Malawi and about the day he met the Snake Man. It was good to remember the old times.

After a few hours of chatting Richard and I excused ourselves, and after saying goodnight to Tom we both headed next door. Richard produced a bottle of Bacardi Rum and sitting in front of the gas fire we chatted well into the night, while slowly consuming the rum.

At the time I was a bit surprised to see Richard have such an appetite for the rum but I suppose at college I had drunk a few more beers than I had when Richard and I were kids so thought nothing of it at the time. I would remember that evening many years later but for now I was just glad to see Richard and talk about Africa that right now as we sat in front of the fire to stay warm, seemed a million miles away.

The next day was spent chatting and having lunch with Tom. Later in the afternoon we went to the local pub for a beer and then around 3pm Richard caught the bus into Halifax and then the train back down to Sussex. It had been a flying visit but it was good to see him.

Soon the Christmas break was over and it was back to college, at least now it was the home stretch, the end was in sight. Only six months to go and I'd be back in Malawi.

No much really happened of any significance. I continued to

feel like I was from a different planet compared to the rest of my fellow students. Oh, I did get a letter from an ex-pupil from St Andrews called Suzanna. She was in the Far East. At first, I was shocked to get her letter, sure I knew who she was, she had been one of the sexiest girls in school; well in my opinion anyway, but why was she writing to me? I wrote back but I didn't ask that question, just assumed that my record at the 100m backstroke still carried a certain amount of kudos but I can't be sure. We continued to write to each other for the rest of my year at Askham Bryan. Her letters ended in more and more kisses each time she wrote. I started to think that maybe she wanted more than just being a pen pal.

The time for the final exams eventually arrived. I thought I had done enough studying and although at times the course seemed totally pointless, I remembered Dave Ball's words and knuckled down. So after the exams I felt quietly confident that I would pass the course. A few days after my final exam the vice principal called me into his office, I hadn't threatened to punch anyone lately so wasn't quite sure why he wanted to see me.

"I've just been checking your file and it appears that you only completed nine months of the required twelve months on a farm before you came to this college." He said without even looking up from the file. "We require twelve months, not eleven, ten or nine, TWELVE MONTHS Mr Prickett. Do you understand?"

I really didn't know what to say so in true Yorkshire fashion I said "nout".

He continued, "So what I have decided to do in this unusual case is hold onto your results. You will leave here and work on a farm in the UK for three months. When you have completed three months you will present to me a letter from the Farm Manager stating that you have completed without a break THREE MONTHS. I will then release your results and possible certificate to you."

I stood there and within seconds had my speech prepared, and it went like this.

"You listen to me shit-head, and listen good. I spent nine months in Namwera, most of it working alongside Africans, matching them hoe stroke for hoe stroke in temperatures of 120 degrees Fahrenheit. I worked for 3 months without a day off and without seeing another European except the owners of the farm. I have walked through forests full of elephants while counting "firewood mendals". I'd been on a farm where lions ate our cattle. I have eaten battered cows' brain and intestine soup for lunch. I have done more in my nine months in Namwera than any of these other students whose time was done on daddies' farm, where they probably didn't even lift a bloody shovel. So, if you think you are going to hold on to my results while I go and work on some "poxy" farm in North Yorkshire, well you can shove it up your arse!"

Reality caught hold of me for a second and at the same time Dave Ball spoke in my ear. "You need to get qualified". He was right, so I rearranged the words slightly and said,

"Are you going to find the farm for me to work on or do I have to find my own?" I asked.

"No, you have to find your own, and you can't do one month on one farm and then one month on another. It was to be three months without a break, so if you get fired from one farm you will have to start the three months again on a new farm. Oh by the way, you will have to do the three months whether you have passed or failed, even though I have your results right here." He grinned.

I pushed away the thought of leaping across his desk and giving him a good thumping.

"Fine, no problem, sounds good to me!" I said, "Can I go now?" and walked out before he could reply and before I changed my mind about punching him.

A few days later the term ended, the college photo taken.

The rest of my class graduated without me. I said my goodbyes and I headed off to Greetland to search for a farm to work on for three months.

Number 27 Briscoe Lane, and No 29 where my grandfather lived.

Digging the garden at No 27

CHAPTER 51

MANHOOD

Finding a farm to work on was not easy but Grandad Tom made a few enquiries and I managed to find a place. I won't bore you with the whole story of this farm but just a few details. It was on the other side of Halifax at Park Nook Farm, Southowram run by a Mr J.H Boyle. He also ran a haulage business and was hardly on the farm, thus the farm was in the hands of his wife, who spent most of her time on the sun bed or shopping. I therefore got my orders from Boyles' fifteen-year-old son. The hours were six till six although the kid found work for me to do that kept me on the farm till sometimes ten at night. I worked six days a week and for this I got £15 per week, no food, or accommodation! I stayed at number 27 Briscoe Lane, which was owned by my parents and next door to my grandad. I could only afford the bus fare one way, so would walk the four miles there in the morning and get the bus home at the end of the day.

The £15 was just enough to last 7 days for bus fare and food. Food was bread, butter and jam, some cheese and that was about all. By the end of the week I would have a couple of pence change in my pocket. I would fill my pockets with grains of wheat from the grain shed on the farm and eat this as I worked. After milking the dairy herd, I would wait a few hours for the milk and cream to separate out, then using a litre jug I would lift a few jugs of the cream off and drink it there and then before the milk tanker arrived to siphon the milk from the tank.

On one Saturday Mr Boyle had not returned to the farm so I went to see his wife to collect my wages.

"Oh, I'm sorry. He didn't leave anything with me. He will be back on Tuesday so he will pay you then." and she closed the door.

That was it, I had no money, and Mr Boyle didn't actually come back till Thursday. I had to walk both ways to the farm and live on the grain and cream for the four days till then.

There were times when I just wanted to punch the son, but couldn't, I'd gone through too much to throw it all away. I had lived in Namwera so I wasn't going to let this family of bastards get me down. Even when young Boyle took the farm car with me as a passenger and drove us headlong into a dry-stone wall at 40 mph I kept my cool, well almost. My knee dented the dashboard and the stones from the top of the wall were thrown almost thirty feet. I did a lot of swearing and threatening but managed to keep my hands from wringing his neck there and then.

I just got on with the work till the day finally arrived when my three months were up. Mr Boyle gave me my letter and my final week's wages of £15 and not a penny more. I never visited the farm again but I always planned to go back and give him a piece of my mind but I don't think it's worth it. He will get his dues and so will his delinquent son.

I sent the Boyle's letter off to the college and about a week later I got an envelope through the mail, postmarked York. It was my exam results and I went next door to see grandad Tom.

"Well by jingo open it lad!" he said with great excitement.

I was not as excited as he was, I was actually feeling sick inside in case all the time at Jorge's, all the year at college and the three months at Boyle's had been a total waste of time.

With my Granddad there I opened the large brown envelope. Inside was a certificate, I had passed my National Certificate in Agriculture! I had also passed and received the College Certificate. Yes, I felt pleased, my Grandfather was pleased too, saying he had no doubts in me, but the VP's attitude towards me, and the three months he had just made me endure had spoilt the relief of passing in a way. There was no real celebration that day, but at least now I could go back to Malawi and the year had not been a waste of time.

A few days later I got another letter from Suzanna; she was back in England and was going to be visiting her grandmother in Halifax next week with her mum and dad. She asked if I'd like to meet her in town to spend the day together. Of course, I would, I wasn't stupid, so I wrote back straightaway.

Finally, the day arrived to meet Susanna in town. She hadn't changed a bit, although it had been two years since I'd seen her. We walked around town for a bit and chatted.

"I've arranged with my mother and dad to collect me from your house at 5pm, I hope that's ok?" she said as she put her hand in mine. I looked at my watch, it was one o'clock so I nervously suggested we catch the bus and go to my house now. She agreed and off we went. One thing led to another and we ended up in bed. This was the first time I had slept with a woman and I remember looking in the mirror afterwards to see if I could see a change in me, if my face looked different. It didn't, except I had this stupid grin on my face that stayed there for weeks. The afternoon flew by and soon it was 5pm so I walked her to the top of the road to wait for her parents. I never saw Susanna again but a few years ago we did communicate via email and I thought it time that I came clean about the afternoon and apologised if I was disappointing. She wrote back a kind and reassuring letter saying as she remembered she was far from disappointed. I did blush.

So now armed with my qualification and a real sense of being a man I wrote to mother and Jim. In their reply they enclosed a cheque to pay for the flight back to Malawi. Looking back now I am amazed they sent the money; it was so unlike them. As soon as the cheque had cleared, I bought my ticket and bid my farewells to my Grandfather.

Now here is a funny story. I again had gone through college under the name of Rupert Prickett and was by now so accustomed to it that when I booked the flight back to Malawi, I purchased the airline ticket in the name of Rupert Prickett, as you obviously would. After all it had been my name all through school. It was the name I had used at College, the name that was on my certificates. A few days before my flight my grandfather Tom handed me a brown envelope.

"You'll be needing this, its your passport." he said.

It was only when I arrived at Heathrow, did I realise that my passport said James Rupert Wilkey. Don't ask me how but for some reason the check-in girl didn't pick up on it and I soon found myself sitting on the plane with a ticket in one hand saying Prickett and a passport in the other saying Wilkey. I certainly wouldn't get away with that now.

I also sat there again with my agricultural qualification in the name of Prickett. All this illegal name change by my parents would certainly cause me some problems later in life. But for now I sat on a plane on my way back to Malawi.

A year or two later mother and Jim came back to England to sell the house in Greetland before they moved to South Africa. While clearing the house they found my old farming jacket and were intrigued to find the pockets full of wheat. It was only then that I told them of what life had been like on the Boyle's farm and the lengths I had gone to stave off hunger. I don't think they were too concerned.

In 1989 Amy made the comment to me that "at least mum and Jim paid for you to go to agricultural college!". She was surprised when I told her that the county of Yorkshire had paid for me to go through college, not mother and Jim.

1982-1983

TOBACCO FARMING

NAMWERA

The tobacco industry in Namwera as grown substantially. In 1910 there were just 40 hectares, but rose to 423 ha by 1937. In 1974 nearly 9,300 ha was under tobacco, rising to 38,510 ha by 1982 and is currently about 50,207 ha.

At present, tobacco contributes about 13 percent to the total gross domestic product and generates 23 percent of total tax revenues, accounting for more than 70 percent of the country's export earnings (FAO 2003). Figures for tobacco-related employment range from 650,000 to 2 million out of a total workforce of 5 million (FAO 2003), and estimates show that 70 percent of the working population are indirectly employed in tobacco.

There are three auction houses Malawi - Blantyre-Limbe (south), Lilongwe (central) and Mzuzu (north) and these so far provide the main markets for estate-grown tobacco. Since 1962, the auction houses are under the umbrella of AHL (with ADMARC, TCC and TEAM as board members). AHL asks for a membership fee of US$100,000 so that most of the aspiring Malawian entrepreneurs are denied from participating which is a crying shame.

For the past half decade, prices realised from tobacco on the auction floors have been low. In 2005, government officials and an international lawyer have accused the leaf buying companies in Malawi of price-fixing and monopolistic buying practices (World Bank 2005)

A bigger calamity for Malawi is the dependancy on the natural forests as a source of fire-wood for curing the tobacco. For example, in Namwera where large flue and burley estates concentrate close to forest reserves and the international border, *Brachystegia* forests have drastically reduced from 191,000 to 29,000 ha within 20 years .

CHAPTER 52

FOLLOWING BUFFALO ON FOOT

As the plane touched down at Chileka I thought, "I'm home." But there was no big homecoming.

While I had been at college, Mother and Jim had moved from the house in Sunnyside to a house nearer the school in Nyambadwe. What really annoyed me was that they had emptied my bedroom in the old house but not much of it had seemed to have made it to the new house. This was absolutely typical of them. Stuff I had collected from first arriving in Malawi, skins of snakes, seed pods, an eagle's talon that Richard had given me, it had all be thrown out. They had kept stupid stuff like an old colouring book I had when I was eleven. Maybe it was my fault, maybe I should have been there to tell them what I wanted and what could be thrown away. But hey wait a minute; I couldn't because I was away in England for a year being thrown in duck ponds and eating bloody wheat grains!

I again felt uncomfortable in the house, isolated and alone, like I didn't belong there. I felt even more removed from the family circle than I had before going to Namwera or even college. The family, it seemed, had grown closer together and there was no room for me. I think if they had still been at the old house things would have been different, things would have been familiar to me. But the new house only had three bedrooms so I had to share a room with Isabel. I felt unwanted but kept quiet as usual.

I needed to get away from the house and would normally have gone down the Mudi River to catch snakes but with Richard in the UK I couldn't bring myself to go down there; plus, it would have been a heck of a walk from Nyambadwe! So, I put my thinking cap on and called Mr Bevis at the Primary School as I had heard he was running a school trip that weekend down to Lengwe Game Park in the Lower Shire. I asked if I could catch a lift into the park with the school bus and he agreed so I quickly packed a few things and grabbed my camera and headed off to the park with Mr Bevis and his pupils. Once at the accommodation block within the park I bid my farewell and headed off on foot into the park, which was illegal but Malawi being Malawi, a quick chat to the guards and nobody said a thing. I spent almost all the first day at the main hide over-looking the waterhole and got some great photos of Nyala. I slept that night in the hide and apart from the mosquitos it was a good night. Next morning, I headed off on foot to explore the park.

As I walked through the Lengwe bush I thought about my hero, C. J. P. Ionides. He had been asked by the museum in Nairobi to provide a specimen of an Nyala for the museum. Lengwe is where he chose to come. I imagined him walking here in the same bush and shooting his bull Nyala on the 9th of September 1944. He had sort a guide from a village called Nafisi, near a dense forest. I wondered how Malawi, of Nyasaland must have been all those years ago.

As I walked I picked up lion spoor quite quickly beside a large baobab tree but did not follow it. I then stumbled upon two buffalo bulls and using the dry earth to test the wind direction I was able to get close enough for a photo. I then headed into some thicket bush and stumbled across a lone bull buffalo. It lifted its head to catch the wind and I decided to slowly climb a nearby tree, which I was glad I did. The buffalo slowly walked straight to the tree sniffing the air as it went. From the safety of the tree I was able to look down and get the photo that appears here. Looking back now I guess it was a little mad, to be on foot, and unarmed, following buffalo but it didn't seem an issue to me then.

At the end of the weekend I made my way back to the accommodation block and climbed aboard the mini-bus back to Blantyre. It had been a nice break and a great "welcome back to Africa".

It didn't take Jorge long to find out that I was back in Malawi and he rang me at home. His first question was "had I passed?" He sounded genuinely happy and pleased for me. He then answered my prayers.

"There is a job with me in Namwera if you'd like it?" he said.

"Err, yes please, wow that's tremendous, thanks." I said down the phone. I must have sounded very apologetic but I hadn't meant to sound that way, it was just that I hardly expected Jorge to offer me a "real" job on the farm when I got back. It was my first real job.

"Good, when can you be ready, it's just the Peugeot 504 is at Stansfield Motors and needs to be brought back to the farm? Can you collect it, pick up some bathroom tiles and other bits and bobs then come up to the farm?" he asked.

Wow Jorge was giving me one of his cars to drive, and on my own. I realised things were going to be different now. I was no longer the rookie farmhand; I was now a qualified farmer; I'd done my time and proved myself to Jorge and now was my rewards. Things had changed.

"Sure, no probs." I said, "I'll go and get it this afternoon."

So, I collected the car, picked up the list of supplies that Jorge had read out to me, and brought the car back to the house.

"Whose car's that? Hope it's not going to be sat on the drive for too long!" mother asked with her usual scowl.

"It's Jorge's, he's given me a job back on the farm, I'm leaving in the morning." I said proudly but they did not appear to share my happiness.

"Hope he feeds you better than dried fish this time." She snapped and then walked off. Thank you, mother, for your support.

Within a day or two I was ready and packed. I was glad to leave the house and again felt at peace to be behind the wheel and driving back up to Namwera.

When I arrived at the farm it was like a hero's welcome, the farm ground to a halt. Those Africans who had been there while I was there all came to greet me. The Africans who were new to the farm strained to get a view of me, and asked the old hands who I was. I could see the familiar faces turning to unknown faces and saying "He's Chikwandala."

It was a very emotional day for me.

The old buffalo photographed from up the tree

CHAPTER 53

STUCK IN THE MUD

Most of the Greek farmers were ok to me; they respected me for what I had done in my first eight months on the farm, working alongside the Africans. But there were one or two who disliked me for whatever reason.

One such farmer was a guy nicknamed Bazooki; I knew nothing about him, he had a farm somewhere and by all accounts wasn't that good a farmer, he was also extremely arrogant. Jorge and Chililie had left me alone on the farm to go to town for the week and as I crossed the yard Bazooki pulled up in his vehicle. I greeted him and he just asked where Jorge was. I started to tell him that Jorge was in town, but as I was in mid sentence he just turned his back on me, walked to his car and drove off. I was livid. What an ignorant bastard I thought to myself. Namwera had taught me that all out fights are not worth it and that bidding one's time would always throw up the opportunity to get even and get even with Bazooki I did.

The rains were in full swing, rivers were flooded, and bridges were three to four feet under water, many being washed away. The roads, being dirt, so turned to red sticky mud and if you weren't careful you could very easily wind up in the ditch up to your axles in mud. I had gone to the post office in Namwera to pick up the mail and was about three miles from the farm. The rain was pouring down, real monsoon stuff. As I came around a corner, through the driving rain that the wipers were struggling to clear I saw this 4x4 stuck in the mud. It had taken the corner too fast and the back end had swung out and in trying to correct it the driver had lost the front end and had ploughed the front wheels up to the axels in the mud on the edge of the road. As I peer through the rain, I could see Bazooki stood at the side of his cruiser, covered in mud and waving me down.

"Oh, now the bugger needs me does he?" I thought.

I rolled down my window, stuck my arm out and waved at him back, with a big grin on my face and drove straight past. Jorge's Land Cruiser had a winch so I could have easily pulled him out of the mire that he had got himself into but "fuck-it" and I drove straight past him and back to the farm with the mail.

A few days later Bazooki steamed into the farm at a shocking rate of speed and skidded to a halt in front of the workshop and jumped out. As he marched towards me, I could see he was boiling and I knew what it was about.

"Why the hell did you drive past me the other day? You could see I was stuck in the mud. Why didn't you stop when I waved you down?" he yelled.

I couldn't help myself, this bloke really had no clue, so I said "Waved me down? I just thought you were waving hello."

He almost exploded with rage. "I wasn't waving bloody hello, I was stuck up to my bloody axles, I was there fucking hours! You could have pulled me out!" he yelled again.

The workshop had now stopped work to see what the noise was.

"Yes, I could have. But you know what, next time don't

bloody turn your back on me when I'm talking to you!" and I turned around and walked off.

He just stood there in total disbelief. He then went and found Jorge to give him his sob story. Jorge found it hilarious and didn't really help matters by telling Bazooki "It was your own fault, I warned you not to fuck with him."

Bazooki avoided me after that, which suited me just fine.

CHAPTER 54

LIONS ARE BACK

L ittle had changed on the farm while I was away. The lions were still terrorising the cattle and one night came the familiar tap at the bedroom door "Rupe, get up, lions".

I quickly dressed and followed Jorge out of the house and into the Land Cruiser. This time we waited for the lioness to return to the cow she had killed but after a few hours without success we called it a night and headed back to the house.

The next morning, we went down to survey the scene. Jorge then arranged for the dead cow to be dragged into the open and tied to a tree. A platform was then built about twenty foot in the air between two "A" frames. The plan was to sit on the platform all night and wait for the lioness to come back that night. Having left orders for the platform Jorge and I headed off to other parts of the farm for the day's work.

That evening the government hunter arrived and I took him down to look at the platform. He was suitably impressed so I left him to make arrangements for an evening meal etc and went up to the house for supper.

After supper the hunter climbed up onto the platform and

made himself comfortable and waited. When the lioness finally returned, she was not alone but accompanied by three young lions. To the hunter a lion was a lion and he fired at one of the young ones. Thankfully he missed, allowing all four lions to dash into the long grass at the edge of the clearing. Time passed and eventually the lioness returned. This time the hunter fired at her. The bullet must have hit her because she leapt off the ground vertically until she was level with the platform that the hunter was on and she was not best pleased. Now picture this, it's dark you are blinded by the muzzle flash from the rifle and the next thing you see twenty feet up level with your face illuminated by your head-torch is the snarling face of one very angry lion not more than a few feet from your face. The hunter nearly fell off the platform backwards in fright. The lion then dropped to the ground and dashed for the grass again. This time she did not come back. It was then decided that all platforms in future should be twenty-five feet high!

The next day the lioness was eventually shot.

A few weeks later lions bothered us again. Jorge had recently bought a new tractor, a Massey Ferguson 290, a beast of a thing. It came with a large harrow and Jorge wanted to do some contract cultivating for other farmers in the area. This would mean almost cultivating twenty-four hours a day. To work out if this was feasible Jorge decided to try it out on the farm first and set about putting a team of drivers, and mechanics together who would be based in the field with the tractor. This meant that all fuel fill-ups and servicing would be carried out in the field without the need for the tractor to come back to the workshop.

A tented camp was set up on the edge of a large field where the tractor would be working and everyone made themselves at home. That night Jorge dropped me off for the night-shift with the rest of the workforce. Before he left, he handed me the shot-gun and the ammunition belt "in case you get disturbed by lions".

As it got dark the tractor switched on its lights and continued cultivating the field. Every few hours it would come back to the tented area for a quick grease, dust down and driver change then back out.

A large fire was established for cooking and warmth and we all sat around the fire chatting about this and that. At about ten o'clock all chatting suddenly stopped as we heard the faint roar of a lion. "Mkango" whispered someone around the fire. As we strained our ears there came another roar but this time louder... or closer!

I slowly got up and went to the main tent and picked up the gun and belt and sat myself down by the fire again. A few minutes later came another roar and this time it was very close.

I now loaded two LG grade cartridges into the shot-gun and placed it across my lap. The next roar sounded like it is right amongst us and I quickly flicked the safety off and held the gun in readiness, expecting a lion to leap from the darkness at the edge of our vision. I think everyone around that camp fire held their breath as they waited.

The next roar came from the right and was more distant, so it looked like the lion had just passed by. I kept the gun loaded and placed it across my lap for the next hour and a half but the lion did not return and I retired to the tent to get some sleep.

CHAPTER 55

STRANGE THINGS IN THE SKY

I had been to one of the fields to check on a team of boys we had working. As I approached the field, I could see that none of the team was working. They were all standing still staring up at the sky. Even my arrival didn't cause any response from them. I turned and looked up in the sky as well and there was this silver bell just hanging there.

It was hard to judge how high it was or how big it was but it was motionless. It had white lights around the base of the bell, which appeared to be flashing in sequence. I just stood there for a while starring up at it. Then I heard a car approaching and turned to see Jorge arriving, he had seen it from the house. I jumped in the car and the two of us drove towards the bell.

It appeared to be on the other side of the main road so Jorge headed that direction. As we drove it didn't seem to be getting any larger. As we drove along Tony sounded his horn behind us, he had seen it from his farm. We all pulled over and stepped out of the vehicles. We chatted about what it might be. Weather balloon, UFO, no one really knew. I took my trusty note book from my pocket and quickly drew what I could see. After an hour or so of watching this "thing" we realised that we all had farms to run so headed back. Throughout the afternoon we kept looking up at the sky and there it was in exactly the same spot. By the evening it was still there. As you can imagine it was the only thing we talked about all night. When we woke next morning, it was gone.

Three things I do want to mention. Firstly, over 1000 staff on the estate saw it that day, not to mention the other farms. Secondly the previous night there had been a huge battle across in Mozambique between Frelimo and Renamo. The explosions had woken us all up and the night sky was like a sunset with the bombardment that was going on just over the boarder not 15 miles from the farm. We wondered that if this was an alien craft, maybe they had come to see just how barbaric us humans are to one another. The third thing was that as we drove back to the farm from watching the bell I glanced at my watch and it had stopped. I shook it and checked that it was wound, which it was.

On my next trip to town I took the watch to the watch repairer. When I collected the watch a few days later the watch repairer was mystified. Two gears in the watch had fused together, but not just fused, it was as if they were welded together. The repairer gave them to me and I couldn't even see the join between the two gears. He had replaced the gears and the watch now worked fine. I had the gears till a few years ago. Again, I have no explanation; all I can do is tell you what I saw that day and what happened to my watch.

CHAPTER 56

A TRIP TO THE HOSPITAL

I t was just after the strange bell in the sky that the Boss had a party at his house and I was invited. I hadn't been to parties in Namwera on my own before; in the past I'd always gone with Jorge, so I wasn't sure really what to expect.

When I got there, I soon realised that it was a male only party and as soon as I walked through the door a beer was thrust into my hand. All the usual suspects were there – Pancake, the "Baker", JT, to name but a few. It basically turned into a drinking party, with more and more alcohol being consumed, and by the time a bottle of 40% Aquavit had been brought out, there was dancing on tables and quite a bit of broken furniture.

At some point in the night I retired to one of the many bedrooms in the Boss's house and hadn't been asleep long when the door opened and someone pushed a young African girl into the room. At first, I thought I was dreaming and turned over to resume my drunken sleep.

The next thing I remember was a naked body climbing into the bed with me and attempting to cuddle up to me. Almost immediately I was hit by the strong aroma of bodily sweat and pushed her away. I staggered out of bed and gathered up her clothes and instructed her to get dressed and leave the room, which she did. As I opened the bedroom door for her I could see from the corridor light that she must have been thirteen or fourteen. It was a rude awakening to Namwera male parties.

After she was gone, I staggered to the bathroom. As I opened the bathroom door, there on the floor was the Boss, passed out. He was face up, stark naked with a toilet seat still in his right hand. His wig was on the floor in the corner of the room. I'd never seen the Boss without his wig. I went back to my room and gathered up a blanket and covered the Boss as best I could and placed his wig on his head and went back to bed.

When I eventually woke, I felt awful, sick as a dog but managed to get back to Jorge's farm. The rest of the day I just kept getting more and more ill. I was eventually taken to the mission hospital in Namwera and the long and short of it was, I was kept there for three days on a drip and taken care of by the amazing Italian nuns. I was diagnosed with alcohol poisoning but don't remember much of the three days. I have to say that the nuns were wonderful and I was grateful for their care.

The only person that came to visit me while I was in the hospital was Thanasi Pantazis and I never forgot that; he was a good man.

CHAPTER 57

PANCAKE

One weekend Jorge arranged a fishing trip to Makanjera, an area on the eastern side of Lake Malawi that belongs to Malawi but is just inches from the Mozambique border. It has always been a "hot-spot" for fishermen in two ways. First it is a renowned place for large Sungwa fish, as very few people fish the area. And second is those European fishermen tend to get arrested by Mozambique patrol boats for "straying" into Mozambique waters. Two friends of mine had spent a few days in a Mozambique jail for drifting into "Mozambique" while fishing. It was like the Bermuda Triangle but the fishing was worth it, or so I was told.

The trip was organised into two teams. Team "A" was Jorge and Pano Calavrias; Team "B" was Chililie and I.

I am not sure where to begin to explain Pano Calavrias. Maybe first by saying that nobody actually called him Pano, due to his dyed blonde hair he was known as Pancake. Jorge also called him D9, after the largest size of Bulldozer available in Malawi at the time, as Pancake's stories took some believing and he had a reputation for talking "bull-shit" sometimes. I think his heart was kind of in the right place although you had to keep your wits about you with him all the time. Nobody knew how old Pancake actually was, he said thirty-eight, I met his mother once and she nearly choked on her coffee when she heard thirty-eight and told me to add ten years to that!

He lived life as young as he could get away with. He always had a bronze sun tan no matter what the weather! Some said it was bottle, some said tablets. His shirt was always unbuttoned down to his belly, and he wore a lion's claw mounted in gold on a gold chain round his neck.

The story was that he had driven in both the Safari and the Coca-Cola Rally's. At the time everyone didn't believe a word of it but he was the fastest driver I had ever seen. Someone met him in a bar in Lilongwe and bet him that he couldn't drive to Blantyre in a given time. I can't remember the time but Pancake beat the time by quite a margin. A race was organised between Lilongwe and Salima for the quickest time using the least fuel, Pancake entered and the photo in the Daily Times newspaper confirmed he won! I think he was just totally fearless behind the wheel. He scared the hell out of me and if I saw his truck in my rear-view mirror, I just pulled off the road as quick as possible and let him past.

I had first met him when he held a party at his house in Namwera. I was offered a drink and asked for coke, working next morning etc. The coke arrived in a glass and as I took a sip coke dribbled down the front of my shirt. I wiped my chin and tried again. Still coke dribbled down my front. I looked at the glass expecting to see a crack or something, but the glass was fine. I turned the glass round 180 degrees and sipped, again coke down my front. I then looked around the room and there was Pancake and friends watching me from a corner of the room. The glass was a trick glass! They had had their laugh. Pancake slapped me on the back and ordered another glass, which was a normal one. As I say, you had to have your wits about you with him.

The weekend of the Makanjera trip arrived, Chililie and I loaded up the Estate Land Cruiser. Chililie being Chililie loaded a full tool box, because "you never know". We also took Chililie's Zodiac inflatable and outboard.

Pancake would take his Land Cruiser and would be towing his boat. Jorge would be his "navigator". On the Friday morning Pancake arrived in a cloud of dust at the Estate towing his boat. It was a bright yellow thing, looked like a dart! It was some kind of jet-boat, sucked water in at the front and thrust it out the back under pressure that sped the boat forward. It looked an incredible machine!

We all climbed aboard our vehicles and it was like being under starters orders. With a blast of his horn, Pancake disappeared in another cloud of dust, leaving Chililie and I to eat dust for a few miles till Pancake was so far ahead that the dust had settled and we never saw him again.

"I hope God breaks his trailer hitch for him! That will slow the bugger down" Chililie said as Pancake's white land cruiser disappeared from view.

As you come down the hills from Namwera, just as you hit the tarmac before the bridge at Mangochi there is a turning on your right to Malinde and then on to Makanjera. Just as Chililie and I turned onto this road there was Pancake's Cruiser pulled up on the side of the road. Both Jorge and Pancake were inspecting the back axle of the boat trailer.

"Looks like God works very fast" I said.

"Bet the buggers bust the axle! Not bloody surprised travelling at that speed over the dirt road!" Chililie muttered as he pulled up behind the trailer.

"The wheel bearing's shot, I think. Have you got any tools?" Pancake asked Chililie. "I've got a spare wheel bearing but no tools."

"Yeah, sure, they are in my truck, I'll get them." And Chililie and I head back to our Cruiser.

"Stupid arse-hole, not even got any tools!" muttered Chililie. "And my tool box is right under all our stuff, right at the fucking bottom. We will have to unload almost everything!"

So, Chililie and I started to off-load the Zodiac, the tents, chairs, tables, the works. After about fifteen minutes in the baking sun Chililie lifted the heavy steel toolbox out of the back of the Cruiser and walked towards the boat trailer. Just as he got about five feet from the back of it, Jorge and Pancake jumped into the front of the Land Cruiser, and drove off in a cloud of dust leaving Chililie standing there holding the toolbox. There had been nothing wrong with the axle at all.

"Bastards!" he yelled out after them but they were gone! He walked back to our cruiser.

I have to say that I actually found the trick quite funny but Chililie just did not have a sense of humour and the joke was wasted on him. Twenty minutes later we had reloaded the cruiser and headed off up the road in pursuit of Pancake. When we finally arrived at the designated "camp site", Jorge and Pancake had already set up their camp, chairs and tables set up, they'd caught some fish and were now drinking beers! Chililie was fuming in the car but when he got out, he was like a volcano! Jorge and Pancake still thought it was funny and actually so did I. I think it took Chililie most of the weekend to calm down.

It did appear though that God had not finished with Pano yet. While he and Jorge were out fishing, leaving us to play catch-up, Pancake's boat had developed a real mechanical problem. Pancake spent most of the afternoon with his head buried deep in the engine bay with a screw-driver and a hammer. After much knocking and banging Pancake takes "Pan-lin" out for a test flight! (Pan after Pano and Lin after Linda, Pancake's girlfriend). He screamed the boat round and round the bay at full throttle.

"Hope he blows the thing up." Mutterd Chililie.

No sooner had the words left his mouth when there is an almighty loud explosion from the back of Pan-lin, and a flame shot high up into the air. Seconds later the back of the boat is filled with white foam from Pancakes on-board automatic fire-extinguishers and Pancake dived from the boat into the Lake!

"Bloody good!" celebrated Chililie.

The burnt-out Pan-lin had to be towed back to shore and sadly pulled onto the trailer. Now Jorge and Pancake looked at Chililie's Zodiac.

"No fucking way, you two left me at the bloody roadside!" fumed Chililie but he was never going to win, not against his elder brother anyway.

That evening baths are in order so the four of us head for the water's edge. Jorge saw a group of hippos close to the shore and suggested that maybe going into the water is not such a good idea.

Pancake then had an idea, "Guys, let's go out into the lake in the Zodiac and bath in the deep water. Hippos don't go into the deep water; they stay in the shallows. We will be fine."

After we all had a discussion about the merits of this theory, it is then agreed that we have all heard this rumour too and therefore it must be true so we all pile into the Zodiac and chug out past the hippos and into the deeper waters of the lake. When Pancake has given his expert opinion that we are in deep enough water to be safe we all strip off and drive into the Lake with our bars of soap.

As I lathered up my hair there is a yell of "Rupe, HIPPO!" from the boat. Through my stinging soapy eyes, I could see that Pancake, SC and Chililie are all sat back in the boat.

"Shit, I'm the only fool in the water! They must have seen the hippo and climbed back in as I was washing" and I started to swim for the Zodiac to the encouragement of my three "mates".

"Swim Rupe, quick, don't look back, just swim" came the orders.

I swam for my life and finally reached the boat. I leaped out of the water and grabbed the side of the inflatable zodiac but my hands slipped right off and I fell back into the water. The three of them were yelling even louder now and I made another grab for the boat but again my hands slipped off and I couldn't get a grip. Then the yells turn to laughs. Pancake had rubbed soap all over the sides of the Zodiac to make it as slippery as an eel!

Oh yes and there was no hippo. They reached a hand out and dragged me into the boat and we headed back to shore.

Bath time was over, much to my relief.

CHAPTER 58

COFFEE & HORNBILLS

J orge was always open to new ideas and not scared to try something new. There had been rumblings around Namwera as to whether coffee would grow well in the area. Jorge suggested that we give it a try.

We selected a four-acre field hidden away from prying eyes behind some trees close to the stream that flowed through the farm. If it all went wrong Jorge didn't want visiting Greek farmers having any excuse to mock him.

Jorge and I went down to the cleared field one morning to measure out the rows and spacing of the planting holes. At each plant spacing, a short stick was pushed into the ground to mark the point in which Jorge wanted each hole dug that would accommodate four seedlings. The idea of the four seedlings was in case one or two seedlings died.

Once Jorge had marked a few rows he left me and one assistant to mark out the planting positions, which took us most of the day. At the end the entire plot had been conveniently divided into blocks with footpaths between the rows for maintaining the plants and harvesting. Now it would be a simple task of sending a team of chaps down the following morning to start digging the holes.

The holes would be more like pits, roughly 1m square and 1m deep. The soil removed from the hole would be placed to one side of the excavated hole; to be mixed with fertiliser and farmyard manure. The whole lot would then be used to back-fill the hole during planting.

The next morning a team of hole diggers were dispatched by trailer to the coffee field and by about 10am Jorge went down to the field to check on progress.

He wasn't gone long before I was sent for.

"Bwana Jorge wants you to come to the coffee field, quickly!" was the message so I hot footed it down to the field.

"I thought you said you had finished marking all the holes like I asked you" he said before I even got within thirty feet of him.

"I did Jorge" I said, wondering what I had done wrong.

"So where are the sticks?" he asked, pointing to the field.

I gazed across the rows and there was not a stick in sight. A cold sweat passed over me. "But Jorge, I did it all, ask Albert" I said looking for reassurance to my story.

Jorge turned to Albert and my version of events was confirmed. Jorge was still not too happy as the boys had arrived at the field, saw that there were no sticks and just sat down for a couple of hours smoking and chatting. It was a total waste of a day and I was really as angry as Jorge.

"I'll get to it straight away", without being asked. Albert and I then set about inserting the sticks again as Jorge marched out of the field.

That evening I reported to Jorge that the task had been done.

Next morning, I decided to catch a lift on the trailer with the boys to make sure that all went well that day, as I didn't want the same problems twice. As the tractor rounded the corner and the field came into view my heart sank. There was not a stick in sight!

"Shit!" I said and called for the driver to stop. I jumped off the trailer and sent the digging team back, there was nothing they could do here. I set about pushing the sticks back into the designated positions. It took Jorge about ten minutes to turn up. "For fucks sake Rupe, what's the story?" he demanded.

"I don't know Jorge, but I will find out what's going on" and got back to marking my holes.

The next morning, I was up before the sun and crept down to the field. I was relieved to find every stick standing just as I had laid them out the day before. What a result! But I decided to conceal myself in the long grass behind some trees and just wait to see if I had just simply got up before the phantom stick remover. I wanted revenge and boy was this bloke or kid going to get a thrashing when he turned up to vandalise all my hard work.

I must have sat there for about an hour, staining my ears to every sound in case a lion was approaching for an easy meal. Just as the sun hit the mountain top, I heard the call of a flock of hornbills. I thought this is it, someone has disturbed them and that someone is my phantom stick criminal. I hoped that they had not taken flight because of a lion.

Just then eight large Southern Ground-hornbills (*Bucorvus leadbeateri*) flew over the trees on the edge of the field and came to rest in amongst the sticks.

They were a nice sight so I continued my wait while gazing at these large, turkey sized birds. Suddenly one of the birds strutted up to a stick and pulled it out of the ground with its strong bill, threw it to one side. It then walked onto the next stick in the same row and proceeded to pull that one out. Then the rest of hornbills started doing the same, each one picking a separate row.

My jaw just dropped. I almost stood up straight away in

anger but then I saw the funny side of it and decided to watch them as they purposefully pulled each stick out. They obviously didn't want the coffee planted in their field.

After a few minutes I stood up and walked out of the trees into the field; at which point the birds lumbered into the air and over the trees. Then as I replaced the discarded sticks, I noticed that the birds' foot prints were clearly visible in the soft soil, something I had not seen the days before.

So, the riddle was solved and I was vindicated. I proudly went back to the house to tell Jorge the news. By the end of the day the digging team had all the holes dug and now we just had to wait for the seedlings to arrive, which they did, a few weeks later. The seedlings were about 16-18 months old, standing about a foot high in their dark rich soil filled black plastic sleeves. When they were all planted it certainly looked a lovely sight. We decided to post a watchman at the field in case the Hornbills returned to rip out the seedlings. It would be three years of tender loving care before the plants would be mature enough to produce beans so time would tell whether the effort was worth it.

As it happens, I later found out that the coffee was not a success and the coffee was up-rooted and hardwood trees planted in their place.

CHAPTER 59

TIME TO LEAVE NAMWERA AGAIN

Things had not been going well between Chililie and me for a while. I can't really say what caused the problems but I guess like most things they started off with something very minor. I had moved across from the main house at Estate One to Dave and Doreen's old house at Estate Two with Chililie.

Lunch times were at no fixed time really, if I was honest but I was accustomed to Jorge's timing where we would eat and have our afternoon thirty-minute nap before heading back out into the fields. Chililie, since he was one of the owners of the farm like Jorge, didn't really have to answer to anyone. I, on the other hand, was an employee and I felt that my lunch hour was an hour, no more, no less. Chililie started coming back to the house at lunch times later and later. Initially I would wait for Chililie to arrive then we would both sit down for lunch; but the problem was that this was starting to mean there was no point in me even attempting to lay down since I had about fifteen minutes before I needed to go back to work.

Eventually, after a week or so, I decided to start lunch when

I got back to the house whether Chililie was home or not. A few days went by and Chililie suddenly flipped!

"I think it's rude that you are eating without me. This is my house and you should be respectful and wait for me to arrive......blar, blar, blar!"

I tried to explain that I meant no offence but Chililie was already steamed about it. Anyway, that was when I realised that we had a problem. The next thing that happened was Jorge's elder brother arrived from South Africa and the long and short of it was that he took Chililie's side and basically two votes against one and it was time for me to go.

Jorge was quite upset at the time as he didn't want to lose me. He said he would do what he could to find me a job and within a few days came back with the news that he may have found me a job with a man I will call Bob in Namadzi.

So again, I said my goodbyes to the workers on the farm. This time they knew that I would not be coming back to the farm. With each handshake came a torrent of blessing and good wishes for the future, pleas that I should not forget them. Each handshake got longer and longer, I had to break my hand away otherwise we would have been there all day. Finally, Chief Spring arrived to say goodbye.

"Chief Spring, its time," I said. His eyes were red and he didn't say too much.

He just held my hand and looked to the sky as if talking to god. When he did lower his head to look at me, he was crying.

It was a very sad day for me and for most of the Africans. Jorge looked pretty upset too and neither of us said a great deal in the car on the way to town on that day in July 1983.

I remembered that Jorge had not given me a reference so I called him the day before I was due to go and see Bob for my job interview. He said he would sort it out and asked when I was going to see Bob.

"Next Tuesday," I said, "Around eleven."

"Stop by the house on your way, I'll sort it out." Jorge said.

So, on the Tuesday morning I arrived at Jorge's town house in Limbe to collect the letter.

"Morning Jorge, I've come to pick up the letter for Bob." I said as Jorge gestured me to come into the house. I followed him into the lounge and we sat down in silence.

Jorge pulled a set of keys from his pocket and handed them to me. I looked at the keys and saw that they were the keys to Jorge's Mercedes.

I looked up, "but I don't understand, is the letter in the car?"

"No," Jorge said, "I want you to go to see Bob in my Merc, that's the best recommendation I can give you. Bob knows I don't let anyone drive my car and he will understand. It will say far more than any letter I can write."

I was dumbfounded and knew that there was no point in declining his offer so I just thanked him and told him that I would take care of it.

"I know you will." He replied.

I then, scared as hell, drove Jorge's Mercedes from Limbe to Namadzi to my job interview with Bob. As I turned into the yard in front of the estate office Bob was on the steps waiting.

"Where's Jorge?" Bob asked, looking past me towards the parked Mercedes.

"He is at his house in town." I said trying to sound very matter of fact.

"What and he gave you his car to come here!" he said.

This was a statement not a question. I could see his mind going through the thought process. "Come inside," was all he said and I followed him up the steps and into the farm office.

After about fifteen minutes we shock hands and I got back into the Mercedes and drove back to town.

"Well, how did it go?" Jorge asked as I got out of the car.

"I got the job!" I said with a beaming smile.

"Great! What did he say about the car? I bet his face was a

picture, wished I'd been there to see it! Jorge said with a face like he had just won a hand of poker. "You want a coffee?"

Jorge called for coffee and then reached down inside his brief-case and produced an envelope which he handed to me.

"What's this?" I asked.

"Open it."

It was a letter of reference. "You'll need it later in life." he said.

I read the letter. "…Rupert worked hard and never once disobeyed an order from his superiors. His manner is very responsible and his honesty unquestionable…If his qualities are used correctly, Rupert will go a long way…"

As I read it there was a lump in my throat. Jorge must have seen my feelings because he abruptly changed the subject to a lighter topic. I didn't make the mistake of showing the letter to the family this time.

On the night of the 15th of May 2018, up to five armed assailants entered the main house at the farm and demanded that Chililie handed over money that was held in the estate safe. Sadly they then attacked him with machetes, before making off with K14,000,000 ($20,000) that was in the safe. Chililie was rushed to Mangochi District Hospital but died on arrival. He was 62 years old.

1983-1984

TOBACCO FARMING

NAMADZI

Namadzi is located on the Namadzi stream on the Blantyre to Zomba road. It is located adjacent to Magomero and is inhabited by the Mang'anja, Yao and Lomwe people. Today it is surrounded by tobacco estates, most of which are owned by European famers, whose families go back generations. People like Wallace, Henderson, Thornycroft and Lewis.

CHAPTER 60

"CHIMIMBA"

I don't really remember how I arrived at "Bob's" or even the date but it was sometime in July 1983. What I do remember was how, in an instant, I disliked Bob's sidekick Jimmy. Jimmy was a Rhodesian, in his mid to late sixties, who allegedly ran a farm that neighboured Bob, although I never saw this farm or him doing much work.

Jimmy was a total drunk and a pig. He treated the Africans like dirt, which was something that really got my back up and for it they gave him the name "Chimimba", which translates as Mr Belly, due to his large beer belly. He was like a cartoon character of a drunk; he had this huge beer belly and these little thin short legs under it that you thought would never hold the weight. He was as arrogant as Bob was; maybe that was why they got on so well. I tried to have as little to do with him as possible but it was difficult.

A few years previous, Bob had had a motorbike accident on the farm and broken his leg. For some reason there were complications that required him to undergo numerous operations, usually in Germany; so once or twice a year Bob would go off on one of his trips to the hospital in Germany, sometimes with his wife, sometimes alone. Although I was in effect Bob's assistant manager, Chimimba was always left in charge, much to my and the Africans dismay.

Chimimba would swan about in Bob' cars and spend hours up at the house like it was his own. I felt like a visitor and would spend hours at the estate office rather than go up to the house if Chimimba was there. I had a few run-ins with Chimimba, most ended in me walking off before I punched him.

When Bob left his wife on the farm while he went off to Germany, things were a little better. Chimimba couldn't have total run of the farm, the house and drinks cabinet with her there !

I was bored on the farm, not that there was a lack of work far from it, but because work was all there was. The boredom was broken from time to time by a few "exciting" moments on the farm.

One I do recall was when the Head Kapital was organising the felling of a large Blue Gum, it must have been a good eighty foot high. I was in a field doing something or other and a "runner" came to fetch me with the usual request.

"Bwana, you should come quickly!" but then refusing to tell me what for, or what had happened.

When I got to the farm buildings there was the large Blue Gum laying smack bang across one of the farm buildings. A large crowd had gathered and I waded through them shouting "is anyone hurt, was there anyone in the building?" Luckily there wasn't. I found the Head Kapital who was pale to say the least. I think he thought he was going to get a revving from me.

"What happened, besides the tree fell on the building?" I asked, aiming to get the obvious out of the way first.

"Don't know Bwana. We cut the wedge out so it would fall the other way, but before we had cut through the other side, the tree just went over."

Well that was his story and he was sticking to it. These

things happen and luckily nobody was killed or injured. Bob saw it differently and went absolutely mad with rage. I did manage to take a photo of the tree laying across the building, but I can't seem to locate it now.

The second time was slightly more a near death experience for me. The mechanics at the farm workshop had been replacing the brakes on the Range Rover and were in a rush to get the job finished before lunchtime as I had to go into Zomba to pick Bob' kids up from school.

"It's ready Bwana." The mechanic said with delight as he wiped his hands on an oily rag. So I jumped in and drove out of the farm down to the main Blantyre to Zomba road. The farm road descends quite steeply just before the junction so I applied the brakes and as I did the vehicle pulls aggressively to the right so I lifted off the brakes and tried to correct by turning left. The road is now coming up fast so again I was forced to apply the brakes but again the car lunged to the right. By now the junction is less than 50m away and things are getting serious so I correct the steering again but with no real way of slowing down, the Range Rover was now fish-tailing towards the junction with me turning the wheel from left to right and I was running out of road. With options running out I decided to drive the vehicle into a ploughed field to my right and allow the soft earth to slow me to a halt. The problem was that I had misjudged the angle that I was approaching the ridges of the ploughed field and the back wheels hit a ridge broadside and the whole Range Rover flipped over on to its side, then roof and then side again; a full 270 degrees. Suddenly I felt liquid all over me and memories of hearing of Range Rovers catching fire filled my mind and I punched myself through the windscreen and out onto the ploughed field.

I just stood there for a few minutes staring at the Range Rover laying there on its side; a real crumpled mess like a sculptor admires his work.

"Shit, this is going to make Bob's day!" I say aloud.

I checked myself over and there wasn't even a scratch, which I guess was a result of the speed I was going or lack of it to be more precise, and thankfully the children were not in the car at the time. We were all lucky.

Bob of course appreciated none of this but you know what….fuck it, I was passed caring with the miserable man. The good news was that the insurance paid out and a body shop in Blantyre were able to make the Range Rover as good as new, you would never have known it had rolled.

The dirt road to "Bob's" place

CHAPTER 61

SCORPIONS IN THE BED

The next bolt of excitement was a little more worrying. I was laid in bed one night; I was asleep but as I am a light sleeper, the slightest noise or movement will wake me. I felt something lightly touch the back of my neck, which I took to be a mosquito. As usual with mosquitos, I gave the back of my neck a good slap to kill the offending insect. Instantly a red-hot-needle like pain shot into my right thumb! I was now fully awake. I felt something larger than a mosquito between the palm of my hand and my neck and instinctively squashed the "creature", which gave a crunching sound as I clenched my fist around it and then threw it across the room. All this happened in a fraction of a second and all in one movement.

I sat up in bed, in pain and in total darkness. The farm ran on a generator that had long been switched off for the night. My thumb was throbbing and on fire. I stumbled to the bathroom clutching my thumb that felt the size of a football and ran it under the cold tap. My thumb pulsed away under the cold tap for quite a while. I couldn't see my thumb but it felt like one of those Tom and Jerry cartoons when Tom hits his thumb with a hammer, it was total agony. Slowly with the cold water the pain started to ease and I went back to bed and dozed off to sleep in the early hours.

In the morning I woke and inspected my thumb. It was still very red and very swollen, and there was a single pin-prick mark on the underside of the thumb. I then remembered throwing the creature across the room and so I got up to search for its crushed corpse. I had a good look round but couldn't see anything. Finally, I found a single front pincer of a large scorpion. The scary thing was that that's all I found, something else had eaten its body while I was asleep, which was kind of disconcerting. Anyway, I lived and was stung a few more times by scorpions in the coming years but none of them hurt as much as that one.

It was while at Namadzi that I bought a Yamaha XJ650 motorcycle. Seeing as I hadn't officially been given a vehicle for use on the farm I had to keep asking if I could take the old 404 pick-up if I needed to go to town. If Bob felt spiteful, he would simply say no and I'd be farm bound in the evenings, which was my only real time off. The bike meant that I would be independent. Also, I could be in Limbe in minutes which meant I had more of the evening to spend. Even on the Blantyre to Zomba road I could often hit 105mph on stretches. I'd knock off work, have a shower, get changed and be in town by seven in the evening. I could catch a movie, have some supper and meet friends and then be back for a sleep and fresh the next morning for work. It really helped me get through the week.

I remember one weekend when some friends were going to the Lake for the weekend and I had arranged to meet them at Club Mak on the Sunday. I told Bob I was off on Sunday to go to the Lake for the day, to which he announced that there was work on Sunday.

"What work?" We had nothing to do on that Sunday.

"I need you to check the ploughing of the field" he said with a smirk. This was bloody unbelievable. We never checked the ploughing. He was doing this on purpose and there wasn't a lot I could say.

So, on Sunday I was in the field with the driver ploughing. In the afternoon Bob pulled up next to the field.

"Eh, Rupert, you can knock off now." He grinned. I looked at my watch, it was 3pm. "Too late to go to the Lake now isn't it?" he said with an even bigger grin.

"No!" and I stormed back to the house, quickly changed and tore out of the farm on the bike. Bob's face was a picture.

It was going to be dark at 5.30pm and I didn't know how long my friends were going to wait so there was only one thing for it, I had to open the bike right up. To avoid the risk of goats I drove down the centre of the road, my thinking was that if a herd of goats did run out of the grass on the side, I had equal space to swerve the bike and try and avoid them. As I tore up the road alongside Lake Malombe I saw a policeman sitting under a Mango tree on a small folding chair. He heard the bike and got up from his chair and walked towards the edge of the road to wave me down. I was past him before he made the edge! When I arrived at Club Mak it was very late in the afternoon and I think we only had time for a coke, a quick chat. I stayed at Club Mak for the rest of the evening and had supper there before riding back to Namadzi.

CHAPTER 62

I TURN TWENTY-ONE

It was while I was at Namadzi that I reached the age of twenty one and to be honest I wasn't looking forward to it very much. I knew I would have to work and there was no way I was going to say anything to Bob or his wife. As it happened the tobacco sales were in full swing at the auction floors in Limbe, so I had to go into town for that. While I was at the floors I bumped into Tony Calavrias and The Boss during the sale and when they found out it was my birthday said that they were going to take me for lunch and there would be no arguments. Well a free lunch and with the Boss and Tony, sounded good to me. Boy was I in for a shock; they took me to the 21 Grill at the Ryalls Hotel, which at the time was the best and most expensive restaurant in Blantyre, if not Malawi. I sat down to a starter of snails in garlic sauce followed by a great beef dish. I ate like a king, thanks to the great heart of both those guys. My family did not acknowledge my birthday so it meant a lot to me that these guys had treated me to this slap-up meal.

A few weeks later Tony Calavrias and his family arrived at the farm one weekend and I thought Tony would be a good person to talk to about Bob and conditions on the farm. I had heard how badly Tony had been treated when he worked for Bob, and they were brother-in-laws. I found the time to catch hold of Tony alone and we had a chat.

"I'll tell you what Rupe," Tony started, "I'm just surprised you have lasted this long. Bob is a complete bastard with no thought for anyone but himself. I have to say one thing." he paused.

"What?" I asked.

"I admire you; you lasted longer than I did! We have been having bets in Namwera how long you'd last."

Tony made me feel better. "Only you know what you need to do, no one can decide for you." He said and he was right.

After Tony and his family had left on the Sunday to go back to Namwera I took time to think of how the farm had been to me, the things that had happened. Okay so I rolled his Range Rover, but it wasn't my fault. I could have been killed. In my opinion he just had his priorities all wrong. The Africans said that before his bike accident and his broken leg he was a nicer person, not much nicer, but nicer none the less.

I had given twelve months plus to the job, yes, I'd been paid, but I'd worked six days a week, sometimes six and a half.

A few weeks later I went to see Bob about the annual bonus he had promised me when I first started and since the auction floors had closed and sales were complete, I thought it would be a good time to chat about how much bonus I was likely to get.

Bob looked straight at me across his desk and said "What bonus?"

Fucking unbelievable! I reminded him about the meeting we had when the bonus was discussed, the day I had driven to the farm in Jorge's Merc.

"I don't remember discussing any bonus that day. Does it mention it anywhere in your contract?" he said with his little brown pig-eyes glistening like he had just check-mated me in chess.

Then it dawned on me that I had never signed a contract, I'd not even been offered a contract to sign.

"We shook hands." I said looking straight into his eyes.

"Did we? I don't remember that." he replied without a flinch.

He sat there with the arrogance that only he had and that smarmy grin on his face as if to say I'm shafting you and there's nothing you can do about it, I was boiling. I don't remember whether it was at that moment or a few days later that I decided to quit. I was still angry, there I was leaving while his favourite Chimimba slept with any available girl on the farm, whether they were willing or not, beat up Bob's watchman on a regular basis and often fell asleep at the side of the road because he was so drunk. I never found out what hold Chimimba had on Bob but there was something.

A few days later I packed up my things and went to find Bob, who was in the estate office; he didn't even get up from his desk to shake my hand to say goodbye. I think I said something like "that's it, I'm off now", at which point Bob asked if I wanted a reference.

"I don't need one, thanks." And I turned around, got on the bike and rode off down the long dirt road to the main tarmac road.

As I pulled off the estate dirt road and on to the tarmac main road down to Blantyre, I saw Laki just turning into his estate. We both stopped for a chat.

"So, you've left then? We were all having bets at how long you'd last, but you did better than we all thought. What you going to do now?" he asked.

"Yes, I heard there were bets going, Tony told me. Don't know what I'll do, I'll find something." I said, "I couldn't stay much longer, he's a right bastard! If I don't leave now I'll kill him!"

"Roger at FES is looking for a new guy at Namwera, Elia has

left. Why don't you drop in and see him? I have called him and told him about you."

"Cheers Laki, I'll do that." And we said our goodbyes and I headed for town.

As Namadzi disappeared out of view I remembered the words of Jorges' reference letter.

"If his qualities are used correctly, Rupert will go a long way..."

My qualities had certainly not been used correctly by Bob.

Laki's farm where he told me about the job at FES

1984-1988

FARMING & ENGINEERING SERVICES

NAMWERA

Farming and Engineering Services - FES was established in 1967. It's Head Office was in Blantyre, with branches in Lilongwe, Mzuzu and Namwera.

Today FES only has branches in Blantyre and Lilongwe, plus depots in Dwangwa and Nchalo. The branches of Namwera and Mzuzu have since been closed.

FES is the single largest investor in the Agricultural equipment industry and specialise in precision agriculture. FES is also the distributing agents for Massey Ferguson products, Komatsu Plant and Equipment, Toyota Forklifts, Challenger Equipment, Agrico irrigation equipment and Baldan implements. The company has been two time "Africa Distributor of the Year" and "World Distributor of the Year".

CHAPTER 63

I'M YOUR COOK

As I pulled up outside Farming & Engineering Services in 1984 I looked at the large wording on the white wall above the large showroom window and at the tractors parked inside. I really needed this job. There wasn't a lot of opportunity in Malawi and I didn't have many options.

The meeting with Roger went well. He told me a little of the history of FES Namwera, how the branch was due for closure but that he had decided to give it one last chance. He mentioned the salary and the benefits; I tried to hide my enthusiasm. Finally, he said that he would be in touch and I left, not really knowing whether I had the job or not. It was a waiting game. I remember walking across the road to the Ryalls Hotel to grab myself a lunch in the Dugout Restaurant to contemplate my life.

A few days later I got a call from Roger at my parents' house.

"Hello son, I pleased to say you've got the job." said Roger. "Can you come in the office tomorrow afternoon to sort out some paperwork?"

I was over the moon to say the least and I don't even think I slept a wink that night.

As I arrived at the office, I was a few minutes early so looked around the buildings and the street. I looked at the large wording that said Farming & Engineering Services, I again looked at the tractors and the four-wheel drive vehicles parked outside. I then looked across the street at the Ryalls Hotel and then it hit me. This was the place I had watched from the hotel window when we had first arrived in Malawi, when I was eleven years old. I looked up at the window that was the room where we had stayed, all those years ago in 1975. I had done it, without remembering, I had done it! I was working for that company I had watched from the window as a boy. A smile came on my face and I walked in through the doors to see Roger.

A while later I walked back out into the sun as the new Branch Manager of FES Namwera, it was the 1st of December – Merry Christmas! A good salary, and my own house, things had certainly improved for me, finally a job without family politics being involved, oh yes and the keys to a company car – it was a great Christmas present; and all at the age of twenty-one. The company car was a five door Toyota Land Cruiser station wagon that had previously been owned by the Branch Manager of FES Mzuzu, a man called Gordon as I recall. As Roger handed me the keys he said it was just a temporary vehicle while they sorted a new one out for me from Mobil Motors.

As I drove back to my parents' house, I felt happy for the first time in a long time. The happiness was dashed when there was little enthusiasm from Mother and Jim. Mothers' comments to the car were "I hope it's not going to be outside the house too long?" You could always rely on mother to put the damper on things.

I spent the next couple of weeks at Jim and mothers house while contracts were drawn up and signed, I didn't fall for that trick again, Bob had taught me one thing at least!

The day before I was due to leave Blantyre for Namwera there was a knock at the folk's house. Stood at the door was

Samuel, Bob's cook. I was a bit taken aback as he was the last person I expected to see. Had I forgotten something at Bob's and the bastard had sent Samuel on the bus with it, it wouldn't have surprised me? I invited Samual in and we went out onto the veranda and had a cup of tea. It turned out that he had left Bob's employment a few days ago and had heard that I was going up to Namwera.

"Bwana, you need a cook, and I need a job, I'm your new cook." He informed me with a smile in a way that was more of a statement than a request for work.

He had a point, it suddenly dawned on me that here I was going up to Namwera, to a house and a job and no cook. I thought for a second; how was Bob going to be when he found out Samuel was now working for me? He would assume that I had cooked this plan up before leaving Namadzi, he would go mad! I thought for a second more about Bob. Stuff Bob I said inside my head and Samuel was hired!

I sat down to discuss terms with Samuel and was shocked to find that Bob had only paid him a monthly salary of thirty Kwacha, plus the standard accommodation etc. I told Samuel I'd double that and that every time I got a salary increase so would he, to the exact same percentage as I received. Samuel was over the moon. I guess there are very few times in your life when you change jobs for double the salary; but Jorge had taught me that "you are only as good as your staff and if you pay peanuts, you'll get monkeys". Samuel would prove to be worth his money and more in the coming years and became a close friend, who I miss dearly today.

As he promised, Samuel turned up the next day, with his belongings, which included a "Gumba-Gumba". For those of you who don't know, a Gumba-Gumba is a sort of a mobile disco - come stereo that runs on a car battery. The music is different but the sound that comes out of the speakers is generally the same, very poor quality, very tinny, din. I didn't say anything as he loaded it in the back of the Land Cruiser.

I said my goodbyes to the family and we headed off to Nam. I think we both must have looked like two demented idiots as I'm sure we smiled all the way on the three-hour trip to Namwera. We both glanced left as we passed the turning at Namadzi for Bob's estate. I was hoping that Bob would be coming out of his turning as we drove past so we could smile and wave or stick two fingers up, depending what took our fancy, but he wasn't.

CHAPTER 64

MY STAFF

FES Namwera had a small number of staff. In charge of stock control, sales and first point of contact for customers was Elias. He was a joyful character, always greeting you with a smile. His father worked as the paint sprayer in the body shop at FES in Blantyre so he had obviously followed his father into working for the company.

In the workshop I had Chilangwe, who was my welder and general manufacturer of all things metal. He was extremely qualified and experienced; even welding thin aluminium with such grace that it looked like it had been done by a robotic machine. He increased my knowledge of welding, brazing, and soldering in the years I was there.

In charge of mechanics was Kawale, a beast of a man. He also had the name Eros, not named after the Greek god of love but I was told, after Jorge's huge Brahman bull, and that gave you an idea of the build of this man. Kawale used to joke and say it was because they shared the same size in testicles. He had a passion for drink, the ladies, and the combination of which usually ending in a fight, as not all the women that he romanced were single at the time. Kawale had an assistant in the workshop, whose name escapes me sadly.

I was happy to have such a good bunch of guys in my charge. I really don't think that we had any problems or difficulties in all the time I was there. Sure, Kawale would be hung over a few days a month but always showed up for work, whether he had a sore head or not.

Since I demanded honesty, no matter what the subject, Kawale would often come straight to my office at 7.00am after a night of heavy drinking reporting,

"Today Bwana, I'm sick. Can I not do anything too difficult like gearboxes or engine work? Oh, and please don't send me out driving. Light duties today Bwana."

I appreciated him being honest, he could have stayed in bed and shamed malaria but no, he had come to work. My lessons from Jorge's school of farm management had paid off and I knew how to treat people to get the best out of them.

With the three of them in the workshop there was always some sort banter coming from behind the office. Kawale was a bit of a joker and would always find a way of having a laugh with somebody. The workshop always had people coming and going, people just coming in for a chat, others collecting or dropping stuff off. Most of the Greek farmers that came daily would have a few of their own workers with them along for the ride. Kawale would often ask the help of these Africans on a small workshop job, while their boss had a coffee and a chat with me in the office. I'd be sat there in my office chatting and drinking coffee when I'd hear a yell, followed by roars of laughter.

"Don't worry," I would tell the farmer, "that's just Kawale testing the ignition system by asking one of your unsuspecting boys to stick his finger in the spark-plug cap while he cranks the engine over." He always had a steady stream of fools who had no mechanical knowledge to inflict pain on.

By the end of the first month at FES I realised that I was going to cause some ripples. I reconciled my petty cash for the month end and it came to about thirty-eight kwacha. I filled in the petty cash form and sent it off to Head Office and a few days later I got a call from Roger.

"I've got your petty cash form here and there seems to be a mistake, thirty-eight kwacha?" He said.

"There can't be a mistake, I checked it a few times, it is thirty-eight kwacha." I reassured him, as a hot feeling came over me thinking that I had got my figures wrong.

"But previous petty cash was always around much more than that, considerably more a month, and every month!" Roger announced giving the indication that I had sold myself short somewhere in my calculations.

"No, mine is thirty-eight." I adamantly stood by my maths.

All Roger said was "Mmmmmm" and the call ended.

FES Namwera is now a Bakery

CHAPTER 65

BEWARE OF GREEKS BEARING GIFTS

The Greeks who had not given me the time of day when I was at Jorge's, suddenly came out of the wood-work now that I was in charge of FES Namwera, like woodworms. I had never been so popular, but as the saying goes, "Beware of Greeks bearing gifts" and I always bore this in mind. I also remembered what Jorge had told me about them being nice to you when they were just about to shaft you. Before I tell you a few stories let me just add that none of my real friends ever tried to get anything for free while I was at FES, they were the first to pay. But it was funny that these friends of mine were the people that all the other Greeks warned me about, funny that.

One of the first woodworms to try his luck was a farmer called Chris. We had taken an engine out of a customer's tractor and replaced it with a larger horse powered-reconditioned one at his request. The old engine lay on a bench in the workshop and Chris had seen it and asked Kawale what the story was with it. Kawale had probably been made an offer but had wisely declined so Chris came to see me for "a quiet word".

"Rupert, you don't have a video player, do you?" he stated. I didn't, and told him so. They had just become available in the country and were for sale in the Indian electrical stores in town at nearly half a year's salary so quite out of my reach at that time.

"Would you like one?" he continued.

"I don't quite follow you. What do you mean?" I enquired.

"Well you have that tractor engine in the workshop that you don't need and you would like a video player. I will give you a video player and you give me the engine. A done deal." He said making it sound easy.

"No problem,............" I told him and his face lit up.

There was no way I was going to give him the engine but I wanted to lay the reason why at his feet rather than give him a slap in the face NO, so I continued,

"............the only problem is that when Roger fires me will you give me a job?"

"Er, no of course not, I can't do that." He said backing out of a corner.

"Well I can't give you the engine either." I said and indicated that the conversation was at an end. He wasn't best pleased.

A few weeks later I got a call from Roger.

"Rupert, I've been hearing that you have been welding African bicycles. Is this true?" he said getting straight to the point.

"No, brazing actually, bicycle frame's are too thin to weld and brazing holds better because it withstands the vibration of riding over the corrugated dirt roads..."

Roger cut me off "I don't want a bloody technical report - why are you fixing African bicycles, we are Farming & Engineering Services, not Ruperts' Bicycle Repair Shop!" he demanded.

I explained my reasoning behind it.

"The guys who come in here with their bikes are smallholder tobacco farmers; their bicycle is their only form of transport.

They work their small tobacco field by hand. My thought is that if we take care of them now, they will remember our kindness in the future. This year he has a good crop and makes some money and decides to buy a tractor where do you think he is going to come? To FES, who repaired their bicycle when they were poor, or to Ford, who turned them away telling them that they were not a bicycle repair shop?" These Africans get invoiced for the work Chilangwe does and my orders are that if a tractor or trailer come in then they take priority over the bicycle." I stopped.

There was a short silence from Roger, "You charge them for the work?" he asked.

"Yes, rods, and labour, you can see the head office invoice copies up in accounts."

There was another pause from Roger.

"Well that's all right then, keep up the good work, and as soon as that guy makes some money you get over there and sell him a Massey before we lose him to Ford!" he said.

"You got it Roger" and the call was over.

It appeared that a Greek farmer had been at my branch when an African brought in the two halves of his bicycle. The farmer did not know who the African was, and had not been in a position to see if the African had been charged. He just got straight on the phone running tales to Roger. Roger did what a good boss should do and that was to follow it up. Roger could see my thinking behind it and now that he knew the money was going into the accounts department, he was happy. Roger did finally tell me who the Greek was and it turned out to be Chris, the bloke whose offer of an "engine for a video player swap" I had refused to accept. It was just a case of sour grapes, I guess. In my second year, one of the farmers whose bike I had fixed did have a bumper harvest and did in fact buy a tractor from us.

It would not be the last time that a Greek farmer would run

to discredit me to Roger. I was sat at my desk one Friday when the phone rang. "Good afternoon FES." I said

"Rupert, you're there?" it was Roger.

"Yes, I'm here, why?" I replied

"No nothing, sorry, never mind" and he hung up. Very strange I thought. A couple of weeks Roger called again, this time it was Saturday morning. Again, he sounded surprised to hear me on the other end of the line. The third time it happened I asked Roger what the hell was going on.

"A Greek farmer keeps phoning me saying that he has just been to your office and you're not there, and the boys told him that you had gone to the Lake fishing. He has done this three or four times, on Fridays, Saturdays and Mondays, claiming you are taking long weekends when you should be at work." He explained.

"But I'm not, I'm here. I haven't been to the Lake for weeks. Who is the Greek?" I asked but Roger wouldn't tell me.

"Sorry Rupert, don't worry about it all, I just needed to check. Just carry on and forget I called".

A few weeks later Roger rang and asked if I could come to Blantyre to see him the next day, being Friday, so I drove down to Blantyre that evening and went into Rogers office on the Friday morning.

"What's up?" I asked, waiting to have to justify myself again because of Greeks making up stories.

"Can you leave your car here," he started.

I thought oh god I'm being fired! But he continued, "and take the white Daihatsu that's parked outside. Note the mileage and the diesel you use. Just drive it around and let me know what it does to the gallon. Bring it back in a week."

It seemed a bit of a strange request but he was the boss so I took the keys from him. We then chatted for a while over a cup of coffee. Just then Roger's phone rang and he took the call.

"Oh hello, … fine, ….fine, …..Oh really, …. yes, oh, is he? Well that's funny because he is sitting here in front of me in my office. Now listen to me, let Rupert get on with his job and you concentrate on your farming, is that understood? Thank you. Good Bye." And he put the phone down. I just sat there staring at Roger. "Who was that?" I asked finally.

"That was so-and-so, reporting you again for being at the Lake fishing!" he told me. The penny finally dropped with me too. This Greek farmer had made it known in Namwera that he had hoped to get me fired from the branch so that he could get his son given the job, presumably so the pair of them could run it for their own benefit, stealing parts and the son doing welding and mechanical work for his farther for free and charging it to other farmers accounts. This was a practice that had been rumoured to have gone on prior to my arrival there. Roger was fuming, but I never had any more trouble and Roger didn't get any more phone calls.

I drove the Daihatsu around for a week and delivered it back to Roger the following Friday.

"Well what does it do?" he tentatively asked me as I gave him the keys. When I told him he just said two words - "The Bastard!"

It was one of the few times that I ever heard Roger swear. I gathered later that a manager from one of the other branches had been siphoning off the diesel to use in his personal vehicle. Roger would often give me jobs like this, I felt pleased that he trusted me and I'm sure Roger felt happier knowing that someone was on his side.

CHAPTER 66

ENGLISH LESSONS

R oger didn't visit the branch often. As long as it was making a profit, then that's all he was really worried about, and left me to get on with my job. The only time he visited was if he was coming up to the lake in the company Range Rover and we urgently needed a spare part. I remember such a time and seeing as Roger was the Managing Director of FES, I called all the staff into my office to warn them to be on their best behaviour. I ran a clean branch but we gave the place a thorough clean, even checking behind boxes and under cupboards to make sure the place was spotless.

"Let me do all the talking, just say hello to him if he comes into the workshop, don't try and have a conversation with him." I had advised.

I didn't want Kawale asking Roger to stick his finger in the spark-plug cap while he cranked the engine over to see if it was sparking or anything stupid like that.

The day came and Roger pulled in through the gates of the yard in his Range Rover. Roger was his usual happy, cheeky self and automatically made you feel at ease. I went out to meet him and together we walked through the show room to my office where I made him a coffee and talked about how things were going. After a while he asked to meet the boys so we went to the store to introduce Elias.

"Morning Bwana Ling." Elias said very official like.

"Morning Elias, your father is fine and asked me to give you his greetings. Wow, are those new shoes? Where did you get them? How much were they?" he replied making conversation with Elias.

Elias was beaming, first to get told about his father and second that the big boss had admired his new shoes and answered Roger.

"Yes, Bwana Ling, they are new, I got them in Mangochi, they cost me forty fucks!" he beamed. Roger was silent and so was I. Roger turned to me as if to ask for an explanation.

"He means Bucks, don't you Elias? Let's go and see the workshop." I said, trying to smooth over the miss placed word and led Roger back through the showroom and out into the workshop. His chat with Chilangwe was technical and I thought "That went well."

Roger then moved onto where Kawale and his assistant were working on the Daihatsu cruiser that was our Field Service Vehicle. It had snapped its rocker shaft clean in half. Kawale was in the process of stripping the engine to establish whether the mistimed push rods had caused any damage to the pistons and cylinders. Roger leaned into the engine bay knowledgeably and asked Kawale what was wrong with the engine. Roger knew engines inside out so I was confident that he would not be out of his depth if Kawale got technical. I had no worries here I thought.

"It's FUCKED Bwana!" informed Kawale.

Roger spluttered in shock and I think I just buried my head in my hands as I turned away from Roger. I just wanted to die.

As Roger walked to his car he said "I know it's important for them to have a grasp of the English language but can we please stick to the Queen's English where possible?"

I hadn't realised that they had been picking up the odd word here and there. I gave them a crash course of the words they were not to use on Roger's future visits to Namwera.

CHAPTER 67

UNCLES

I had first met Denis Phocas while I was at Jorge's place. We had chatted a bit but never really had the time to become friends. When I became the Manager at FES Denis came in a few times and over coffee in my office a friendship was struck. He was a joyful guy, always-seemed on top of the world, not a worry. He loved Africa and Namwera and had all the Greeks sussed. He was very good at doing impressions of the other Greeks and often had me in stitches. He also had a habit of talking in an Indian/Asian accent that was really amusing.

Over one of our coffees he invited me for supper at his farm. As was usual with supper invitations you would always go in the late afternoon, never arriving in the evening. On this particular occasion it had been raining and the roads were muddy and treacherous. I rounded one corner in the long-wheel based Land Cruiser and the back end slid out to my left. The road was just too slippery and if I'm honest I was going a tad fast so there was no way to correct it. The Cruiser was now going sideways, literally ninety degrees to the direction of the road. Time stood still as I looked out over the bonnet at the fields flashing past. I then looked to my left at the road I was sliding down.

"Oh, here we bloody go again!" I thought as I remembered Chris's Range Rover. I just had to sit there hoping that the tyres would not catch a rock or something that would flip the vehicle over onto its roof. Thankfully there weren't any rocks and eventually the Cruiser slid to a halt. I gingerly reversed the car back onto the road and straightened it up and continued on my way to Denis's place, at a more sensible speed now I might add.

As I pulled up to his farmhouse, I was stunned for a second. Denis's house was two-storey, never had I ever seen a two-storey house in Namwera. What a place, I loved it. As I stood there taking the house in, I heard Denis shout in his Indian accent from the balcony.

"Uncle, velcom to my humble abode. May Mohamed shine down on you and bless you with a thousand children who all have the faces of Baboons!" said Denis, followed by this belly laugh that he had that had a sinister evil tone to it, the kind of laugh the villain has in a movie just after he announces his plans for world domination.

When I got to the top of the wide stairs on the side of the house and on to the balcony there was Denis laid in a hammock, strung between two of the balcony's pillars, dressed only in shorts and a straw sombrero. On his feet he had a pair of Chelsea boots and was playing a guitar. Why was I shocked, this was Namwera!

We talked about all sorts, drinking beers and listening to Al Stewart. Denis' cook then appeared to announce that supper was served. And what a meal, it was absolutely great. Denis's cook was called Carrotie, an old African who must have been in his eighties. Carrotie had worked for Denis's father before he retired back to Greece so Carrotie had been taught all of Denis's mothers' Greek recipes.

One evening I arrived again at Denis's for supper and was greeted with the usual yell of "Uncle, come on up" from somewhere upstairs. As I came into the lounge there is Denis getting a foot massage from Carrotie. Johnny Clegg and Juluka were playing in the background.

"Uncle, you got to have one of Carroties' massages, they're the best."

Denis waited for me to remove my shoes, but I passed on that occasion. Another time I would arrive at Denis's and wasn't greeted by the usual Indian greeting. On entering the house and calling if anyone was home, Denis called from the bathroom, "I'm in here, come in." I found Denis laying in the bath with Carrotie scrubbing his back. Johnny Clegg and Juluka were again playing in the background. I have all Johnny Cleggs' albums now and listening to them now always reminds me of Denis and that sight of him being massaged and washed by his cook.

Denis and I would often share trips to town, once going in my car and the next time in Denis'. He was a good mechanic and loved modifying things to get more performance. He had an immaculate Rover 3500, that had once been Roger's company car and when it was replaced Denis had bought it. It used to go like a rocket and at night with all its dashboard lights lit up, it was like sitting in a jet fighter and just as fast. However, Denis felt that the rear springs were a little weak and were a design fault.

"Uncle, I've changed the springs on the Rover and put in Range Rover springs to lift the back up a bit more and force the nose down, for high speed driving!"

The car had the resemblance of a dragster at Santa Pod. You needed to wear your seatbelt just to stay in your seat when the car was stationary so that you didn't slide into the foot well, but when you accelerated you could unfasten the seat belt as you were going nowhere except into the back of the seat. It was awesome.

CHAPTER 68

I ALMOST SHOOT MY DOG

A few weeks later I received a call from Roger asking me to come to town as my new car was ready, so I headed to town in some excitement.

When I pulled up outside FES in Blantyre, there outside the showroom window was a gleaming Toyota Tercel 4x4 in white. It was fantastic. I exchange keys with Roger and handed the old Land Cruiser back to Roger.

I was still staying at home with my parents when I came to town so drove out to their house in the new car. My feelings of pride were again dashed by another cutting comment from mother. I think I returned to Namwera the next day.

One evening I had invited Denis round for supper and on such occasions had arranged for the gates to be left open ready for Denis's arrival and it wasn't long before I heard the throaty rumbling of the Range Rover V8 that announced his arrival. The next thing I see is Denis running up to the house, white as a sheet.

"Rupe, I'm so sorry, I have run over Namson!"

Namson was one of my dogs, named such because he was the Son of Nam, a name that Denis had given him. When we got to Namson he was in a poor state. It appeared that he had just run out from the bushes and straight under the front wheel of the Range Rover. The front tyre had gone over his head, and it looked like the jaw was broken.

A vet was out of the question in Namwera so I went up to the house to fetch my .22 rifle and say goodbye to poor Namson. By the time I got back to him though Kawale, who had heard the yelp, had arrived and was inspecting Namson.

"No bwana, don't kill him, he will be fine, He will recover!" he said knowledgeably.

"Ok I'll give him till tomorrow and if he is no better in the morning he's gone" I said not believing that Namson would even make it through the night.

So next morning to everyone's amazement Namson was much improved and Kawale agreed to take him to his house to care for him. I think he was worried I was still going to shoot the dog.

The good news was that Namson did make a full recovery and was taken by the local agricultural liaison office from ComBank in Namwera. I'd often see the Bank pick-up driving through Namwera with Namson stood up in the open back with his ears flapping in the wind. He had certainly not known how close he had come to not making it that day. Now I feel so glad I was prevented from shooting him. It scares me now to think what I was prepared to do; maybe Namwera was starting to get to me.

CHAPTER 69

CAR MODIFICATIONS

T he months went by and Denis and I would spend most evenings together, either at my house or at his. We were two bachelors and after a few beers the subject often turned to car modifications. One evening while I was round at his place for supper he started to discuss how to increase the octane in the Malawian petrol.

"Uncle, our petrol is around 82 octane at best, we really need to bump that up to 92-95, that way we would get more miles per gallon and more performance."

I gave the usual "Mmmms" in-between sipping my beer, trying to imagine what was coming next.

"If we fill the tank, then chuck some moth balls in, they will dissolve and the chemicals in the moth balls will increase the octane, I reckon two or three balls should do it".

More "MMmmmmmssss" from me.

"The engine might heat up a little so if we chuck in half a litre of 2-stroke oil to each full tank of petrol that should keep everything lubbed up!" he said with a big grin on his face.

At this point I made the small suggestion that seeing as my car was a company car and that I didn't think Roger would be too pleased if I blow the thing up, that maybe we should try this first on one of Denis' cars to see what happened.

A few more beers later......

"If I remove the air cleaner intake pipe and attach a length of hose to it, then at the open end fix a funnel; then as you drive along the wind will shoot into the funnel and build up a pressure, then when the carb-butterfly opens to take in air, the pressurised air will shoot in at whatever speed the car is doing, instead of the engine having to suck it in. A sort of a Turbo cross Supercharger. What do you think Uncle?"

"What do I think? I think you're nuts, that's what I think!"

To cut a long story short, Denis did his modifications on his Rover 3500 and decided we needed a test run one evening to Club Mak. The trip on the dirt road from my house to Mangochi was just to see if the engine blew up from the mothballs. All went well, the temperature didn't go above normal. We crossed the bridge and turned right onto the Lake road and Denis floored the Rover. The Rover accelerated normally as it always had done, then at about forty miles per hour the car suddenly bolted forward like it had been kicked up the backside. I was pushed back in my seat.

"Uncle did you feel the funnel kick in!!!" Denis screamed with joy.

He was sat there like a kid who had just built his first chemical fuelled rocket, which I guess he had. The following weekend I was at Denis' farm making the necessary modifications to my Tercel. I could get about another ten miles per gallon out of it on a run to town and no one could catch me off the lights when I hit forty miles per hour. We never told anyone about our mothball/funnel secret, but in 2003 on a visit to Malawi I saw my old white Tercel driving around Mzuzu so the beast still lives!

CHAPTER 70

NIGHT RIDERS

You must remember that, at the time, we were all young guys; I had just turned twenty-three. The nearest anything was either Blantyre, over 140 miles to the south or Lilongwe, almost 170 miles northwest. Making the round trip was close to 300 miles whichever way you went.

Sure, you get used to living so far from a cinema, a restaurant, a bar, or a night on the town. But every once in a while, a trip to town was necessary, or you would go around the twist.

One afternoon Thanasi came into my office and said that he and Costa were going to town that evening, just for the night to catch a movie, get something to eat then back to Namwera in the early hours, ready for work the next morning. Was I interested? I thought about it for a while, and thought there was no harm in it, sure I'd go. The plot then thickened.

"We are going in Costas' car, so can I leave my car at your house? Also, my dad doesn't know we are going to town so if you see him in the week, which you will, we stayed at your house watching videos." he explained.

"So, you want to go all the way to town, in the night, without your dad's finding out and be bright-eyed and bushy-tailed for work in the morning? This is nuts, you'll never get away with it." I reasoned with Thanasi.

"Sure we will." he said with that slight curled up on one side smile and a twinkle in his eyes.

So that evening around 6pm the two of them converged on my house and we all piled into Costa's car and bolted for town. With Costa driving we made it to town in under three hours, but I'm not sure how, my eyes were closed tightly for most of the trip. Most of the dirt road from my house to Mangochi was either sideways or with all four wheels off the road! I lost count how many close shaves we had, although I do remember in particular a Land Rover that we nearly hit broadside on a bend coming into Zomba as it pulled out of a junction. I have no idea how Costa managed to swerve but he did. We enjoyed the evening, we had a meal, Thanasi went to see a girl, creeping into her house as her mother slept. All the time I was just thinking about the return trip. Finally, Costa hooted outside at the agreed time and we "flew" back to Namwera, literally. We had to get back to my place before 4.30am so that Thanasi had time to let his car cool down and get into the house before Taki or his mother woke up and we just made it.

That afternoon Taki stopped into my office for his daily coffee on his way to the Post Office. "Did you youngsters have a good time last night?" he asked over his coffee and cigarettes.

"Yes, it was a good evening." I said realising that we had not agreed on a video that we were supposed to have watching. Luckily, he didn't press me with any more questions or ask for details.

A few days later Thanasi was back in my office. "Sorry buddy, we got to go to town again, but we gotta go in your car this time, Dad just serviced my car and knows the mileage"

"What about Costa, can't we take his car?" I asked.

"No, we used his car last time."

When he put it like that, I couldn't find a reason to say no, so off to town we went again.

The next week Thanasi is back in the office, as I see him arrive I just shout "NO!" but it has no effect. At least this time it was in his car.

We were all starting to get fatigued by the driving and the lack of sleep; this trip in seven days brought our collective mileage to nearly 1000 miles. Thanasi was as mad a driver as Costa was. On the way back I looked at his oil pressure gauge and the needle was shaking so much it was flicking between the minimum and the maximum like a high-speed pendulum. As we turned off onto the Lake Road at the Balaka turn-off Thanasi said he had to stop as he was falling asleep. I didn't argue since I didn't fancy the chance of him not being in full control of the wheel as he ran into a herd of goats at over 100mph. He stopped the car, jumped out and ran to the front of the car and starred at the headlights for a few minutes. He then got back in the car and off we sped. After about fifteen minutes he was feeling the strain again so we pulled over.

"Rupe, pull the wiper washer button for me" and then he got out and stuck his head in the washer jet and sprayed his face with water.

When he was refreshed, off we dashed again. We just got home in the nick-of-time but it was close.

These runs went on for a few months, one trip in my car, one in Thanasi's and the next with Costa. Driving at night on the Lake Road was hellish since even at 3.30 or 4.00am goats would still run into the road. I decided that drastic actions needed to be taken.

During moments of "free time" in the workshop, when the guys didn't have any work, we set about constructing a "crash-bar" for the front of the Tercel. Since it wasn't a large 4x4 the bars had to be tastefully constructed, light, but strong enough to hold-up if we did hit a herd of goats. After a few days we had the bars made and fitted and I was really pleased with the results. Since the car was white, I decided to paint the bars white and I have to say they looked pretty good. The bars were bolted directly onto the car's chassis and the hope was that if the force hitting the bars was too great that the bolts would sheer and therefore not cause any serious damage to the chassis. I then invested in four powerful spot lights which I had Gordon Williamson wire in because my knowledge of electrics was dangerous.

The result was amazing; the Tercel looked like it had just been entered into the Safari Rally. The day finally came when the bars proved their worth. I was doing a late afternoon run from town back to Namwera and was just passing Lake Malombe, where all the racks of dried fish are on the side of the road, where the smell paralyses your lungs, you know the place. A herd of goats ran across a patch of cultivated land at the side of the road, all the goats came up to the edge of the tarmac and then veered away back into the field.....except one goat! He came straight into the road. Swerving was suicidal at the speed I was doing so I just remember holding the steering wheel straight and locking my arms and thinking "this is it, he goes".

The goat disappeared in front of the right front wing and then there was a thud! The car jolted on hitting the goat as if I had just changed down a gear. Then I saw the goat fly off the bar into the air and land on the left hand side of the road....stone dead.

In situations like this it is always best to not stop, otherwise you are there for hours while the owner of the goat is found. He then demands payment of six hundred kwacha for a thirty kwacha goat and then won't let you keep the dead goat either, even though you've paid for it and you wouldn't mind it roasted on a Brai at the weekend with a couple of mates.

So, rule is, Keep Driving, if your car is drivable!

When I was a good few miles up the road I pulled over and

got out to inspect the damage.........there wasn't a dent or scratch on the bars. I think I even punched the air with my fist and jumped for joy. I never hit another goat but I had confidence that if I did the car would be ok, not the same would be said for the goat!

In all those Night-Rider trips we were never discovered and the identity to who were the Night-Riders remained a mystery.

One day I was sitting in my office and I could hear the sound of this car coming down the road at high speed. I glanced out of my window to see Costa shoot past. His car was easily two feet off the ground and in a flash, he was gone. A few minutes later Kawale came into my office.

"Bwana, did you see Costa? His car was in the air!"

"Yes, I saw him, he's mad. One of these days he is going to kill someone". But we both had a laugh about it.

Minutes later, hordes of people were flooding out of the roadside stores and heading down the road in the direction of the Post Office. They were all shouting to others in the street. Elias left the stores and went to the fence to see what was going on and then came back to the office.

"Costa has just had an accident. He has hit a woman." Elias said quietly.

I got up from my chair and walked out onto the road. I couldn't see anything. Just then Taki came down the road in his Land Cruiser. He looked concerned as he waved to me. I thought of following him down in the direction of the accident but there was not going to be much I could do and anyway Taki was there and he would handle any situation.

About an hour later Taki came back up the road and pulled in through the gate. I got up to meet him and asked if Costa was ok.

"He's ok, he's not hurt but he killed the woman".

"You're joking? Oh my god!" I thought back to my comment to Kawale.

Taki was shaken. "This is a bit of a mess; his dad is on his way up to try and sort this out. Let's have a coffee." And we retired to talk in my office.

It had to happen I guess, it's the law of averages. Your luck can't hold out for too long doing anything without due care or with total disregard for your safety or that of others. Time always catches up with you. Costas's dad arrived and after a cash settlement with the woman's family and the Police no charges were brought and the matter was closed. I don't condone the payment but, in a way, Costa going to court and possible prison in the worst case would not help the woman's family. The cash payment would. And the money to the Police, well that's just Africa.

Both Taki and I agreed that afternoon in the office that maybe Costa needed for this to happen and that maybe it would now make him slow his driving down. Sadly, and horrifically it didn't.

A year or so later Costa got married to a lovely Greek girl. One night they were driving down the Chileka Road to his dad's place and they drove into the back of a broken-down lorry. As is the case in most of Africa it was just over the brow of a hill and had no back lights. His wife was killed; she was a few months pregnant.

The Night-Riders were officially disbanded as neither Thanasi nor I felt up to Costa driving.

CHAPTER 71

200 MILES FOR A COKE

A few months later JT pulled through the FES gate one afternoon.

"Hey Bud!" he beamed as he walked through the showroom towards the open door of my office. He never called me "Bud" so I knew straightaway that he wanted something from me.

"Ok what do you need?"

"No nothing, I just need a favour. I have got to go to Lilongwe to see Sharon tonight and wondered if you would come with me to share the driving?"

"Oh, so you do want something?" I thought.

Lilongwe is a bloody long way but hey, I was a Night-Rider, I could do this. But hang on a second, JT was the guy who only a year ago hated my guts for dating his cousin. But saying no wasn't going to help our inter-family relations.

"Ok I'll come, except I can't leave till after work and I have to be back in time for work, no jokes!"

"Hey, no problem, trust me." said JT. Well that comment didn't really fill me with confidence.

So that evening after work JT arrives in his dad's Merc and we head off to Lilongwe. It was a tedious journey, sat next to the guy who not so long ago was threatening the hell out of me, was difficult to say the least. As the miles clicked by things started to get a bit better and but I was glad when we reached Lilongwe. Sharon's dad was the Manager of a large bank in Malawi and they lived in a gigantic house in a posh area of the Capital. Her parents were away for the night, so I was beginning to see why JT was so keen to make this visit.

I soon started to feel like a bone in a chicken sandwich and wished I said no to this favour. I decided to have a bath and head to bed to get some sleep at least before we had to head back to Nam. While I was in my bath, I thought I heard another person's voice in the lounge but didn't really want to know what was going on in there so headed off to get some kip. I hadn't been in bed long when the door was gently opened and Sharon's friend Sarah entered with obvious plans for the night. I thought about it for a second then made my excuses and Sarah left me to sleep.

A few hours later I woke, JT and I said our goodbyes and headed out into the night for the drive back to Namwera.

"Rupe, why didn't you sleep with Sarah, she wanted you?" JT just asked after a long period of silence.

"JT, I'm going out with your cousin or have you forgotten."

"It's ok Rupe, I wouldn't have told her. You should have done it, I heard she's great in bed."

I muttered something and settled down to drive us home. JT soon fell asleep which was great, I didn't feel much like talking anyway. When we got back to my house, I woke JT up and got out of the car and he drove home.

I spent a few days thinking about the Sarah incident. The saint in me being glad I hadn't slept with her and the devil wishing I had. I just knew that if I had JT would have blabbed, even if he hadn't, he would have had it over me for the rest of my life. I was glad I hadn't, I didn't really trust him.

A few weeks later JT pulled into the gates again.

"Hey Bud!"

"No way, no bloody way. Not again!" I yelled.

"Hey come on, I need this, I'll owe you. Hey Rupe, we are almost family now."

Family! Shit things were moving on fast. A few weeks ago he was trying to get me to be unfaithful to his cousin with his birds mate!

"Ok, when?" I asked.

"This Thursday, only I can't take my car so you'll have to take yours but I'll pay for petrol".

Finally, I agreed. "But I'm still not fucking Sarah!" I stated, which he agreed to so on Thursday we again headed off to the bright lights of the Capital City.

JT had arranged to meet Sharon at a bar in Lilongwe which made me feel a little more at ease. Sharon was already there when we arrived and I ordered the drinks while JT and Sharon sat down at a table. Before the barman had even finished pouring the drinks, JT and Sharon had started yelling at each other about something. I took their drinks across to them and headed back to my barstool to keep out of the way. No sooner had I picked up my coke to take a sip than JT grabs my shoulder.

"That's it we're leaving, that bitch is nuts!"

"Leaving? Are you nuts? We only just bloody got here!"

"Yeah, I know but I've had enough of her, come on let's go".

So, I down my coke and hurry to catch JT who is already standing by my car. I unlock the doors and we both jump in and drive off out of town. We hadn't gone far when JT nods off to sleep.

"Oh, fucking great, so I have to drive there and back right? It's a fucking long way for a coke!" and I drive off towards Namwera.

I was right, it was four hundred miles but JT did at least reimburse me the petrol. Some small favours, I guess. I never took him to Lilongwe again or did him another favour.

CHAPTER 72

BETWEEN A "ROC" AND A CLUTCH

Roger was keen to expand Massey Fergusons' control of the Malawian market by taking business away from Ford. Finally, a plan was hatched.

FES came up with the idea of fitting Massey engines into Fords. To enable this a plate was developed that bolted onto the bell-housing of the Ford gear-box, the Massey engine was then bolted onto the plate and bobs your uncle. Well, of course it wasn't just that simple, there were a few technical items and magic but it worked. FES called this "Frankenstein" marriage ROC. I seem to remember Roger saying once that it stood for Recycled Old Crap, the crap being the Ford tractor the engine was in.

This all meant that farmers who had old Ford tractors could have a Massey engine installed and FES had a foot-hold in the market that they wouldn't have had normally. It was genius.

Roger then set about trying to get as many "buggered old Fords" as he could to put these engines in. He scoured the country for willing farmers who would buy into the scheme.

One day Roger rang me from town.

"Hello dear boy. Are you well? I'm coming up to the Lake

Cottage for the weekend with the family and I've got a little trip planned for you!" he said with a chuckle.

"I need to go and pick up an old Ford tractor that we are going to ROC. I'm sending the lorry up from here to meet us at the guy's farm. You noticed I said WE?"

"Mmmmmm carry on" I said not really knowing what I was getting myself into.

"Well I'm coming up in the Rover (by this he didn't mean Land Rover, or Range Rover, he meant his saloon car!) and obviously I cant take that into the bush where this guy lives…….." there was a pause……." so I wondered if you could pick me up and drive out to the farm and the two of us can put the tractor on the lorry?"

"Sure. Does the tractor run?"

"Don't be bloody stupid lad, it's a Ford!" and there was more chuckling.

So we agreed a time and place, and I was there to pick Roger up and as I recall the FES lorry followed behind us as we drove mile after mile along dirt tracks through the bush, hoping that the directions Roger had been given would eventually lead us to the Malawians farm and the deceased Ford tractor.

After a good many hours, we arrived at the farm, if you could call it that. The tractor was in a field and had certainly seen better days, it was a wreck. I think Roger, the lorry driver and I just stood there looking at the tractor for a few minutes not really knowing where to start.

Our first attempt from memory involved us all trying to push the tractor onto the back of the lorry, but to be honest it was a lost hope, so Roger made a plan.

"Rupe, attach this chain onto the back of your car and we will thread the chain through the side of the lorry and fix it to the front of the tractor. You can then pull the tractor on to the lorry."

"Ok, I'll give it a go." I said, trying to look enthusiastic.

Well even with the rest of them pushing the tractor and me pulling it with my car, it wasn't going well. After a few attempts the familiar smell of my clutch pad started to fill the car.

"Roger, my clutch is burning"

"Bugger the clutch keep going" he said desperately.

"If you're sure?????" I needed confirmation on this.

"Yes man, I'll buy you a new car!"

So, I kept pulling the tractor onto the lorry and finally it rolled up the planks on to the truck. There was a roar of "yes" and much clapping.

We still chuckle about that old tractor when Roger and I catch up almost thirty years later.

A few weeks after the clutch vs ROC incident I was down in Blantyre for the month end, when I handed in the monthly accounts, picked up a few urgent spares for the stores and did my monthly shop for groceries.

I had parked on the road outside FES, as all the staff spaces were taken. As usual after seeing Roger in his office to give him an update on how the Branch was doing, the two of us took a walk into the workshop area. These walks were a chance for Roger to show me any new developments they were trying. It also gave me a chance to catch up with Elias' father who working in the Paint Shop.

As we were walking around the workshop, there was an almighty crash outside on the road, like two cars had collided.

"That sounds like someone's car's a right-off" Roger said with a smile and we continued our walk.

A few minutes later one of the FES staff came running into the workshop....

"Bwana Rupert, your car is in an accident!"

Roger and I rushed out of the workshop gates and on to the road. There was a Toyota Land Cruiser firmly crumpled into the back of my car, which had been shoved about ten feet. Stood by both cars was a gentleman who was most apologetic.

"I parked my car outside the Ryalls Hotel and I thought I had put the hand-brake on but I hadn't and the car rolled down the street into yours. I'm so sorry!"

As we all stood there surveying the damage it suddenly dawned on Roger that had my car not been parked where it was, that the Land Cruiser would have continued to roll down the road, gaining speed and would have eventually driven straight into the side of Rogers' new metallic gold Rover 3500.

"Well that was bloody lucky!" he said and slapped me on the back. "Never mind, yours needed a new clutch anyway!"

My car was towed away to Mobil Motors in Limbe for repair and Roger sorted me out a vehicle while it was being fixed. I have to say, they did a great job and you would never have known it had been shunted halfway down Hanover Avenue.

CHAPTER 73

TAKI

In Africa there are some good old characters, people who have been there, seen it and done it. People who were fast disappearing and Taki Pantazis was one of those people. I had first met Taki when he had come to Jorge's field day some years ago. He was probably very early fifties and fit for his age. He was an educated man who had seen a lot in his time. While he was not popular he was respected if that makes sense. As Jorge said, when they hate you it's because you are doing better than them and I think this was true of Taki. He was one of the first farmers in Namwera to try and grow coffee on a large scale, and he was successful. He was married to a delightful Portuguese lady called Louisa. They had one son, Thanasi and two daughters. When I was sick in the mission hospital in Namwera with alcohol poisoning and Malaria at the same time, Thanasi was the only person other than Jorge and his family to visit me out of 200 farmers. They were a good family.

During my time at FES Taki would always drop in for a strong, double strength black coffee on his way into Namwera or on his way home. We spent many, many hours chatting about all sorts of things and we became very close. He would often stop by to invite me to their home for supper that night and the invitations got so frequent that I was there probably twice a week, every week.

Taki was a most entertaining man, he was a great story teller, an art that is almost dead now. The evenings were great fun. Thanasi used to get bored, at having heard the stories so many times but I have to say that in the three years that I went for supper with Taki's family I never heard the same story twice, which says a lot.

Most of the stories were about Taki's time in Portuguese East Africa and later when it became Mozambique. He had been there when Africa was still wild and unspoilt. He had been a Professional Hunter taking out rich clients, especially Americans hunting. He had also spent a lot of time hunting crocodiles, and rumour was that this was where he had made most of his money. Two walls of his lounge were floor to ceiling framed black and white photos of every possible animal Taki had shot in his career as a hunter, everything from elephant and rhino to porcupine and pangolin. It was an impressive collection.

Taki told me literally hundreds of stories over that 3 year period but I will try to mention a few to give you an idea of this man. But before I do, I just want to recount an incident that happened to me one afternoon when I went around to see him.

On entering the house, I greeted his wife Louisa and asked if Taki was about. She said he was in his bedroom but said I should knock loudly and not to go in till he called me in. Seemed a bit strange but when you knock on a man's bedroom door you don't know what to expect. So, I knocked loudly and said it was me.

"Rupe! Great to see you, come in but quickly close the door behind you" his voice came from inside.

I slowly opened the door, stepped inside and closed it after me. I was not expecting the sight I saw. There sat in the middle of the double bed was Taki, cross-legged and holding a rifle! He must have seen the look of disbelief on my face and quickly and in a whisper explained.

"I have a bloody mouse problem. I'm just waiting for him to show his face. Anyway, come and sit on the bed, howzit going? You're staying for supper right?" he asked not taking his eyes off scanning the floor area.

I should not have been shocked; this was after all Namwera. Most people with a mouse problem would get a cat or put down a mouse trap but this was Nam. Here we sat crossed legged on our beds and waited for the rodent to show its face and then we blasted the little rodent with a gun!

Thankfully the mouse knew what was good for it and declined to make an appearance so after we had chatted a while Taki suggested we retire to the lounge. I was glad really, I just wondered what it would be like to have a bullet whizzing round the room, ricocheting off walls while we sat on the bed. It would have been like a bizarre form of Rodent Roulette. The lounge was a far safer place.

The best story was of when Taki and Louisa went for a meal at a fancy restaurant in town. The meal was going well when something suddenly catches Taki's eye.

"That guy across there is looking at you." he says to Louisa.

Louisa looked gingerly over to the corner but can't see anyone looking. Now Louisa was a very glamorous woman and Taki was taking no chances so he glanced across again at the guy in the corner.

"He's bloody looking again, the bastard, can't he see I'm sat here with you?"

Louisa again glanced across to the corner but can't see a man. "I can't see anyone amour, which guy?" she asked.

"Oh, you can't see him? Maybe you know him, is he a friend of yours, is that what it is?"

Louisa told Taki to stop being silly and to just get on with the meal. Taki tried to calm his temper but every time he looked up and across to the corner this guy is starring back at their table.

"He's bloody looking again! Either he's gay and looking at me or he's looking at you? I'm going to sort him out".

Louisa tried again to calm her husband who by now is firing on all cylinders.

"If he looks again, I'm going to the car to get my gun and I'll shoot the bastard! There, he's looking again, that's it!" and with that Taki pushed his chair away from the table and stands up. It's only when the guy pushes his chair away from his table and also stands up at the very same moment that Taki realises that the man across the room is actually his own reflection on a mirrored wall. The worrying thing is that had it been another guy Taki might well have shot him!

Not only was he a great story teller of true events but sometimes he would tell what you thought was a story only to realise at the last moment that it was a joke. A story that comes to mind was the hunter and the fisherman story. I can't tell it like Taki told it at the time so I'll shorten it and tell it as a joke.

A hunter and a fisherman are drinking in a bar and comparing tales. The hunter tells the fisherman of a huge python that he saw in the Congo in the 1940's. It was a monster. Not to be out done the fisherman recalls a shark fishing trip in the Indian Ocean when he hooked a monster of a fish.

The hunter then tells how the python must have been as thick as a tree! The fisherman continues how he hooked what he thought was a huge shark, but couldn't see it, but it just took line out and the fisherman was unable to wind any line back on the reel. The hunter tells of how he wrestled with the snake for half a day before he finally had it beat. The fisherman says that's nothing and explains how he fought the fish for 8 hours, eventually tying the line to the back of the boat and heading for shore. The hunter continued to tell how at first they thought the snake was 30 feet long. The fisherman is unimpressed and says that when they got to harbour, he then attached the line to a winch to haul the brute in. When the thing finally came to the shore it was a sunken Spanish galleon ship. The hunter says that that's nothing, when they actually measured the snake it was 60 feet long. Again not to be outdone the fisherman announces that the lamp on the galleons crows-nest was still alight!

The hunter thinks for a while and then finally says "Put out the lamp and I'll cut 40 feet off my python".

Some stories were about things that had happened to other people, like the Branding Iron Incident.

This European farmer was branding his steers one day with the help of a few of his African staff. Two guys were binding the legs of the steers and then holding them down while the farmer branded them, the steers not the staff! Helping him with the branding irons was a chap called Boniface. It had all been going well for a few hours; Boniface was passing the hot irons to the farmer without incident…........until the farmer stuck his hand out for Boniface to place the handle of the hot iron into his hand for the next steer when instead of grabbing the handle the farmer's hand closed around the hot end of the branding iron!

The farmer exploded in pain and anger "What the hell are you fucking doing?" but Boniface just looked at the anguished farmer blankly.

The farmer decided to go to the hospital as the burn looked bad. Thinking that the pain may increase the farmer decided to take Boniface with him as Boniface was also a driver. The farmer with Boniface next to him drove off to the hospital without incident. On arrival the farmer had his burn dressed and was given a shot of pain killer to help with the agony. The nurse asked the farmer if he had anyone who could drive him home as the pain-killer may make him feel a bit drowsy. "Yes, I have my driver with me so if I start to feel sleepy, he can drive."

So, the two men headed off back to the farm, the farmer at the wheel. After about 30 minutes into the journey and without warning the farmer falls asleep. As he awakes, he sees trees and bushes coming at him through the windscreen and in total panic he jumps on the breaks and brings the vehicle to a stop. He then turns to his left to look at Boniface, he is sat with his arms folded looking out of the windscreen like nothing had happened.

"What the fuck are you doing, couldn't you see we had left the road, why didn't you grab the wheel?"

"You're driving Bwana, not me".

The farmer didn't bother to say anymore but fired Boniface the next morning.

It was about this time when Thanasi decided to get married it was to Heather Johnston, a girl that I had gone to school with but she was originally from Zimbabwe. Her father was the Agricultural Officer for the Commercial Bank (he was killed in a car accident while I was still in Malawi). The strange thing was for most of the farming community was that she was not a Greek girl. I think most of the farmers had Thanasi marked as marrying one of their daughters and were put out by his choice. They were also put out when he announced that he was getting married in Lilongwe and not at the Greek Church in Blantyre. None of the Greeks agreed to go to the wedding. The excuse from most of them was it was too far to go.

Thanasi and I had known each other for a long time. As I have already said he was the only Greek to visit me in hospital at a time when I really hardly knew him, I hadn't forgotten that, so when the invitation came for the wedding there was no a question of me not going. In the early hours of the morning of the wedding I drove up to Lilongwe, went to the service, then the reception and then afterwards drove all the way back to Namwera.

Thanasi was pretty angry with the Greeks for shunning his

wedding and used me as an example. "Rupert drove all the way up for the wedding and all the way home again that night. If he could make the effort, why couldn't you?" They had no answers. The answer, if they had known, would have been "Well it's ok for Rupert, he's a Night-Rider!"

Me when I worked at FES

CHAPTER 74

GRASS TYRES

Working for FES was fantastic; I loved every day, and was happy to go to work. I was valued, respected and rewarded for my efforts. Roger was a great boss. I had my own house, my own car. Life was good.

For the first time in my life I was earning enough money to enjoy myself. Money was hard to spend in Namwera if you didn't play poker, which I didn't so my bank balance was getting quite healthy. I had, as everybody does in Malawi, enjoyed weekends at the lake. I enjoyed the fishing and the water-skiing but up till now I had relied on the hospitality of friends who had boats. I was grateful for their continued offers and invitations but decided that I really needed a boat of my own. Boats are not easy to find in Malawi and it is always a case of who you know before someone else does. By chance I heard of a "Konde Sale" at an American missionary's house where they had a fish tank for sale so went along that Saturday to see.

By the time I got there the fish tank had gone but parked in the drive was a speed boat, which was for sale! It was a small four-seater boat made of wood but with a fibreglass skin on the hull. It had a 40hp Johnson outboard on the back and sat on a light trailer. All in working order so the owner said. I bought the boat there and then for K2,500 and took it up to Namwera.

It needed a bit of a tidy up but all in all I was thrilled with it. The only downside was the condition of the tyres on the trailer, they were perished beyond belief but hey, they had got me to Namwera so the next weekend Samuel and I headed off to the lake with the boat to see how it went.

We didn't get more than about 20 miles down the hills towards Mangochi when I got a flat tyre on the trailer. I didn't have a spare or any way of repairing it so had to think of something as it was getting dark. I decided to remove the inner-tube and then pack the tyre with grass as full as I could. It kind of worked and got us to Mangochi.

We limped into a small local garage to get the tube repaired professionally. The African was in stitches when he saw the grass sticking out of the tyre.

"How far did you come like this?" he asked.

"Just from Namwera" I replied.

"Namwera?" was all he said but gave a look that said he wasn't surprised as nothing was out of the ordinary in Namwera.

We paid for the repair and continued on to Cape Maclear.

The next morning, we launched the boat. The pull-start was a demon, and took me a while of exhausting pulls to work out the knack but finally we got the engine fired up.

Samuel and I climbed aboard, he had never seen the lake before, let alone been in a boat, so his face was a picture as we tore across the bay towards the island and back again.

The boat worked!!! I was like a cat with two tails. I was independent and could now go fishing whenever I wanted, life was good.

On Sunday we packed up the tent and gingerly headed back to Namwera with the boat and trailer. We made it!

Over the next week or so I got busy constructing another, stronger trailer with large 750x16 wheels from an old Land Cruiser. It was a fairly easy job in the FES workshop; Kawale and I just turned the boat upside down and constructed the trailer on top of the hull. We used galvanised poles to construct the trailer so there was little chance of it rusting and then gave it a coat of paint just to be sure. I think the trailer would have outlasted the boat and probably did!

There were a few other jobs I wanted to do on the boat while I had it at the workshop. One was an engine service since we did not know how long it had been since the last one. Also, while at the lake I had noticed that there was no way of knowing if the water pump that took water from the Lake and pumped it around the engine to cool it was working or not. This was slightly worrying to say the least. Modern engines dispel the water out of a small jet at the side of the engine that can be easily seen with a quick glance over your shoulder as you are driving the boat.

The two of us pondered this for a few minutes before reaching for a drill! We then made a small 5mm hole in the engine casing, which we then threaded with a tap. We then took a common or garden grease nipple and drilled out the sealing ball so that there was a hole straight through the middle of the grease nipple. Then we simply screwed the grease nipple into our threaded hole.

To test the engine, we placed the engine into a water filled 200 litre drum and fired up the engine. Water now squirted out of our grease nipple, showing that the water pump was pushing water around the engine, job done! The other thing was to fit an electric start as the rope pull one was a pig to say the least. I made a phone call to a sister company of ours, who just happened to be the Evinrude dealership. My engine was a Johnson but the engines were identical.

With the next delivery of spares for my branch I had a

reconditioned electric start for a 40hp Evinrude. It took Kawale about 30 minutes to get it fitted and another 30 minutes to get an old tractor key start fitted to the dashboard of the boat and wired in. No more pulling on the rope!

A proud moment - my first boat

CHAPTER 75

I'LL BUY YOU A BAR

O n one of my trips to town I bumped into an old school friend named Gordon who mentioned in passing that he had two old motorcycles he was trying to get rid of. I was immediately interested and arranged to view the bikes that afternoon at his house.

When I got there, I was a little disappointed at the condition of the bikes. One was an old single cylinder Royal Enfield with a single bicycle type sprung seat; the only problem was it was rust from end to end.

The other was a 1954 single cylinder AJS 350cc that was a little worse for wear also. It was covered in black oil that looked like it had been burnt on. It didn't have an exhaust and the tank was a dull scratched red.

"It runs" said Gordon trying to seal the deal.

I ummmmed and scratched my head, wondering if the AJS might be worth trying to do up. Eventually we struck a deal and I collected the two bikes and loaded them on the back of the FES pickup and drove to my parents' house.

When Jim saw the two dilapidated wrecks and said "you will never get them running again, waste of money!"

"Well, we will see" I said trying to not get too deflated at my purchases.

At the end of the weekend I decided to leave the Royal Enfield for another day and just loaded the AJS on the FES pickup and headed back to Namwera to see what Kawale would make of it.

I needn't have worried, Kawale was ecstatic!

"Bwana, we will have this running by the end of the day!" he boasted.

"If you do, then there are a few beers in it for you" I said.

"No problem Bwana" and he skipped off to the workshop, in a manly kind of way obviously.

I then set about tending to some paperwork and dealing with a few customers. Suddenly I am shaken from the paperwork by a loud throaty growl from the workshop, followed by whoops and hollers from Kawale.

"Bloody hell, he's got the beast started!" I shouted as I got up from my desk and headed out to the workshop, followed by Elias who wanted to know what the excitement was.

Kawale was beaming as he sat astride the bike. "Told you Bwana, one hour!" he said tapping the top of his bare wrist where his watch would have been if he had owned one.

"You're bloody amazing" I say slapping him on his back.

Since it didn't have an exhaust, half of Namwera as far as the Post Office were now coming up the road to see what the noise is about so we decided to shut the engine off.

I turned again to Kawale, "We need to work out how we are going to sort an exhaust out."

"Don't worry Bwana" and with that he disappears out of the gate and down the street.

About 30 minutes later he comes back into my office holding a complete exhaust, foot rests and hand grips all for an AJS. Well I nearly fell off my chair.

"More beer Bwana?" he beamed.

"I'll say, I think I'm going to buy you a bar!" I reply, inspecting the goods.

It turned out there is an old AJS behind the market in Namwera and the guy who owned it was more than happy to sell it as parts so I quickly sent Kawale back to purchase what remained of the second AJS.

I was tempted to call Jim there and then to report my success but decided that it was all a little premature at this stage as we may have got it started but that was far from a road legal bike so I retired back to the house for lunch and to savour my success in private.

At 1.30pm I arrived back at the workshop to find Kawale sitting stride, not the AJS, but a cream Lambretta.

"Bwana, look what I found!" he beamed. "The same man had this also, I told him you would buy it".

"Oh, did you? Does this work?" I asked with some doubt.

"Not yet Bwana, but give me an hour!"

I then told Kawale to hang on a minute, I was not about to buy every rundown bike in Namwera and get the reputation of the stupid Mzungu who will spend good money on junk. I had a quick look at the Lambretta, it certainly was a cool looking scooter, it even had a spare wheel on a small luggage rack behind the seat. After scraping the dirt off an old plate, we discover that it has a 150cc engine and was made in 1968. Finally, I agreed to buy it on the condition that if Kawale can't get it running then it goes straight back.

"No problem Bwana, I told you, one hour, Bwana, one hour!" he laughed, again tapping his wrist and I left him to work his magic for a second time and I retired to my office to do some work.

Again, within the hour Kawale got the Scooter spluttering into life.

Over the next few weeks, I spent lunchtimes and quiet periods of the day stripping the AJS down to the frame with

369

Kawale's help, checking each part as we went. We then rubbed the frame down, checked for cracks and then these were welded up by Chilangwe's expert hand.

Once the frame was cleaned and repaired, we hand painted the frame with black gloss paint. Then we started to clean the bike components and refitted them onto the bike. The donor AJS supplied us with many of the parts that we were missing. Wiring was replaced and within the month the bike was starting to look great.

We spent a few days rubbing the tank and side covers down with fine wet and dry paper till the surfaces were smooth. I realised that even with a tin of spray paint we were not going to get a professional finish on the tank or covers so decided to take them to Mandala Motors and let their body shop guy do his stuff. I decided on British Racing Green with gold pin striping and I have to say when they came back the finish was amazing; you could see your face in the reflection. The spray painter had even put a coat of clear on, I was thrilled to bits.

Now we could get the bike completed and it looked a masterpiece. We had it sitting in the small showroom we had at FES for a few weeks before I took the bike to town again to show Jim.

When Jim saw the bike, his jaw dropped. He was speechless.

The nice end to the AJS was that Gordon, who had sold me the bike in the first place, put me in touch with a guy from England who collected vintage motorcycles and he bought the bike, shipping it back to England.

After all his help with the AJS I decided to give the Lambretta to Kawale, who, as you can imagine, was beside himself. We did discover once we opened the engine that the piston rings were worn so Kawale dug around in the stores and found some piston rings from a Briggs & Stratton lawnmower that were the exact same size and the engine ran like a charm. Kawale was very resourceful like that.

CHAPTER 76

"SNEAK THE GREEK"

I've already spoken about Tony Calavrias, from my time in Namadzi. Tony was one of those guys who very few people get the chance to meet, let alone get to know and become friends with. You meet his type once in your life, if ever and it has a lasting effect on you. Even after all these years I still feel honoured to have known Tony, although knowing his modesty he would be embarrassed at me saying it. Unlike his brother, Pancake, he was quiet, modest and unassuming.

He was born in Arusha, Tanzania, where his mother ran a hotel. He'd had numerous jobs around the world and was well travelled. He had worked on the ships in the Far East and been a diver in Indonesia.

He later went to Rhodesia and joined the army to fight the terrorist incursions, signing up in the Rhodesian Light Infantry (RLI). He soon became a tracker for them and later for the Selous Scouts. You have to keep in mind that this was Africa where nobody knows the bush like an African and for this Greek to work as a tracker over an African just about goes half way to telling you what Tony was like in the bush, his nickname as a tracker was "Sneak the Greek"! There was a rumour that he had gone AWOL from the RLI whilst on operations in Zambia, but I wasn't sure how true this was.

Tony was a tall bloke, over six-foot with long thin gangly legs. His waist was small but from there upwards he just widened like a triangle placed on its point to these broad shoulders and bulging tattooed biceps. He looked like a superhero character in a boy's comic, Captain America or as someone once said in Namwera he is like "Arnold Schwarzenegger meets Tarzan". His facial features were Romanesque, with his forehead coming straight down level with the bridge of his nose and a square jaw. He sported a close-cropped black beard or a moustache, depending how he felt at the time. He presented quite an imposing figure.

Tony never wore socks with his shoes and more often than not would wear African "car-tyre shoes" that he had specially made for him in Tanzania.

Tony had a fascination for knives, and throwing knives in particular, and he commissioned Jim to make a number of hand-made knives for him. Most of the knives were either bush knives with hardwood handles, but one was a dagger with a brass and ivory handle. Tony also had a set of three throwing knives made by Jim that were weighted and balanced to Tony's hands as per his instruction. The handles were made from non-slip black impact rubber. Tony was over the moon with the knives; the use of which I saw on many occasions and Tony was deadly with them. He was one of the few men I have seen who was able to accurately throw an axe. It was frightening.

He never really said much about his time in Rhodesia and I never saw any medals although in a quiet corner of his house hung a framed Mentioned in Despatches surrounded by assorted memorabilia from the war. Pancake used to use Tony's time in the army to full effect with the ladies, and was able, through his intimate knowledge of his brothers' time in the war, to convince them that he had been with the Selous Scouts also. I would often listen to Pancake at one of the Sports Club bars chatting to an unsuspecting lady dropping the names General Walls, Schulie, and others into conversation in an attempt to impress her with his war hero stories; even though Pancake had never even joined the army. Such was the difference between the two brothers.

I guess the years in the Rhodesian Army had a lasting effect on Tony as he used to write his name on EVERYTHING. If it was made of wood, he would carve his name into it, if it was metal, he would punch his name into it with dots. He even punched his name into the side of his Seiko stainless steel watch with a hole-punch.

I used to joke with him, "Is that so that if you forget who you are you can look at your watch?"

His white Land Cruiser was a work of art. On the bonnet and on door was a large silver eagle transfer with wings spread. Inside he had replaced the internal plastic door panels with genuine leopard skin. The glove compartment door was also covered in leopard skin. Around every knob, switch and button he had painted a fine red pin-striping. He had also fitted a horn-sound system that you could adjust for different tunes from within the cab. The centre of each wheel hub was painted red. It probably sounds hideous but it was actually very well done and I loved it. While I was working for Bob, Tony had gone to Greece on holiday with his family and had left me the keys of the "CITIS violation" on wheels.

"When you go to town or the lake, take my car, keep the battery charged." He told me. When did I ever get a chance to go to the lake? This was Bob I'd been working for don't forget!

Tony was like that; he was a very generous guy and had a heart of gold and if he liked you would do anything for you. But if he hated you, that was a different story. Samuel told me how Tony had dealt with Bob's dog.

Tony, it seemed, had a small dog, a Sausage Dog I think, called Trixi and he loved this little dog. One day Tony had come back to the house after a few hours in the fields and Trixi didn't run to meet him as she usually did. Tony called and called and then asked the cook if he had seen the sausage dog.

"Sorry Bwana," Samuel said with sorrow "Bob's dog attacked Trixi this morning and killed her."

Tony didn't say a word; he just went quietly to the kitchen drawer and grabbed a large kitchen knife. He then went to the freezer and grabbed a piece of meat. He then called Bob's Alsatian into the kitchen and held the meat out. When the dog came to take the meat, Tony grabbed it by the scruff of the neck and cut its throat right there in the kitchen leaving the dog dead in a pool of blood on the kitchen floor. Tony then got up and walked out of the kitchen without saying a word.

Samuel said that as far as he knew Tony never spoke to Bob about the incident and Bob knew better than to mention it, in case he met the same fate as his Alsatian.

On another occasion I met a man in Limbe who had been in a restaurant or an African bar where food was served, when Tony had a disagreement with some African bloke over something. I think the bloke was either the owner or at least worked there because Tony tracked him down in the kitchen, maybe Tony always settled his grievances in the kitchen, I don't know. Anyhow, Tony only hit this African once, with a half uppercut. It sent the bloke, who was not small by any means, flying into the air and landing in the top tray of a six-foot high vegetable rack. It is important to know that Tony had only hit the bloke once and it was with his left. The story is that Tony still held his bottle of beer in his right hand and that's why he hit him with his left. Knowing Tony, I believe the story.

Thankfully Tony and I never had a cross word. You would certainly want him in your corner in a bar fight!

Tony was a great father to his two sons. When he went into the bush with his young sons, as soon as the camp area was decided he would go to the Land Cruiser and bring three 6-inch nails and a hammer. He would then hammer the three nails into a near-by tree at different heights. Then he would return to the vehicle and get three tin mugs with their names painted on them. On the lowest nail he would hang Jerry's mug. On the middle nail hung Terry's mug and on the highest nail went Tony's mug. Camp was now established!

It was at one of these bush camps that Taki had shot a kudu at some considerable distance and in thick bush. The shot had not been clean and the Kudu's back end started to go down but then the animal seemed regain its strength and was clearly going to get to its feet again. Before it could get to its feet and make a dash for it Tony had sprinted to the animal and with his Panga, slashed the tendons in its back legs. The Kudu was not going anywhere and Tony then dispatched the animal with his sheath knife! All this apparently happened in the blink of an eye and before Taki could fire a second round into the Kudu.

The Africans were always very wary of Tony. They used to tell me that it was because of the fact that he had fought in the Rhodesian Bush War and that meant to them that he had probably killed lots of Africans and that he would have no hesitation in killing them if they upset him. Due to the rebel war going on in neighbouring Mozambique, and the excess of guns being given to both sides by the Russians, Africans often crossed the border into Malawi in the hope of selling some of these guns to the Europeans. The Africans on Tony's farm were convinced that he had bought a number of AK47 and hundreds of rounds of ammunition and that he thus had the ability to shoot any African who upset him. I never saw these AK47 but it would not have surprised me that he had them, not that he would shoot his workforce!

The Africans in Namwera gave him the name Bwana Kalemba, which means Mr Writing, due to the mass of tattoos he displayed on both arms. The Africans were intrigued by his tattooed arms. My gardener Giabu, asked me once after Tony had come to visit me at home, "Did Bwana Tony's parents never give him any paper to write on when he was a child? Is that why he wrote on his arms?"

When Tony next came around I told Tony what Giabu had asked. Tony was really amused by this and went out into the garden to find Giabu. He then explained what the drawings were and how they were done. Giabu nearly passed out with a look of horror. He couldn't believe that Tony had let someone "punch nails into his arms with ink for hours." It only reinforced Giabu's belief that Tony was an even tougher and crazier man than he had first thought.

It is difficult to mention Tony without mentioning a crazy old man in Namwera called Ke'ke. It wasn't his name but he was unable to talk properly and used to just make the sound ke'ke all the time. He would just arrive every few days at FES much to the amusement of the staff and me if I'm honest. You'd look up and there he'd be saluting, marching up and down and carrying a stick that he would pretend was a gun and he'd be performing drill. He always had a pipe in his mouth and a huge smile on his face. He was the jolliest of men. I never gave him any money but I would give him my old clothes which he would wear the next time he came to visit to show you. Ke'ke must have covered some miles during the week because he was often on Tony's farm at Mandimba which was quite a walk. You knew when he had been to Tony's because he'd be wearing some of Tony's old shirts or a worn-out bit of ex-Rhodesian army uniform.

It was always a happy day when Ke'ke arrived. Kawale used to march up and down with him and the more Kawale marched the more Ke'ke marched, till Kawale was worn out and Ke'ke would then wave goodbye and head down to one of the shops in Namwera to do the whole routine again.

Sadly, Tony passed away after a long illness in June 2013. It was a great shame. I had always hoped to write Tony's life story one day but now I guess that chance is gone.

CHAPTER 77

I LOSE MY BEST FRIEND

I was driving through Blantyre and was stopped at the traffic lights on the Kamuzu Highway, at the junction for the Queen Elizabeth Hospital. A newspaper seller was approaching the car window, I waved him past as I waited for the lights to change to green. Just then I thought of Richard, I don't know why, he just came into my mind. I turned to my friend who was in the car at the time and said "I must call Richard and see how he is; I haven't heard from him for a while." The lights finally changed to green and I never actually called Richard.

About a week later I got a call from my mother. It was a Saturday afternoon in late September and I knew that it was either good news for them or bad news for me. In all of the three years that I was at FES my parents had never called me. Come to think about it they had never called me all the time I was in Namwera or at Namadzi.

"Richard has died." My mother said almost instantly. "He committed suicide in England. I just thought you should know".

My mind flashed back to the week previous when I was at

the traffic lights. I suddenly realised that I had never made the call to him that I said I would. My thoughts came back to the phone and my mother who was at the other end of the line. I didn't have time to think of what to say. I felt a strange peace wash over me, and it made me laugh, in a way I felt happy for him. "Way to go Richard," I said, "thanks for letting me know" and we said our good byes and I put the phone down.

I stood there for a while looking out of the lounge window. I called to Samuel to make a cup of coffee and I went and sat outside on my veranda. I was upset, like I'd been kicked in the stomach. Richard was gone and I hadn't even had a chance to help him. If I had made that call maybe we could have talked about what was upsetting him so much. I knew he hated being in Brighton; Africa was where he wanted to be. I thought about all I wish I had done, I wished I had booked him a flight, got him out to Namwera to stay with me. We could have gone "snaking" together. Samuel brought the coffee and as I drank it, I looked out west from my veranda across the bush to the hills beyond. The hills rose and then fell down to the shores of Lake Malombe. Richard would have loved them. I started to cry and all the things that we hadn't done, all the places we said we would go, the places we had talked and dreamt of exploring when we were kids. I was crying because I thought we would have all the time in the world to go to those places.

Sure, in those last few years we hadn't spent as much time together as when we were younger but that didn't matter, we were still pals. Richard had been doing his A-levels and later university in England. I had been on the farms without much holiday but when we had met it was like we had never been apart. Friendship is not measured by the amount of time one spends together but by the bond you have that distance or time cannot break.

You may think that when hearing news that your childhood

friend was dead that it would have helped to talk more openly with your mother but in my case I had laughed on the phone not because his death was funny or meant nothing to me, but because I wanted to hide that I was upset from my mother. I had learnt to hide my feelings and not talk to her.

Laughing was to dismiss the fact that I was hurt. I would mourn alone, which is what I did and continue to do to this day. My mother advised me not to contact Richards's parents at the time as "they are very upset", so I didn't. I have regretted not calling them ever since. I wish I had not listened to my mother

Richard was my best friend, and my biggest sadness was that I never had the chance to say goodbye, go on one last snake hunt with him.

As I sat looking out to the hills I said, "Now you can visit anywhere you want. I'll see you on the dark side of the moon mate."

A few years ago, I made contact with Richards's family. It was a hard thing to do but I had to lay some ghosts to rest on the circumstances of his death, mainly because I still blamed myself for not being there when he needed me.

Mrs Terrell told me that Richard was cremated and that they scattered his ashes in Kasungu National Park. He loved that place and they thought he would like to be with the animals he loved so much. It still brings a tear to my eye when I remember Richard always saying he wanted his body to be fed to the lions. Well that didn't happen but he got pretty close. I think he would be happy.

I often wish I had something of his, something to hold and look at. But I do have something of his, I have great memories. When I close my eyes, even in England, Richard and I are walking down the Mudi River, scanning the bushes for snakes. I can hear the trickling of the stream as it flows between boulders. I can hear the birds singing. I can smell the smoke from his cigarette when we stop to rest at a comfortable spot. I can hear his voice.

All I need to do is close my eyes.

There is a James Taylor song called Fire and Rain that always takes me back to Richard:

Just yesterday morning, they let me know you were gone.
Suzanne, the plans they made put an end to you.
I walked out this morning and I wrote down this song,
I just can't remember who to send it to.
I've seen fire and I've seen rain. I've seen sunny days that I thought
would never end.
I've seen lonely times when I could not find a friend, but I always
thought that I'd see you again.
Won't you look down upon me, Jesus, You've got to help me make a
stand.
You've just got to see me through another day.
My body's aching and my time is at hand and I won't make it any
other way.
Been walking my mind to an easy time, my back turned towards
the sun.
Lord knows when the cold wind blows it'll turn your head around.
Well, there's hours of time on the telephone line to talk about things to
come.
Sweet dreams and flying machines in pieces on the ground.
Oh, I've seen fire and I've seen rain. I've seen sunny days that I
thought would never end.
I've seen lonely times when I could not find a friend,
but I always thought that I'd see you baby, one more time again, now.
Thought I'd see you one more time again.
There's just a few things coming my way this time around, now.
Thought I'd see you, thought I'd see you, fire and rain, now.

Shortly after Richards death I did suffer what I think was a nervous breakdown. I was at my mothers house on Brereton Drive and one evening I just had a melt-down and collapsed outside by the car.

CHAPTER 78

KITTEN FOR LUNCH

I had started to get quite a collection of animals. I started off by having Cassey, then I acquired two more small dogs. They were both Dachshund cross Terrier that were named Tambala and Florence. These were their names when I inherited them from some people who were leaving the country. A few months later Taki arrived with a baby duiker that he had rescued and asked me to take care of since my house had a six-foot chain-link fence all the way around. I also had a few chickens that I hoped would provide eggs but it never really came to much.

It was about this time that the cats arrived. The first was Ella, a small black cat. She was lovely but was only at the house when I was there. If I left the house in the car for any reason she would walk out of the gate behind the car and go off into the bush by the house and would not come back till she heard the car; be it a day, a week or a month.

One day I was coming back from town and I saw a man who used to be the watchman for the Chibuku depot in Namwera but he had recently been laid off. I would have just waved to him as I passed but he was carrying a sack, and as you know I can't let a sack go past unopened so I stopped and asked him what he had in the sack.

"It's kittens bwana". He said and began to open the sack. Inside were three very small kittens probably a few weeks old.

"What are you doing with these?" I asked. He replied that he was going to eat them.

You must not make judgement here; I know it's awful to you and me but in Africa food is food. However, I was keen to exchange money for the kittens so he could buy a few fish instead. We chatted a bit and immediately he broke down in tears saying that since he had lost his job he and his family were really suffering.

"Right, you come and work for me as my watchman" I said straightaway and he and the kittens got in the car and I drove to the house.

So, he got a new job, I got a new watchman and three small kittens; sounded like everyone was happy. Sadly, only one of the kittens survived the night and I named her Smudge.

The watchman whose name I can't remember for the life of me was first rate. I armed him with a beret, a baseball bat and a pair of army boots so he looked the part and every evening when he came to work, he would march up the drive and come to attention on the veranda and salute, then stand there till he was dismissed. I know he spent all night asleep as all watchmen did but it was good to help his family out and it did give the house some added security.

CHAPTER 79

BAREFOOT-BUSHMAN

O ne Saturday morning as I sat in my office a red box-body pulled up and a guy got out whom I didn't know and had never seen before. The first thing that I noticed about him was that he was bare-foot. He didn't seem to acknowledge my staff in the workshop or Elias as he walked towards the office. I got up from my chair to meet him.

"Howzit, I'm Dave Bradshaw, I farm out at Katuli." he said.

"Katuli?" I said "that's the back of beyond!" Which it was, even by Namwera standards. Everyone knew where it was but no one had ever been there or wanted to go there.

"How you finding Namwera?" I asked.

"Oh, it's ok, I've been here three years, but the people are a bit strange, present company excluded." he replied with a slight smile.

"THREE YEARS!!!!! I've not seen you around?" I was shocked. I don't think he even replied.

We sat and chatted for a while over several coffees. It turned out that he ran one of President Banda's farms at Katuli, right on the border with Mozambique. It appeared that the Greek farmers didn't really know what to make of Dave so either avoided him or when they did come into contact with him, ignored him, which made Dave more solitary.

You looked at Dave and thought "Drunk idiot" or "Fool" but you would be wrong, yes, he would drink and he would get very drunk but he was no idiot. He was a Rhodesian and had been in the Police during Rhodesia's Bush War. He never wore shoes, even when visiting his Bank Manager in Blantyre he still didn't wear shoes; he wore trousers instead of shorts obviously, it was a business meeting after all. Rumour had it that even when he had meetings with the President's representative, he didn't wear shoes then either, although I don't know how true that was.

I did hear a funny story once. Dave had come to Namwera to buy a couple of drums of petrol at the filling station. The manager at the time was a Greek guy named Nick "The Disco King", nothing was meant by the name, although you never called it to his face. Anyway, Dave walked into Nicks' office to pay for the fuel. Nick was sat behind his large wooden desk. The usual chitchat occurred and Nick asked where Dave farmed.

"Out at Katuli" Dave replied with the look of here we go again.

"Oh god, do you know that crazy drunk bloke with the tasty wife, oh what's his name? You must know him; the idiot never wears shoes."

With that Dave lifted a bare-foot off the floor and planted it down on Nicks desk.

"Yes, that's me!" he said, signed the delivery note and walked out. Nick said he just wanted to curl up under a stone.

Nick was right, Dave's wife, Gennie was tasty, an absolute stunner, what we would call a total "Rhodie Babe" and it baffled me how he could leave her alone on the farm while he went into town, got blind drunk, sober up and then make his way back to the farm days later. Then again if someone did try to muscle in on his wife, Dave would probably shoot him, so I guess he had no worries really. Sometimes when I would visit Dave on his farm, I'd arrive at the house and Ginnie would be making jam, she was always making jam, and she'd invite me in. I'd feel drawn to the kitchen by her and the smell of cooking jam but then think better of it.

"No, its okay thanks, I'll see if I can find Dave down at the barns or in the field" and I'd get out of the house as quick as I could.

Although I didn't see Dave often, we became good friends. He was, as most Namwereans were, totally mad!

Dave had this beaten up old red Toyota Hilux 4x4 with a red box on the back. Anyone who has lived in Malawi will know that the Post Office had similar vans so we used to call him "The Postman".

One day he took a trip to town, and as was usual on the farms, when you went to town, you'd always find twenty Africans on the farm who would find an excuse why they needed to go to town with you. I think on this occasion about nine or ten of his staff had convinced Dave that their need was great and into the boxed-back of the pick-up they piled. When they were all in Dave locked the door at the back and headed off to town.

Just before the bridge at Mangochi that crosses the water between Lake Malawi and Lake Malombe Dave's pick-up left the road. Story goes that he had some beers in the front of the pick-up and had drunk a few by the time he reached the bridge. At any rate, he missed the bridge and the pick-up flew almost thirty feet, over the papyrus reeds and plunged into the river.

Well Dave soon sobered up I can tell you!

He managed to open his window and get to the surface and swam to shore. A large group of Africans had now gathered on the river bank and helped Dave get to his feet. As he stood there in his wet clothes thinking how he had survived an African asked if anyone else was in the truck.

There was a look of thoughtfulness as Dave tried to clear his head of beer and river water to think straight.

Suddenly he'd gathered his thoughts, "Shit, my boys are in the back!"

With that Dave dived back into the muddy river. After diving down a few times he managed to finally unlock the back door of the sealed box and freed the, by then, gasping Africans. When the pick-up had gone in nose first into the river, the nose had sunk and as the water started to fill the back of the pick-up the Africans had been forced to hold their heads in a small pocket of air trapped in the roof of the box. Dave said a few more minutes and they would have drowned.

The pick-up was winched from the river and on hearing what happened the President refused to replace the car and ordered Dave to have it repaired.

A few months later Dave was on the same stretch of road heading for the same bridge, on his way to town. He had just been waved through the Police road-block and had only gone about twenty feet when he heard this loud bang that he took for a gun shot. He felt the steering pull hard to the right as the front tyre bursts.

"The Bastard Police are shooting at me!" and he opened his door and piled out and rolls down the embankment on the side of the road and hid in the grass to think about how to resolve his current situation.

He looked for his red pick-up and sees it leaving the road and plunging into the river. "Not a-fucking-gain!" he mutters forlornly.

With that the two Policemen from the road-block ran up to where they saw Dave exit the pick-up and peer into the grass. Dave considered his options; they were armed with old 303's and he was unarmed so he raised himself from the grass and holds his hands high.

"Are you okay Bwana?" asks one of the Policemen.

"No, not really, why the hell are you shooting at me?" he demands.

"We not shooting Bwana, you had a blow-out."

Dave stands and looks at the bubbles coming up from the riverbed where his pick-up now lies. "Shit!"

The President ordered him to repair the "post van" again.

Dave's red "post van"

CHAPTER 80

DAVE'S IN A HOLE

Not all encounters with Dave ended in a vehicle being written off but they all involved water, either Lake Malawi or Lake Malombe.

I spent a few weekends up at Cape Maclear with Dave. We were both into fishing and it was nice to get away from Namwera once in a while. Without a boat fishing on the Lake is almost impossible but Dave's pockets were quite deep so in true Dave fashion he decided to make a boat.

"How hard can it be, I'll knock it together out of flue-pipes, should have it made in a week", and bloody hell he did. He took two flue pipes and capped off the ends, then lashed them either side of a platform. It looked more like a raft than a boat. He painted it blue and called it "4Q", a twist on fuck you.

The maiden voyage showed all its faults, it had no speed because of the capped off ends to the pipes that just acted like a brick wall. The added weight of a few crates of beer that Dave loaded onto the boat each time he went fishing didn't help the performance either. So, it was back to the farm for 4Q where Dave made some minor modifications.

He brought the front of each set of pipes to a point and

found a double seat from an old bus and screwed that at the rear of the wooden platform so he had somewhere to sit. To the back of the seat he mounted a wooden engine plate where he could attach the 4hp seagull outboard he had just acquired.

He renamed this version "4Q2" (fuck you too).

The modifications had helped but the little seagull was wildly underpowered. If we ever decided to go fishing, I would either have to tow 4Q2 behind my boat to the fishing spot or he would have to leave hours earlier than everyone else.

On one occasion a small group of us had decided to go fishing at a spot called "Onions". We had all decided to leave Cape Maclear around 6am, and retired to bed. At around 4am we are woken by the sound of a little seagull engine spluttering into life as Dave heads off into the darkness of the lake. We still managed to catch him up before he got there and tow him the last few miles. Fish at Onions was well worth the trip.

One Easter holiday my mother had gone to the UK on one of her shopping trips or to sell the house, I can't really remember which. Anyway, since Jim had never been to Namwera before, I invited him up to stay with me for a week or so while she was away.

Somehow Dave had got the use of a "cottage" at Cape Maclear for the weekend so the three of us headed off to the lake. Ginnie had again taken the wise option and opted to stay on the farm, maybe she knew something I didn't.

Dave was a hit with Jim straight away. I think that Jim saw Dave as a bit of a rebel, a loner and admired it. Whatever it was Dave was enjoying the company and having a great time soaking up this adoration.

On the Saturday night a few of the youngsters had decided to have a brai on the beach. At about eleven in the evening Taki came down to the beach and he got into story-telling straight-away, as only Taki can. Suddenly he stopped telling his story,

391

looked out into the darkness of the Lake and put his hand on my shoulder.

"Can you hear that Rupe?" he asked.

"Yeah it sounds like a boat engine, what crazy fisherman is out on the lake at this time of night without lights?" I replied.

"It must be an African because it sounds like a seagull, he must be bloody mad. No wait, I can hear singing, Rupe can you hear singing?"

I strained my ears into the darkness and heard the faint sound of voices singing. I tried to make sense of the words, and slowly as the boat engine grew louder, I could make it out.

"Yes, hang on, it's English" I told Taki.

"It is. I can hear it too now".

Then the singing came fully into earshot and we could now make out the words:

"My girlfriends got ginger hair, underneath her underwear, I know because I've been there….." and so on. I won't repeat the rest.

Then it dawned on me. "It's Bradshaw!" I said to Taki.

"Yes, it is, but who's that other voice? Wait a minute; it sounds like your Dad!"

I strained again to make out the other voice, Oh god it was, it was Jim!

Just then 4Q2 came into the light from the beach fire. Sat on the bus seat with their feet on a crate of beer were Dave and Jim, pissed as farts. If I had a shovel, I would have dug a hole to bury myself in. Taki didn't say anything; he just looked at me with that look as if to say I had something to do with this or should have some way of fixing it. I didn't.

I had wished that this was the end of my troubles that weekend, but sadly it wasn't. Dave convinced me to stay Sunday night suggesting that we could leave early on the Monday morning so he could get back to his farm as promised to Ginnie. Foolishly I agreed which was my first mistake.

That afternoon Jim and Dave jumped into the red post office van yelling "We are off to Stevens, see you later" and then wheel spun out of the camp site.

Stevens was a rest house, come bar at Cape MacClear, run by a Malawian called Mr Stevens, oddly enough; I know, how original. It was in the African village at Cape Maclear and was a favourite haunt of European backpackers; which was probably the reason Dave had gone there.

I decided to hop into my boat and spend the afternoon fishing behind Otters Point. At about 5pm I came back and Dave's truck was not outside the cottage so I went off to find some company.

The next time I looked at my watch was around 7pm and still they were not back; so I decided to walk along to Stevens to get a situation report. That was my second mistake.

It is a fairly long walk but about 30 minutes later I got to the bar to find Jim and Dave very much the worse for wear. Jim was sat there almost giggling like a demented child surrounded by empty beer bottles. Dave was trying to chat up some unsuspecting female backpacker with stories of the Rhodesian war.

When Dave saw me, his face lit up. "Rupe, come here, meet Christina, Christina this is Rupe, what a bloke, top bloke. I love this guy." he said putting an arm around me. "Rupe, I'm pissed!" Like I couldn't see that, he only said he loved me when he was drunk.

I wriggled free from his over affectionate embrace and got myself a coke from the bar. I then tried talking to Jim and explaining to him that we needed to head home as we had an early start in the morning but it was like talking to the village idiot. Jim had consumed god knows how many beers too.

After a few more hours Dave made his announcement.

"Rupe, rupe, where are you? Oh, there you are. Christina and I are going back to the cottage now" and he pulled the keys to the red post van out of his pocket. I should have been grateful that he still had the keys, but I wasn't.

"Dave, I think I had better drive, give me the keys." but my words were as wasted as Dave was.

"Rubbish, I can drive, look I can stand up all by myself" as he hung on Christina's neck for support.

I made a few more attempts to gain control of the keys but in the end, I thought "Sod it, if he drives into the lake it might just sober him up" so Dave and Christina climbed into the Hilux and weaved out of sight into the night.

I then turned to my next problem which was getting Jim on his feet and home but again I was wasting my time. As I sat there asking "why me?", a dishevelled Christina appeared at the bar door.

"Rupe Dave needs some help" she said in a slurred speech.

"Shit where is he?" I asked rising to my feet.

"He's stuck in a hole!"

"Fuck and I bet he needs me to push him out, does he?" but I didn't wait for her reply.

I grabbed Jim and all three of us walked down the road in the direction Dave had driven off in. By now it was about 11pm and I was thoroughly pissed off with the whole evening. As we walked along the dirt track, I suddenly heard the hooting of a horn coming from the bush on my left. As I glanced in the direction of the sound, I could see two shafts of light pointing straight up into the air. A second later there was another honk from the hooter so I decided I had better investigate.

After a few minutes of negotiating our way through the low bushes we arrived at the vehicle, it was Dave.

He had done quite well for the first few hundred yards but then he had weaved off the track and driven through the bushes, luckily missing all the large trees. However, the Africans had a dug a large pit about twelve-foot square and about six-foot-deep where they deposited rubbish to burn. Dave had driven straight into the hole. Not to be beaten he tried to drive out the other side but unfortunately, he had jammed the Hilux at an almost seventy-degree angle with the front of the Hilux pointing skyward.

There was no way I and three drunks were going to pull or push the vehicle out of the hole tonight so I extracted Dave from the cab and we all headed back to the cottage, Christina included.

Next morning with the help of someone's Land Cruiser we managed to drag Dave's Hilux from the pit. Dave was very grateful and suggested that to say thanks he would buy everyone a drink at Stevens!

With the feeling of dajavu descending upon me I abandoned the suggestion of celebrations and headed back to pack my car alone. We did finally get to leave the lake but boy, what a struggle.

CHAPTER 81

WATER SKIING - NAM STYLE

A few weekends later Dave, Dave's friend Dave Toft and I had decided to go fishing on Lake Malombe. I know what you're thinking and you'd be right. I should have learnt my lesson from the previous week.

Dave Toft had been in the Police Anti-Terrorist Unit (PATU) during the Rhodesian War, although with his large beard everyone in Namwera thought he was in the Selous Souts. He also went everywhere barefoot, just like Bradshaw and thus often suffered with Jiggers, minute worms that burrow under your toe nails and lay a sack of eggs that you need to remove with a pin, without bursting the sack. This was an operation Dave T often performed at the supper table when he visited my house for dinner, just as one cleans your teeth with a toothpick. He was a quiet, unassuming guy, but I wouldn't have wanted to upset him.

Anyway, back to the events of the weekend. We launched our boats at the slipway just behind the war memorial, south of "Dave's Bridge" at Mangochi. We trawled for fish as we powered down towards Lake Malombe but didn't catch anything. We then fished likely reed inlets on the shores with some success, landing a few good-sized Sungwa. As usual along with the fishing gear, a few crates of Carlsberg were also loaded into Dave Toft's boat and the two of them had now consumed a good few. I was more adult and restricted myself to cokes, it was mid-day and blisteringly hot after all.

Soon Bradshaw had got bored with the fishing, a man can only eat so many fish and produced a pair of water-skis and a rope from the bottom of Dave T's boat. He had this naughty boy grin on his face. "Oh no" I thought, but Bradshaw looked at me as if to say "Oh YES!".

The river between Mangochi and Malombe is full of hippos and crocodiles and we had seen lots of both while we had been fishing. I think my reply in words to Bradshaw's look was "Are you out of your bloody mind?"

He replied by jumping into the water with the skis. Dave T had already hitched the rope to the back of his Jet-Flight so I anchored my boat and jumped into the Jet-Flight. We blasted off down the river towing Bradshaw behind till he realised he couldn't ski and drink beer at the same time so I was nominated as the next on the skis.

I plunged into the water. We were close to the reedy-bank and as I pulled the skis on I felt something brush against my leg. It's only the reeds I told myself and hurriedly got the skis on. The boat had now drifted and had pulled the rope taught so all I needed to do was wait for Bradshaw to start the 70hp engine and get me up and out of the reeds. I gave the thumbs up to say I was ready. I heard the engine turn over but not fire. Then again it turned over. Another "thing" brushed my leg.

"Get it started for god's sake!" I screamed, trying not to sound too scared. The thought of crocs was really starting to give me the heebie-jeebies.

"It won't start" Bradshaw said as the engine turned for a third time.

I then realised that he was messing with me and when he

saw he had been rumbled fired the engine into life and I was up and out of the water in a flash, thank god. I was genuinely worried in those reeds.

The aim of the day was for the boat driver to go flat out down the river then to turn the boat on a six-pence at the highest speed possible causing the skier to swing round at near twice the speed of the boat. When you did come off, and you did, you would bounce on the top of the water several times before slowing down enough to sink into the water or crash into the reeds on the bank. The more painful the landing looked and the more bounces, then the more cheers and applause from the boat!

We were all having a great time when Bradshaw wanted another go. Time to get him back, I thought, for the reed episode. After getting him to fall off on a hair-pin corner I decided to drag him through the water for as long as possible instead of powering the boat fast enough to pull him clear of the water. The force of the water against your chest makes the boat almost pull your arms out of their sockets till you have to just let go.

The river has numerous sand banks just under the surface and it just so happened that Bradshaw had come off just in front of one of these banks. As I slowly dragged him through the water his shouts got louder and more abusive. I turned to Dave T, "should I let him up yet?" "No, let the bastard drown!" was the reply, so I dragged him a bit further.

After a good minute of this I thought he had drunk enough river water and I floored the Jet-Flight and Bradshaw emerged from the river. As he had been dragged across the sandbank he must have gone through a bed of weeds because when he finally stood up on the skis he was covered in green weeds that trailed behind him in the wind.

"Oh look, its bloody Neptune!" roared Dave T.

I was in stitches. As we sped down the river, Africans in their dugouts and those on the river bank cheered and clapped at the sight of Bradshaw. All he needed was a trident. By this time we were almost back at the bridge and as I swung the boat around to head back down the river again with a reed-covered Bradshaw a car crossed the bridge. I looked up and saw that it was Taki and Louisa. I saw him look down at the boat with a look of "Oh God, why I am not surprised?"

On the Monday morning Taki came into my office at FES for his regular coffee and chat. As he walked through the showroom, he held up his hand and said "I don't even want to hear about it!"

Looking back, we were mad, but at least now if my kids ask me if I have ever water-skied down a river in Africa infested with hippos and crocodiles, I can say yes.

Shortly after the skiing in the "Shire River" incident I was up at Katuli visiting Bradshaw at his farm. He had specifically asked me over to look at a house he was building on a hill overlooking the farm. He had designed the house himself and it consisted of two round rondavels separated by an oblong room between them. It had a thatched roof and sat on the edge of the hill with panoramic views, it was spectacular.

He had arranged lunch at the new house in celebration at its near completion and soon had a poki-pot on the go as soon as we got there. A poki-pot is a cast-iron stew pot with a lid where you layer meat, potatoes and vegetables and let it slow cook for a few hours. So, while we waited for the pot to boil, we had a few beers and soaked up the view.

"Rupe, after seeing your boat trailer I had a small idea." He said. I had no idea where this conversation was going so made the usual Namwera Mmmmm noise and took another sip from my bottle of Carlsberg.

"Well how long does it take for you to get to town? Three, three and half hour's, right? Well for me you can add another two to that. What if we built two micro-lights with engines and we flew to town? We could leave a car at Chileka so we had wheels when we got to town. We could be there in what, say twenty, thirty minutes. I built 4Q2, so how hard can a micro-light be!"

I know, most of you would be thinking are you out of your mind, but this was Namwera where last week we had swum with hippos and crocs, so my mind only had one thought which was "ok, lets discuss this".

So, for the next few hours we sat and hatched a plan for these micro-lights. Dave already pointed to an empty field in the distance that he had ear-marked for a runway. As we sat there in the mid-day sun drinking beer (a fatal combination with Bradshaw) the micro-light idea seemed to be do-able.

Over the coming weeks Bradshaw started to do some investigations and caught up with an old friend of his who was a crop-spraying pilot at the tea estates at Mulanje; and was invited down for a lesson in flight! The plane that the guy flew was an old yellow Stearman bi-plane with a piston rotary engine. As with most crop-sprayers it was a single-seater but did not have a canopy so the pilot was open to the elements. Because of this Bradshaw had to sit on the fuselage behind the pilot with his feet wedged down either side of the pilots' seat and hold on to upper wing struts.

When Bradshaw gave the thumbs up the plane rolled down the runway and they were airborne. They did a few low passes of the tea fields and then climbed up over Mulanje Mountain. After a while of flying around the top of the mountain the pilot leaned back and said something to Dave which he didn't hear due to the wind but Bradshaw let go with his right hand and gave the thumbs up to the pilot. What the pilot actually said was "hold on tight" and before Dave could grip the plane again with his right hand the pilot flew over the edge of the mountain and plunged the plane into a steep vertical dive down the sheer rock face of the mountain. Dave said "my arse left the fuselage and luckily my feet were wedged so tight down the side of the pilots seat otherwise I would have flown off the plane. As the plane screamed down to the plains bellow Bradshaw's ear popped bursting an eardrum! Eventually the plane levelled out and headed for the runway and Dave was able to put his feet back down on terraferma. It was a miracle that Dave did not plunge to his death that day. Thankfully this experience put pay to our plane building idea and we continued to make the three-hour trip to town using four wheels.

I hate to imagine how it would have all ended if we had actually started construction and built these two death machines.

Dave Toft went on to manage Mvu Camp on the banks of the Shire River at Liwonde National Park. He was later killed in a car crash on his way to Blantyre not long after I had left Malawi. He was a great guy and it was a great shame.

We didn't read the sign, sorry

Hippos in the Shire River

Mangochi, where we launched the boats

CHAPTER 82

PARA

Tony came into my office at FES one morning holding two video tapes in his hand.

"You gotta watch these films! This one," handing me one tape, "the Three Amigos, is as funny as hell. This one is a documentary about people training for the Parachute Regiment in England, it's excellent". And he hands me the second tape.

"Cheers Tony, thanks, I'll watch them over the weekend." And he climbed back into his Citi's violation and pulled out of the gate.

That evening after supper I sat down to watch the Three Amigos, sadly about three minutes into the film it jammed up my player and I had to dismantle my machine just to get the tape out. The video player cost quite a bit to repair. I gave Tony the video back next time I saw him, unwatched. As for the second tape I took it with me when I went to town to get the video player repaired and convinced Jim to let me watch it in the schools' video room.

I just sat there in silence, spellbound by this documentary. It was about a group of new recruits joining, or attempting to join the Parachute Regiment. As the cameras followed them through the selection process their numbers became less and less. Some through injury, some by failing to meet the required standard and others who simply just threw the towel in and went back to their previous jobs. I must have watched it three times over that weekend.

Joining the army had been a boyhood dream, until mother had put a stop to it, "No son of mine is going to Northern Ireland". But this video rekindled that dream. The documentary had said that you could apply to join the Para's up to the age of 25. I was 23. As I drove back to Namwera that Sunday evening all I could think about was the film, the Para's, the Army, I was tingling.

On the Monday I drove out to Tony's farm to talk to Tony. He had been in the army and seemed a grounded guy. We talked through lunch and he gave me some good advice.

The next time I went to town I dropped in to see Mike Bowler who had done 3 years with the Army Air Corp in England and now ran a security guard company in Blantyre. His advice was mixed, and was as follows.

"Para's? Shit they're fucking nuts! If a bloke in the army locks his keys in his car, he might try to force a wire through the window to reach the lock, or failing that he might go off to find a brick to break the window. A Para won't mess about with any of that, he will just head-butt the window to break the glass, get in and drive off!"

"But if I was honest, if I was joining the army again, I would go straight into the Para's. When they walk down the street with that maroon Beret on, they look the dog's bollocks, no one messes with them. When you get to the recruiting office don't let them try to put you off and don't let them push you into some other namby-pamby unit!"

Ok so they were nuts, so were half the men in Namwera. They got respect, well why shouldn't they, I'd seen the film of their selection and training, it looked tough.

I spoke to a few other people about it, one of them being Gordon, the chap I'd bought the AJS off. Turned out that his parents now lived in England and one of their close friends was a Sergeant in the Para's with twenty odd years' service with the Regiment. Gordon suggested that I went over to England to talk to this guy to get some sound advice and to see what army life is all about.

Within a few weeks I had arranged a month's leave and booked a flight to London.

CHAPTER 83

FRANK THE PYE

England was a culture shock from the moment I came through the arrival's hall at Heathrow. It is terrible looking back now but the first thing that hit me was the white men sweeping the floors in the airport. Hey I had shovelled cow shit for a week, and worked alongside Africans everyday but somehow seeing these men sweeping in what I always thought of as the "Land of Gold" seemed to bring me into reality. I had been in England a few years before when I was at college but for some reason, I saw England with different eyes this time.

In all the crowds of people I managed to find the train into central London and then the train down to Southampton and a taxi to Gordon's parents' house. I kind of knew his parents from when Richard and I used to cycle out to their farm on the Zomba road and spend the day with Gordon. His sister Wendy was in my class at school so these people were not strangers to me.

After a quick cup of coffee and a quick chat Gordon's mum drove me over to Romsey to meet Frank.

I don't know what I was expecting, guess someone from the

documentary. What I wasn't expecting was the man who opened the door. Visually Frank was and still is a very frightening man. He is extremely thick set and has a neck that comes out, well no, let's start again. He has NO neck; his head simply sits on his shoulders. His shoulders sit on this huge chest. Visually he scared the pants off me that day. But when he looked at you and spoke you saw a different side to him.

He invited me in and straightaway we got on like a house on fire. Frank told it how it was, there wasn't any feathering it up, or making it palatable, he spoke his mind and was direct. You knew where you stood with Frank and whether he liked you or not. I spent the afternoon listening to Frank telling me about himself. How he had joined the army at eighteen to escape from the East End gangsters after punching a bloke unconscious in a London club, only to find out that the bloke was a cousin of the Kray twin's. It was suggested that Frank leave the club as soon as possible before he was gunned down or worse. Frank decided that the British Army was his only escape from the East End Gangster Mobs.

I heard about his "tours" in Northern Ireland, where Frank said "you quickly learned to fucking switch-on!" He handed me a Para Company flag that had a large red stain on it, "what's the red stain?" I foolishly asked.

"Oh that's so-and-so's brain, he was killed at such-and-such an IRA bombing and I used the flag to mop up the bits" he said with a smile.

He told me about his time in the Falklands War, which had turned his hair from jet-black to grey almost overnight. There were many occasions in the years that followed that I'd be laid fast asleep in the next bed to Frank, which in itself took some doing as he was a really bad snorer, so bad in fact that you could hear him through walls! Suddenly Frank would dive out of bed; sound asleep and land on me pushing my head into my pillow shout "Get you're fucking head down! Are you trying to get killed?" You'd be gasping for air through your pillow, then as quickly as he had leapt on you, he would get back into bed and go to sleep. In the morning he wouldn't remember a thing. Guess his memories of Ireland and the Falklands were still vivid.

He told me about his selection for the SAS. It was a fascinating story. The selection process had become so real that when it was over Frank just wouldn't switch off from trying to escape and if I remember correctly it had taken the presence of a number of officers to convince him that the course was over and he had passed. The final twist was that the SAS Team had neglected to notice Frank's age, which was in fact over the age limit for acceptance even though he had actually passed the selection course. Frank was devastated, after getting himself super-fit, running miles over the Brecon Beacons every weekend in preparation, doing the selection and passing he had to go back to his Parachute Battalion because he was too old. Again, I think this gives an indication of the man to have passed the toughest course in the British Army, possibly the world when he was "over the age limit". Well done Frank.

He had also been part of the British Army Training Team sent to train the new Zimbabwe Army modern soldiering techniques, "Para Style". He told me how every morning at parade he would bellow at the Zimbabwean Army soldiers, "What's an Astronaut?" In unison the parading African soldiers replied "An Astronaut is a person that Sgt Pye kicks up the arse!"

I remember Frank telling a story that afternoon about an incident at Aldershot that I will recall as Frank told me.

"I nearly got done for racism, not in Africa, in bloody England. I was taking a bunch of recruits on a run when I was at the Depot at a DS (Directing Staff). After the run I was summoned into the CO's office. The Boss had had a report of me shouting racist remarks. I assured the CO that I had not. The CO was adamant, saying that two old ladies had been having afternoon tea together in a garden when the recruits and I had run past and they had heard me shouting racist comments and reported it to the Depot. Well I thought long and hard to try and remember if I had shouted anything like you 'welsh cunt' or 'you Geordie twat' but I couldn't recall anything. I asked the CO what I was alleged to have said. The CO said the ladies had reported 'Move your arse, fucking Black man'. Well I nearly laughed, turned out that there was a 'black man' on the course but his name was in fact Blackman and he was as white as fucking snow".

Frank suddenly stopped his story telling and asked "where are you staying tonight?"

I thought for a second, I hadn't really made any plans and guessed I would head back to the Williamson's house, after all that was where my suitcase was.

"Rubbish, you're staying here, I'll call Sheila at work and she can stop off and pick your case up." So that was it, he called his wife, who brought my case home and I stayed with them.

A few days later Frank took me up to Aldershot to show me the "home" of the Para's. I was introduced to Frank's CO and taken into the Sergeants Mess. I was later shown the Trinazium, a sort of high climbing frame set in a playing field. It was probably the height of a three-storey building and made of scaffolding poles and planks, like an assault course cross obstacle course that tested recruits' nerve.

As we were walking back to one of the buildings Frank pointed out the Sergeant who had been on the documentary. It was like seeing a celebrity for me, I was over the moon. Frank said that the bloke had turned all "fucking religious".

On the drive back to Romsey, Frank asked how I felt now about the Para's, I had no hesitation, I wanted in. He then drove me down to Portsmouth Army Recruitment Office. Frank dropped me outside and said he would pick me up in thirty minutes. That was typical Frank, he wanted me to take that step, unaided, on my decision. Once inside I found the Recruiting Sergeant most unhelpful. He started off with the comment of "Why are you trying to join the British Army, wouldn't you be better joining the Malawi Army?" Obviously he had no bloody clue. He then tried to suggest that the guards would be a better bet. All in all he was being a bit of a prat. Thirty minutes later Frank pulled up outside and I climbed in the car.

"Well howdit go?" Frank asked.

I told Frank what the Sergeant had said and Frank was all for going in and "having a fucking word in his shell-like" as he put it.

"Let's go to Southampton Recruiting Office, they might be more fucking helpful!" he said so that's what we did.

I'll never forget the Sergeant there, Sergeant Darling! It reminded me of Captain Darling in the BBC series Blackadder. Meeting him was like chalk and cheese. He asked me loads of questions about my exam results from school and college. He then tried to suggest a commission which was flattering. He tried, looking at my exam results, to suggest that I consider thinking about the Guards but I told him my mind was made up with the Para's.

"Right then lad, I'll make an appointment for you to have a medical, eyes and hearing tests, then a few written tests, I can book you in for three weeks' time?" and he looked at me.

Gosh, hang on a minute, I thought! "I'm still on contract with my company in Malawi. I have one more year to go on a three-year contract. I'm going back to Malawi in two weeks' time and I will then hand in my notice and twelve months from now I will be back here to start the process."

He looked at me then at his sheet; I could see the thought going through his head. "The bloke is bottling out and he has just wasted all my time writing all these details out!"

"I'll be back" I said, "I just need to honour my commitment

with my employer, that's all." I could see by the look on his face that the sergeant thought I was having him on.

"I will, I'll see you next year" and shook his hand and walked out into the street.

Frank was pleased that I still wanted to join the Army and particular the Parachute Regiment. His wife Shelia told a mutual friend once that "there is a shared admiration between the two of them. As Rupert waits to join the Para's he looks up to and admires Frank for all that he has done in Para's. As Frank comes to the end of his twenty-two years in Para's he admires Rupert for wanting to join the Para's and envies him of all that he will do and achieve. For one the day is ending, for the other the day is just beginning."

Maybe she was right. I did admire Frank and still do, even now. At the time I remember looking at him and thinking I wish, like him, I'd been 18 years old when I was trying to join instead of 23. Whether he admired me I'm not sure. There was one day that I felt I saw pride in his eyes. He had taken me up to Aldershot where he was co-ordinating some shooting at Ash Ranges. The soldiers there that day, for some reason or other were Royal Marines, Franks worst nightmare, "Cabbage Heads" he called them, in reference to their green berets. Anyone who is not "airborne" as far as the Para's are concerned is a "Crap Hat" or simply "hat". RM's Frank especially disliked.

I'm really not sure how it all started but suddenly Frank handed me SLR (self-loading rifle) and told me to jump in the hole at the end of a line of six Royal Marines. As I got in the hole they must have wondered what was going on, "this 'kid' in jeans and denim shirt……Prat!"

"The weapon may not be zeroed so you'll have to listen to me" Frank calmly whispered as he squatted behind me.

"With a magazine of …rounds, load"……. "In your own time….FIRE" shouted the Range Sergeant. The Royal Marines let off a volley of shots. I lowered my index finger down to the trigger.

"Watch your breathing," came Frank's words. "Fire when you're ready, forget those muppets," nodding towards the Marines, "they think it's the bloody O.K. Corral!"

I looked along the rifle, through the open sights to the target in the distance. I aimed in the centre of the "advancing enemy" silhouette and gently squeezed off the first round. The rifle gave me a firm punch into my shoulder as the 7.62 calibre left the rifle.

"High Left" whispered Frank.

I adjusted my aim down and to the right and fired the second round.

"High" said Frank. I again adjusted my aim down and fired the third round.

"On Target" said Frank. I fired the fourth round.

"On Target".

Once the requested rounds had been fired, we were then instructed to remove the magazine, then holding the breach open, tilt the rifle to one side, showing the weapon was clear. The Range Sergeant then waited for the staff in the BUTTS to feed him back with the number of "hits" for each number, obviously I was number 7.

He then called out the scores. "Number 1 - 5, Number 2 - 6, Number 3 - 4, and so on, till they got to me. "Number 7, - 9"

"That's ok, don't worry, you lost two rounds having to zero." Frank said reassuringly.

Next was firing the weapon prone, lying flat. I tried to remember Frank's advice and tried to block out the firing coming from the Royal Marines. Again the scores came in. "Number 1, - 6", "Number 2, - 5", "Number 3, - 7" …. and so on, till they got to me. "Number 7, - 9"

Frank lent forward and patted me on the shoulder, "well done". I felt a little embarrassed, like I shouldn't be doing better than these Royal Marines, kind of guilty I suppose. But I didn't have time to dwell on this guilt as we were ordered to put on our respirators for the final shoot. Frank quickly yelled out, and a respirator was delivered to him immediately. "Here, Get this on." He said handing the respirator to me.

"With a magazine of 20 rounds, load"....... I was still putting on my respirator. "In your own time....FIRE" I was just loading my magazine.

Frank had by this time stood up and left me to get on with it so I aimed the rifle and fired the first round. Then fired the second, it was at this point that I realised that I couldn't hear any of the Marines firing because they had all finished! This got me a bit and my respirator started to steam up as I breathed heavily. As I looked towards the targets, they were very misty to say the least.

I thought to myself "What the hell and aimed through the misted-up lenses of the respirator and squeezed off round number three, then four, five and so on till I was done and the Marines had finished their tea and cake! It was a bloody nightmare. Once the weapon was checked 'clear' I turned to Frank and said "I couldn't see a bloody thing!"

"No, but you fired the whole magazine off anyway. Well done. Always remember, you're not going to hit jack-shit if the rounds stay in your mag! If you're out of ammunition, fix bayonet, hit the bloke with the butt, pick up a brick, anything but the fights not over till you're standing and the enemy is not!"

Just then the scores came in. I thought "hell, this is going to be embarrassing" and looked down at the ground thinking "that's it, the party's over".

"Number 1- 3, Number 2 - 4, Number 3 - 2, and so on, till they got to me. "Number 7, - 6"

In a loud voice so they could hear, Frank said "That's shown the cabbage-heads! Well done Rupe! Give me the weapon, let's go and get a brew".

Frank's chest swelled more than usual that day as he walked me past the open-mouthed Marines, as if to say, "Look, this is my boy!" not in a parental way but in a teacher-pupil way. What it was, was Frank being a good soldier, the fine instructor getting the best results from the man in his charge, and on that day it was me. I wish I'd known what was going through the Marines minds, "who's this fucking kid?" probably and "I wish that bloke wasn't an NCO so I could say something, but I can't, I just have to take the 'cabbage-head' abuse!"

So that was Frank! If he intended to put me off the idea of joining the Para's it didn't work. After I'd spent a few weeks with Frank and his wonderful family I returned to Malawi with my head filled with thoughts of the Para's, the Army and a change of career and a change of country.

CHAPTER 84

I'M JOINING THE ARMY

I sat in Roger's office in Blantyre.

"I'm going to join the Army, I've been to see them and I stand a good chance of getting in."

Roger was clearly taken by surprise.

"The British Army? Well, that's a bit of a shock! Look Rupert, I know some of the Greeks have given you a hard time over the years but can't we work something out?"

"It's not about them, not really, this is something I want to do and if I don't do it now, I won't get another chance and I'll regret it for the rest of my life."

"Ok, I understand. I'm just a bit shocked that's all."

And that was that, for about three days at least, then I got a call from Roger.

"Rupert, I've been thinking. Gordon, the manager at Mzuzu is leaving, how would you like to run the Branch up there? I know you've always wanted to go up north. It would get you away from the Greeks, well?"

"Thanks Roger, I appreciate the offer but..." he cut me off ...."I'll give you a pay rise!"

I said I would need a few days to think about things. Sure,

Namwera was not a great posting. Mzuzu was a dream location for me, Richard and I had always talked of searching for Gaboon Vipers there and now I was being offered the chance to live there. I sat and thought about what I was doing. I was really torn between what to do. I talked again to Tony; I spoke to Dave Bradshaw and Dave Toft. I spoke to Taki. They all wanted to help, but there wasn't a lot they could really say.

At the end of the week I rang Roger who told me to come to town and see him at his home, so I took the long drive to town. All the way over the three hours my mind changed many times, but when I stepped through Rogers' front door my mind was decided.

"I'm going to go to England and join the Army." I said.

Roger stuck out his hand, "If it doesn't work out for whatever reason, there is always a job here for you." He squeezed my hand tighter and looked into my eyes, "do you understand, ALWAYS!"

That probably meant more to me than all the branches and salary increases that he had offered. Probably for the first time in my life I felt valued, like I had done something right in my day to day job. There are not many times when you work for someone that you feel appreciated or valued.

I realise that Roger didn't want me to leave, not really because of the work I did, sure I turned the Branch around from the brink into one that made a profit. But more than that, Roger had a person he could trust, which is rare to find. Employees are always trying to take large companies for what they can. They take advantage of petrol allowances, petty cash floats. They may even see a way to privately sell parts to farmers, pocketing the cash and covering up the lost part in the stock-take. With thousands and thousands of items of stock it would have been easy to do. But from me Roger got honesty and loyalty. That has no price and Roger knew that.

I spent the rest of the weekend in town, thinking about what

I had given up. Life is full of forks in the road and I believe that it doesn't matter which fork we take, your ultimate final destination is the same, it's just one route is the straight and narrow and the other is the rocky road. Maybe I had just decided to take the muddy side of the road. We would see.

The next twelve months were spent trying to get fit again. I had been running 30-35 miles a week in my last year at Saints. I could run the 1500m in 4 minutes 20 seconds but that was a long time ago. I stared running again but it was hard. I made some exercise machines and benches, begged some weights and converted one of my bedrooms into a home gym so I could work out. My friend George Kavourides used to come over three times a week to work out with me in the evenings. He would then stay for supper and a movie. He helped me train when possibly I would have put it off in favour of an early night. I figured that I could get back in shape in a year, plus I had the heat and altitude so running in England at almost sea-level would be a doddle.

CHAPTER 85

I SEE MY DEAD GRANDMOTHER

One weekend my training partner, George Kavourides and I decided to go to the Lake for the weekend. As usual we set up camp at Cape Maclear and launched the boat to do a bit of fishing. It wasn't long before we were joined by Bauka in his boat. Bauka was still at Saints in his final year and was a close friend of George. As I remember the fishing wasn't that good that day so we put our rods away and headed for Otters Point, a small rocky headland on the west of the bay. We anchored the boats and proceeded to find the highest rock on the point to jump off and into the water. It was all good fun, but as with everything there is only so many times you can dive off a high rock into the water below.

"I heard there is a tunnel under that island. It starts here and goes under the island and comes out on the far side" Bauka suddenly announces as he points to a small group of large rocks that makes up a small island just off the point.

Before you could say "lack of oxygen in a water filled tunnel" we were all swimming over to the island. After a few duck dives we managed to find what looked like a tunnel entrance. We then swam around to the far side to locate the exit tunnel, but after much duck-diving we couldn't find it.

"Don't worry, it's there, just maybe a bit deeper." Bauka insists. "Let's give it a go!"

Now I know what you're thinking and you'd be right. We were stark-raving-mad but in those days we didn't ask Why?, we asked Why not! I suppose that because I was older than the two of them by some margin, I was nominated to go first. My only concern was crocs for some reason, although I hadn't really thought of what a croc might be doing in a water filled tunnel, apart from waiting for me to join it for lunch!

After a few deep breaths and much encouragement from my two accomplices, I duck-dived down into the dark hole. Well I couldn't see anything as I groped my way along the rocks, banging my head on the tunnel ceiling and trying to kick my legs. After possibly just a few meters I decided to turn around and head back towards the light.

"I can't see shit!" I announced as I surfaced.

"I've got a waterproof torch in my boat" said Bauka and he swam off to get it.

So now armed with the waterproof torch and renewed confidence I dove down again into the entrance. The torch did help a little but now I had lost the much-needed propulsion of one of my arms. I thought about putting the torch in my mouth but there was no hope of that so I stuck it down the front of my trunks. This worked pretty well as it shone forward and I was able to swim quite well. I realise now that it can't have been long but it felt like minutes had past, which of course they hadn't. A thought suddenly came into my mind. "Where was the point in the tunnel where I would still have enough air to turn around and go back the way I'd come without drowning?"

Then the answer came back. "You've passed that point, now bloody swim you dumb idiot!"

Suddenly as the tunnel turned, I saw light at the end of the end in the distance. Hoping that it was not Saint Peter waiting for me at the pearly gates I felt a surge of energy and pushed towards the light. The words to "We don't need another hero" by Tina Turner plays in my head as I swim. At least it wasn't "Another one bites the dust" by Queen!

I could feel my lungs starting to tighten up and the urge to just open my mouth and take a breath but I would have drowned so I just tried to keep going. At one point I could have sworn I saw my grandmother!

As I came out of the tunnel and hit the surface things were going black and I could see stars. I gasped for air as I broke the surface and I hear a voice in my head, "You bloody stupid bastard!"

After I got my breath back and the darkness faded from my eyes and I could see again and the stars disappeared I shouted out to the boys to tell them I'd made it.

I have to say we spent the rest of the afternoon all going through the tunnel three or four times. I think it was the feeling of the unknown that made the first time so scary.

The following day we all spent water-skiing but again this ended up in a near death experience. We were keen to try some bare-foot skiing but neither of our boats had the power needed to achieve the speed that was needed to barefoot ski so the next best thing was body-surfing. We thought if we lay in the water with our elbows tucked into our stomachs and our hands under our chins and held onto the rope we might be able to use our arms as skis to get us on top of the water. We tried it a few time but the resistance of our bodies in the water was so much that we couldn't hold onto the rope and it was simply wrenched from our hands as the boat sped off.

I decided that instead of just holding the handle on the ski-rope that I would wrap the end of the rope around my wrists a few times then hold on to the handle.

"Ok, I'm ready, GO!" I yelled as George floored the engine.

The unexpected then happened. Instead of flying out of the water and skimming on the surface as I had imagined, I was being pulled through the water causing a huge bow wave as the water hit my head and prevented me from breathing. I tried to turn my head to get some air but the water was all around, so I realised that the time had come to let go......but the rope was wrapped around my wrists and with the force of the boat the rope was digging into my skin. Thankfully after a while George slowed the boat down and I was able to get a breath but once again for the second time in two days I thought I saw my dead grandmother and it was a close thing.

We spent the rest of the day relaxing, fishing and chatting, it was safer. You live and learn as they say.

I'm not sure what happened to Baulka but George became a commercial pilot for the Greek airline Olympic Airways.

Otters Point at Cape Maclear

CHAPTER 86

MY HOUSE IS ON FIRE!

O ne night I was woken by an enormous crash or bang. I stumbled out of bed with thoughts of a stray rocket or mortar from nearby Mozambique landing in the garden. As I staggered down the corridor and into the dining room there lying across the dining table was a roof beam burnt black and still smouldering. I wasn't worried, I was very calm. I looked up and there was a huge round hole in the dining room ceiling, about 6 feet across, the ring of which was still burning. All around the floor of the dining room was burnt embers.

I stood there for a few seconds trying to see how a mortar had done all that without putting a hole in the roof. I thought some more and decided that it wasn't a mortar round. As I stood there looking up at the flaming hole, literally I decided "No, this is a dream, this is not real." And I turned around and went back to bed.

I lay in bed trying to regain my sleep for several minutes, when I suddenly leapt out of my bed.

"Shit, my house is on fire!"

I ran back into the dining room and yes, my house was indeed on fire. I rushed outside to the car to get my fire extinguisher. On the way I stumbled into my watchman, who had heard a bang but couldn't see the cause of the noise.

I discharged the contents of the extinguisher into the flaming hole in my ceiling and put the fire out. There wasn't much I could do right now so I went back to bed.

Next morning, I was woken by Samuel asking what had happened in the night. There wasn't much I could tell him apart from that I thought it might have been caused by wiring as the fire seemed to radiate out in a circle from the light in the ceiling.

I rang Roger who was very good about it all and had the maintenance team up within days to put a new ceiling in, paint the lounge and dining room and to check the wiring. It turned out that a mouse had chewed through the wires in the ceiling causing a short that set fire to the ceiling boards. The mouse had been electrocuted and was found toasted close to where the burnt hole was.

For some reason I found the thought of the mouse funny, …..chomp, chomp, chomp……bang, zap…..sizzle…..!

It was just after the fire that I went to town for my monthly supplies of food and stock for the house. Samuel always came with me to town on these trips and I would drop him at his village in Bvumbwe, then collect him on my way back to Namwera. He would always prepare a shopping list for me, of food we needed for the month and I would go to the National Bank on Livingstone Avenue in Limbe to collect cash to pay for shopping (no credit cards in those days). I always checked my bank balance before making a withdrawal, mainly to make sure I had been paid. To do this you would go to the counter and give the teller your account details and he would go off to another room, then come back with a folded piece of paper that he would hand to you. Written in pencil on the paper was your bank balance. As I unfolded my bit of paper I was staggered at the amount, which was over one and a half million Kwacha.

Keep in mind that at that time you could buy a detached house in town for about fifty thousand kwacha, so over a million was an unbelievable amount. I went back to the teller and gave him back the paper saying there was a mistake and could he check it again; so off he went to the side room.

A few moments later he came back, "No Bwana, its correct." He said with a smile.

"It cant be, go and check again please", and off he went back to the room.

"No Bwana, its correct!"

I stood back from the counter and allowed another customer to be served. I went and sat down on one of the benches by the window and thought for a while. What should I do? Should I ask to draw the full amount and run? Run where? Kwacha's are only good in Malawi. I thought some more. If I took the money, they probably wouldn't even know me, there weren't any cameras in those days. I went back to counter.

"Sorry, can you check this balance one more time please because I'm sure it's not correct?"

By now he was getting a little fed up with me but off he went to the room. Moments later he returned, beaming and laughing.

"Eeeee Bwana, you are indeed right! I made a BIG mistake!" and handed me my folded bit of paper. He had scratched out the millions and written a new number down, that I knew to be closer to the mark. When I looked up the cashier had called his friend, his friend had called his supervisor, who had called everyone else, including the Bank Manager. They were all laughing and shaking my hand. I think the Bank Manager was relieved in a way that I hadn't cleared the money from someone else's account. From then on, they always greeted me by name, and I became a bit of a celebrity after that. I often wonder if I could have robbed the bank that day, without even carrying a gun.

CHAPTER 87

FISHING FOR CROCODILES

I had been in Malawi for almost thirteen years and had never been fishing for Tiger Fish. I guess the reason why was that it had a bit of a mystic to it. Everyone went to the lake fishing, or fly-fishing for Trout either at Zomba or Mulanje, but Tiger fishing was real hard-core fishing. I had heard stories of epic struggles with this great fighting fish, how the caught fish would leap clear out of the water and shake its head. Sometimes it would "tail walk", shaking its head in an attempt to either shake the hook free or break the line. Monster fish could weigh 30lbs.

The Tiger Fish is a predatory fish, occurring in the Zambezi River and hence up the Shire River as far as Kappachera Falls just above Chikwawa. The falls here prevent the fish from continuing up the river into Lake Malombe and then on into Lake Malawi, although there are other falls too further up the river at Kabula that would pose a similar obstacle.

One weekend I decided that I had to give Tiger fishing a go and grabbed some tackle together, large hooks, wire trace and for bait I had some Chambo fillets with the skin left on. I also had some large spinning lures but wasn't too sure how I would fare with these as without a boat, spinning may prove difficult. Armed with all this I headed down to Chikwawa in the Lower Shire at the crack of dawn.

The Lower Shire is like an oven at the best of times and now being October, it was at its hottest. Here tarmac melted in the heat and molten tar was thrown up on to the side of the car. It was a hellish place with temperatures often going into the forties. I had been in nearby Lengwe National Park where I had measured 45 degrees centigrade in the shade. As children we had heard that the mosquitoes were so bad that the bus stops had mosquito nets to protect the waiting passengers; and that there the mosquitos didn't just bite you, a couple of them picked you up and carried you off to eat later! It was not a place that gave any quarter that much I knew.

As I drove down the long and winding escarpment road, I imagined catching one of these infamous fish. I pictured the scene in my mind, the first bite and then the fight. And then the delight at hauling a giant fish ashore. I couldn't wait.

I had no real idea of where I was going to fish but thought that below the falls would be a good place to start, guess that these predatory fish would wait below the falls to pick up any injured fish or animal washed down the river. A few stops at the side of the road to ask the way took me through a quiet village scattered with mango trees. I looked at the trees and thought of how many Green Mambas and Boomslangs they might hold, but then reminded myself that I was here for the fishing and not snakes and drove on along the little dirt track.The track got more and more indistinct and finally the two tracks formed a single track. Luckily there were no trees so I was able to continue along it picking my way around rocks. Finally, the track came to an abrupt end at the bank of a dry river bed. Looking right down the sandy bed I could see the muddy waters of the Shire flowing past about two hundred meters away. Where the dry river bed met the Shire would make an ideal spot to fish so I reversed the car and swung right picking my way towards the flowing river. I managed to park the car on the bank above the river and started to unpack my gear.

I decided to place my fishing chair in the middle of the entrance to the dry river bed about two meters from the waters of the Shire. There was no particular reason for this, it was just level ground and was away from bushes that may hamper my casting. I always carried a panga with me, it just gave me security to be armed and I stabbed this into the sand next to my chair and cast my Chambo baited hook into the fast-flowing river of the Shire and sat down to wait. I looked up at the sun that was burning down, it was hot, I then looked at my watch, it was ten o'clock. As I then looked at the water in front of me a crocodile's head surfaced about four meters in front of me, its eyes cleared and it looked straight at me.

"Shit" I thought, "my knife?" I daren't take my eyes of the croc, I knew that it could come out of the water if it chose at lightning speed and taking one's eyes off it was suicidal.

Very slowly moved my right hand across and down and felt for the panga. After a few seconds my hand touched the handle and I gripped it tightly but did not draw the knife from the sand. Now I felt that I had a chance if the croc made an attack. I looked into the eyes of the croc.

In a whisper I said to it "You come out of that water and you're a dead croc". I wasn't sure how I was going to achieve my threat but I felt I needed to communicate with the beast. The stale-mate continued for a few minutes, the both of us motionless. Then as silently as it had appeared the croc submerged and vanished into the muddy river. After a few more minutes I released my grip on my panga and breathed for the first time in what seemed like hours.

Judging by the length of the head I would guess that the croc was probably seven feet long, probably not a monster but I don't think I would have stood a chance if it had got me into the river, where I would have been exhausted very quickly and would probably have drowned in the struggle.

Before I had time worry about the croc anymore my fishing line suddenly went taught. Line began to squeal off my reel at an alarming rate. I applied the drag to try and prevent my reel being emptied. Still the line sped out. So, this was Tiger fishing I thought, great stuff! My spool was almost empty I decided there was nothing for me to do but to wind the clutch right down and use the rod and my strength to exhaust the fish. As the spool locked the rod was almost wrenched from my hands with the force of the pull. My feet had nothing to grip on to in the sand of the river bed and I was just pulled along the narrow beach like I was water-skiing. It was as if I had just hooked a passing train. God this must be a monster of a Tiger Fish I thought. I was fast running out of beach and heading for the water. Just then there was a foaming splash and a crocodile rose headfirst from the water and snapped its jaws. I caught a glimpse of my Chambo fillet in its mouth before my line snapped and the croc was gone in a swirl of mud and water.

I stood there shaking and sweating at the water's edge. I was just catching my breath when I suddenly realised that I was standing about half a yard from the water's edge and had just had one croc almost pull me into the river and another eye me up from my chair. I leapt back about two yards and grabbed my panga, preparing for a mass of crocodiles to swarm from the river in a sort of Raiders of the Lost Ark movie. The swarm never came. I nervously looked around to see if anyone had been watching my near-miss with the jaws of death. I couldn't see anyone, thankfully. I gathered up my gear and scrambled to the high bank above the river. I wasn't sitting down there a moment longer. As I got to the top of the bank, I had a commanding view of the river in either direction. As I looked upstream, I could see the white foaming water of the falls. I could see some African kids standing on the rocks in amongst the foam so headed off towards them. When I got close enough, I called to them in Chichewa, "Is there any Tiger Fish around here?"

One of the smaller kids beamed at me, "Yes lots," and held up an enormous Tiger about 80cm in length. I went down to the rocks for a closer look. It was an impressive fish; its jaws were full of protruding teeth that were at least 3cm in length. It was a solid, muscular fish.

"Where did you catch it?" I asked.

"Just here." He said, pointing to the white foam in front of the rock he was standing on.

"What you using for bait?"

The kid then produced a thin bamboo stick about a meter in length. Tired to the end of it was a short length of string about two meters long, to the end of that was a piece of bicycle spoke with its end bent and filed into a hook. On the end of the hook where two small minnow sized fish and that was it. I looked at my gear and felt ashamed of myself.

"I was going to try down at the dry river bed." I said nodding back towards where I had been sitting.

"Don't fish there, Bwana, dangerous, too many crocodiles! Here is good." the boy said knowledgeably, pointing down to the white foam again.

Now pay attention, here is a point to remember. When doing anything in a foreign land, always seek the advice of the locals before you get yourself killed. Even children here have a better understanding of the environment they live in than you will ever have.

I placed my fishing gear under a near-by bush and just sat on the bank and watched the kids fishing for the rest of the day. I was just happy to watch them, I felt privileged to watch these kids who were no more than eight or ten years old, dancing from rock to rock, with their bamboo catching these large fighting fish just as their fathers and their fathers before them had. Sports fisherman would pay thousands of dollars to fish this river and there were these boys whose only equipment was what they could scratch together. For these boys the fish was not sport, it was a meal for them and their families. I looked around at the hills and the river, at these boys and it occurred to me that this scene had not changed since Livingstone had come up the Shire on his Zambezi Expedition of 1858-1863 aboard his little steamer, the Ma-Robert. Then Africans had shot poisoned arrows at Livingstone's boat as it steamed up the river. I was almost at the spot where Livingstone had observed a crocodile come out of the water and snatch a woman from the bank, then drag her into the water to eat her. That was in 1859, over a hundred years ago and nothing had really changed.

I felt lucky to be where I was. I was also lucky to be alive after the two croc incidents. A great days fishing was had by all, except me!

The Shire River at Chikwawa

CHAPTER 88

I TAKE TO THE SKY

Another thing that I had always wanted to do was learn to fly. As I kid, I had wanted to be a pilot but maths was never my strong point. I had set the maths exam twice at school and my grade the second time around was worse than my first so gave the idea up as a lost cause.

In 1987 I had the chance to get a flight in a Cessna 150 over Liwonde National Park with a commercial pilot I was hooked again by the bug. It was great, flying up the Shire River, over the barrage at Liwonde and then over the Park, 200 ft above elephants was amazing. The pilot even let me take the controls for about fifteen minutes as we flew over the Park and then back towards the dirt airstrip at Club Makokola.

I made some enquires on where I could learn to fly and as it turned out there was a flight school at Chileka International Airport. Chileka International Airport is at an elevation of 2,555 feet (779 m) above mean sea level about 19 miles from Blantyre. It now has two asphalt paved runways: 10/28 measures 2,325 by 30 metres (7,628 × 98 ft) and 15/33 measures 1,372 × 30 m (4,501 × 98 ft) but at that time there was only one runway.

I arrived at the airport on a Sunday morning to meet my instructor. He was a Malawian who actually worked for Old Mutual Insurance in Blantyre, a hell of a nice chap, and very patient. I seem to remember that his name was Patrick.

The plane was an old 4-seater Piper Cherokee 140, it's call sign was WPR-something or other.

The first lesson started off with an end to end check of the plane. When we reached the tail of the plane the instructor pointed to two screws and said "Check the Tennent Screws".

These two screws had apparently come loose on a plane being flown by Mr Tennent and had jammed the tail flaps causing him a very difficult landing. I checked ours and they were tight. Once the checks had been done, we climbed aboard and once cleared by Chileka Air Traffic Control we taxied along, testing brakes and doing final checks till we finally arrived at the holding point.

"Whisky Papa Romeo you are cleared for take-off, have a pleasant flight." came CATC.

We released the brakes and increased throttle until the plane started to move forward then throttle back as we gained momentum. We trundled along and onto the runway, turning west before making a 180 degree turn at the end of the runway.

"Are you ready?" I was asked. I think I said something like "Oh yeah" and we then applied the throttle and rolled down the runway till we reached our take-off speed and then with a small pull on the stick and we were airborne.

As we cleared the runway and banked left the instructor said "Look out for other idiots, this was an international airport so we don't want to be in the flight path of the VC10!"

The instructor made slight turns left and right telling me how to use the foot pedals at the same time to keep the "ball" in the centre of the Turn & Bank Indicator (sometimes called the turn & slip) on the instrument panel. He then had me make the same turns left and right over and over again until I could keep the ball central when turning.

He then showed how to climb and descend using the throttle control rather than pulling up with the stick and again I had a go at that. He was talking to me all the time, and I was trying to concentrate on everything he was telling me, when suddenly he said "Ok, that's great, now let's go back to the airport, you have the controls."

I looked out of the windows at the African bush below and then I scanned the horizon. Now you would think that a large airport would stand out like a sore thumb but I couldn't see it anywhere. "Shit!" I said aloud.

"Ok, see how easy it is to lose concentration on where you are? Let's look for a landmark."

This was all well and good but for miles the landscape looked all the same from the air. Suddenly the Shire River glistened in the sun light, ok, so I had found the biggest river in Malawi, great, now where? I looked at the fuel gauge and the reality of the situation hit me. Suddenly I became extremely hot, and the sweat poured off me. This was a real situation.

"Ok, I don't know where we are." I said throwing in the towel.

"Ok I have the controls." And he turned the aircraft round and headed straight for the airport.

It was an important lesson. Nowadays we all have GPS and SatNavs but in the mid 1980's in Malawi, it was a compass, a map and always keeping an eye on landmarks like mountains and rivers.

A few days later I was up in the air again. I took off and banked left, "look out for other idiots" I said aloud as I scanned the sky for large jet aircraft. I then looked across to left at the airport and then at the compass and noted the degrees. The lesson was very similar to the previous one, going through turns and climbs. The instructor was talking all the time as he had done before. After about 30 minutes he said "Ok, take us back to the airport".

I looked down at the compass and turned the aircraft round to the opposite bearing that we had flown out on, after a few minutes the Airport came into view.

"Well done, you've learnt your lesson". He beamed.

I continued to take my lessons and do my Ground Training. It was a great feeling flying over Malawi and I loved every hour I spent up there. Sadly, I never had time to take my Private Pilot's Licence before leaving Malawi.

Flying up the Shire River, looking down on Mvu Camp at Liwonde

CHAPTER 89

THREE LITTLE SHEETS

I had decided to hold a leaving party at the house and just to do something different than the usual "let's eat, drink and then play poker" gathering so I arranged a fancy-dress party. I knew that the old guys and their wives would not dress up and that was understandable but the young farmers were all keen.

The party was arranged for the Saturday evening and by midday the heavens opened which was unusual for this time of year. My lawn was swimming in water and without changing the party into a mud bath something had to be done. At that point Tony pulled up into the drive.

"Don't you bloody laugh," I warned him as he got out of his Land Cruiser.

"Jesus, it's going to be mud by the time everyone has walked on it for an hour! We need to do something." He said and in true military fashion in about an hour he had built a large frame from blue gum poles and thrown over the top of it a tarpaulin sheet from his lorry. Another one was placed on the ground under the awning. The party was still on.

As predicted the old timers arrived in shirt and trousers,

they weren't quite ready to let their hair down just yet. But the youngsters or those young at heart made the effort.

Tony reappeared with his wife and kids. He had dressed himself in hessian used for wrapping the tobacco in bales ready for the auction floors. His hat was made from it, his shirt, and his shorts. Around his neck was a sign that read "Farmer of the year 1989." It was his prediction for the future price of tobacco and how poor all the farmers were going to be. The old timers didn't seem to be too amused at the prediction but we all loved it. His son Terry was dressed in camouflage, complete with black face paint.

About an hour into the evening Dave Bradshaw turned up. But he had not brought his wife, instead was accompanied by two other blokes who I didn't know and turned out to be friends of Dave's from Zimbabwe. The three of them were dressed in white bed sheets, toga style, with string belts; each had a cardboard sign hung round their necks with wording on it. All three piled or poured out of Dave's, Red Post Van, each clutching beers so I was surprised that they had found the gate.

The first of Dave's friends, who was a tall bloke, had a sign that said BIG SHEEET. The second bloke's sign said LITTLE SHEEET, for he was indeed the smallest of the bunch. Dave's sign read DIRTY SHEEET, as he had muddy handprints all over his sheet. It was a play on the word sheet/shit and had to be explained to a few of the old Greek ladies, but thankfully not by me. We were all in hysterics.

I did the courteous thing and asked where Ginnie was. I was going to call her TASTY SHEEET, YUMMY SHEEET or I'M IN LOVE WITH YOUR SHEEET but thought better of it. She had stayed on the farm. Guess she didn't want to be witness to the Three Sheets antics. Dave Toft and his wife couldn't make it either which was a shame.

The three sheets certainly got the parties entertainment started by way of downing a few more beers and breaking into song, well a few songs actually which I won't write on these pages.

As well as all the Greek farmers I had also invited my staff, and they all turned up just after supper. I think Kawale was immediately thrown an arm around by Tony and a cold beer thrust into his eager hand. Kawale was in heaven.

I proceeded to get completely hammered and remember at one point dancing on a table with Denis and Kawale, well I don't think it was dancing, it was more like stamping because within a few bars of the song the table gave way and the three of us hit the floor, where we rolled around laughing, as only drunk people can do. I didn't care, I was happy, I was with my friends, and people who thought enough of me to come to the party.

Those that didn't turn up were not a loss to me, except Taki and his wife, who had said "you youngsters have a good time, you don't need us old fogies there" and of course Dave Toft, his wife and Ginnie. It turned out to be one hell of a farewell party and was greatly enjoyed by all.

In the morning I was dragged from my slumber by the sound of frantic knocking at my bedroom door.

"Bwana, wake up, wake up."

I was suffering from a major hangover and wasn't planning on getting up just yet, so enquired first what bloody time it was and second what the problem was.

"It's seven thirty Bwana, but I can't say what the problem is. I think you should come quickly!" Samuel replied.

So I dragged myself from the bed and opened the door, "What is it?"

"Just come Bwana," said Samuel, grasping my arm and leading me along the corridor to the kitchen. "Look" he said and pointed outside.

I stepped to the kitchen door and looked out. There was Giabu the gardener, standing facing the outside wall with his nose pressed up against it.

"Giabu, what is it?" I asked, I felt that this was just one of those bad dreams when nothing made sense.

"I can't look Bwana." He said not moving his head. "Look at what?" I demanded. And with that Giabu indicated with his thumb in the direction of the garden. It was at that point that I heard voices, and laughter coming from the garden so I stepped out of the doorway and around the house. And there it was.

Dave and his two mates running around the garden chasing each other with the hosepipe, completely naked!

I just stood and looked at them for a while like I was Alice watching the Mad Hatters Tea Party. Was I to stop them and risk their attentions being directed at me? No way, I might end up being stripped and sprayed with water or worse.

"Giabu, Samuel, take the day off. I'm going back to bed." And back to bed I went.

Knocking at the bedroom door woke me again.

"Bwana Dave and his friends have gone now. It's twelve o'clock and lunch is ready." I was informed and got out of bed.

CHAPTER 90

A SAD FAREWELL

I was in a well-known Greek Delicatessen in Limbe one day doing some shopping. A European lady came up to me and asked,

"You're Rupert, aren't you? I hear that you're leaving Malawi soon, have you found a home for your little dog?"

I looked down and there was Cassey sat at my feet as usual. "No not yet, why?"

"Well I'm Mrs So-and-so, you don't know me but our eldest boy was killed by a hippo at the lake and our youngest son is devastated at the loss of his brother. I've seen you in town a few times with your dog and he is so well behaved. Our youngest boy always wants to come over and pat the dog and never stops talking about him all the way home. It would mean the world to my son if he could have the dog, it may take his mind off his brother......what's the dogs' name?" she asked as she bent down to stroke Cassey, who was sitting there loving all this attention as usual.

As I told her his name, I felt so sorry for the lady, her family and her son. It must have been an awful time for them all. A few children had been killed by hippos while I was at Saints and I remember the devastation those deaths caused.

"Where is your son now?" I asked.

"He is in the car."

"I'll take Cassey out to meet him if that's ok with you?"

"Oh God, he will be thrilled!" she said openly crying.

I took Cassey out to the car and the little boy was almost beside himself. His mother and I just stood back and couldn't find anything to say to each other, we just watched the two of them. It felt like Cassey knew the heartache the kid was going through.

"Looks like Cassey has found a new home." I finally said.

I agreed with the boys' mother to keep Cassey till the last few days before I was due to leave, so I could have my "good-byes". She wasn't going to tell the little boy that they were having the dog; it would be a surprise on the day. I was happy that Cassey would go to a good home, where he would be loved.

My two other dogs, Tambala and Florence were taken by the Onion family who farmed in Namwera.

Samuel, my cook also needed a new job. He had been with me for almost four years and was a good friend. He had fed me, and kept a good house. He had even slept on the floor at the foot of my bed when I had been down with malaria. He had become family. I made some enquires and eventually, I found him a job as a cook at Mvu Camp on the banks of the Shire River at Liwonde National Park under the watchful eye of my crazy hippo skiing partner Dave Toft.

Samuel had been a godsend and I was going to miss him. I gave him a bonus which he wasn't expecting plus a few things from the house, however all this really didn't matter to either of us. As I started to pack up the house Samuel came into the room.

"Bwana, I've decided to come to England with you instead of working for Bwana Dave."

I was stunned "….but , but you can't" I stuttered.

"Why not, who will cook for you in England? I am your cook! I must come with you." He said in a stern way.

After a long debate I finally went to the kitchen and opened the freezer door. "Put your hand in there" I instructed Samuel, "that's how cold England is every day". There was a look of horror on his face.

"You need to stay here in Malawi and take care of your own family. You will be ok with Bwana Dave at Liwonde. He will treat you well". Samuel seemed a little happier now and we continued to pack the house.

So, with all my affairs now in order said my goodbyes to Samuel, Cassey, and my friends. Emotions were very high at the office, where all the staff had lined up to say goodbye. Elias was clearly upset. "You've been my best boss" he said holding my hand. As I drove out of the gates the wives and children ran forward to wave goodbye with both hands. I was very sad.

As I drove down to Blantyre from Namwera on the last day it suddenly hit me that I had survived living in Africa. I thought about the school friends that had died, people I knew who had not been as lucky as me. I thought also about all the risks Id taken and all the diseases I could have caught. Things like Hepatitis A, Hepatitis E, Typhoid fever, Vectorborne diseases (acquired through the bite of an infected arthropod), Malaria, Dengue fever, Yellow fever, Japanese Encephalitis, African Trypanosomiasis (caused by the bite of the bloodsucking Tsetse flies), Cutaneous Leishmaniasis (caused by the bite of sandflies), Plague (yes still prevalent in Malawi), Crimean-Congo hemor-rhagic fever (tick-borne viral disease), Rift Valley fever, Chikun-gunya (mosquito-borne (*Aedes aegypti*) viral disease), Leptospirosis (bacterial disease that occurs through contact with water contaminated by animal urine), Schistosomiasis (caused by the parasitic trematode flatworm *Schistosoma*), Lassa fever, Meningococcal meningitis, and of course Rabies. I shuddered at the thought of some of them and continued the long drive to town.

I left Malawi in 15th of April 1988 and flew out to the UK to join the Parachute Regiment.

I was just 24 years old.

Cassey was a great companion and I think of him often.

POSTSCRIPT

"You may leave Africa but Africa never leaves you"

BRIDGET DORE

Africa smiled a little when you left.
You cannot leave Africa, Africa said.
It is always with you, there inside your head.
Our rivers run in currents, in the swirl of your thumbprints.
Our drumbeats counting out your pulse.
Our coastline, the silhouette of your soul.
So Africa smiled a little when you left.
We are in you, Africa said.
You have not left us, yet.

CHAPTER 91

YOU'RE NOT EVEN FAMILY

s you will have gathered from reading this book, I always felt like an outsider with my family, as if they were a special club where I couldn't get membership. I always felt that I had had been dealt the wrong hand and just wanted to have a second go at life. If I thought that by ending this life I would be able to come back and give it all another go I would have done it. But life is full of ups and downs and I now realise that life does go on if you wait long enough.

Life has been hard. I have had to rely totally on myself for everything. My twenty first birthday was only really celebrated thanks to "The Boss", it went by as any other birthday at home. I bought my first car, with the money I had earned; no car was bought for me. When I bought my first house I had no help from the family, no help with deposit. I furnished it myself, even though months before mother's late father had left them close to thirty thousand pounds. Don't get me wrong, I don't expect hand-outs, it was their money, it had been left to them but things like "Here, lets help you with your new house, is there anything you need, can we get you a sofa?" would have meant a lot to me. When they did visit the house for the first time I felt like they begrudged me owning it. I half expected them to say, "What have you gone and bought a four bedroom house for, you don't need four bedrooms."

I remember arriving at their house in my brand new car, expecting them to say, "wow, what a car, it looks smashing!" but mother got into it without comment, not a word. It just made me feel guilty for having bought it. At that moment I could have dumped it in the nearest ditch and walked away, I was so hurt. A few months earlier mother had arrived back from visiting Amy in Chicago and couldn't stop telling me about Roberts's new car, it's got this and does that when you press this. But when I got a brand new car, nothing! I hadn't bought it to seek applause but just wanted to hear "we are proud of what you have achieved".

My years of making excuses for my family finally came to a head in 2002 and I ceased speaking to mother and Jim. I was tired of feeling that I was at fault, and taking the blame, even when I was hurt. I would rather not have any contact with them than feel pain.

Within a year I received news from Kenya that Dick had passed away at his house in Nyeri. I spoke to Isabel on the phone and waited to hear through her what Jim had decided to do regarding his fathers' death and funeral. I wasn't surprised to learn that he was adamant he was not going to Kenya for the funeral. I also gathered that both him and mother were leaving arrangements to me. Well there's a bloody surprise I thought. I contacted Dick's firm of solicitors in Cumbria and was surprised to hear that Dick had deposited five hundred pounds with them some years previously to take care of legal matters on his death. The solicitor said he had a copy of Dick's will and would make me aware of the contents in a few days.

I agreed to fly out to Kenya to make arrangements for the funeral seeing as the "Family" appeared to be waiting for me to wave my magic wand. Isabel said she would come with me, accompanied by her boyfriend, so we arranged to convene at my house in a few days' time.

When she arrived I felt that something was adrift. The atmosphere was thick with tension but I just put it down to the upset of Dicks' death and kept myself busy with booking flights, hotels, car hire etc. and arranging the trip for all three of us.

As I sat in my lounge, quiet in thought as I often did, Isabel's boyfriend asked for a few words. Sure not a problem.

He then proceeded to nervously inform me that "Isabel feels that you are taking charge of the situation, when it's not really your place."

Isabel then shouted down from upstairs, "Leave it Liam, please!"

"What do you mean, taking charge?"

"Well you're arranging what needs to be done, and you shouldn't be doing that. You're treating Isabel like a kid."

"Oh really!" now I felt my blood starting to boil. "If Isabel has something to say then let her come down and tell me, what are you her bloody spokesman?"

With that Isabel appeared at the door and started to finish the conversation that Liam has started. Things started to get quite heated with Liam telling me that Isabel is a grown woman, not a child and I should treat her accordingly. I politely ask him to wind his neck in and stay out of this. He then basically insulted me in my own house and I told him to "But-out" and judging by the speed in which he ran upstairs I guess he realised how close he had come to getting a hiding.

I was fuming by this stage and stormed out into the garden to calm down and get some air. It's not long before Isabel came out to join me, I assumed to try and calm things down. I tried to explain to her that with Jim not facing the situation and Dick basically laying there in the mortuary, that someone had to deal with this; and seeing as I was the only boy and the eldest

446

member of the family it was my duty to take charge and deal with this.

"But why do you feel it's your job anyway, you're not even family anyway!"

BOOM!

So there we were, we finally had it. The feeling I had felt for almost forty years, "you're not even family". The first time my "family" had been brave enough to tell me, even if she had blurted it out without realising it.

At the time of writing its been 16 years since I last spoke Mother, Jim, Amy or Isabel - and they have made no contact with me.

Looking back at all this the only thought going through my mind was why had my "family" allowed me to go through school, college and most of my early working life under the surname of Prickett, when at the end of the day it was worth nothing but a name. All my qualifications and most work references were in the name of Prickett and now I sat here and I wasn't "even family". The thing was, they had put me through school with a name that wasn't even legal. What were they hoping for? Why had they done this? I guess now I realise that it provided them with a short-term fix to their problem, but they hadn't really thought about the impact on me. Neither my mother nor Jim had been forced to experience my situation. Their parents had stayed together, they had a stable family. I think they could have handled the whole thing a lot better!

So in 2005 I sat down one day and said, "I'm going to find my father". There wasn't any particular reason that I chose that day over any other. Nothing had happened to spark this off that day, it was just a thought that came from nowhere and entered my head.

I sat there for a few minutes trying to remember the little I had been told that would help me locate him. Mother was forever saying "He was cruel to you, he would tease you with chocolate" and "the court said he could never see you as long as he lived".

I sat and thought some more. I had my birth certificate so dug it out of the drawer. It said Michael Wilkey, occupation Teacher. Well that was a start. Kenya! I'll have to go back to Kenya, not physically but start there. What did I know of him from the Kenya days?

Before he died, Dick had mentioned that my real father was the art teacher at the Prince of Wales. It came out in conversation one evening in Nyeri and I'd commented on a painting of a waterbuck hanging on the wall in the lounge.

"John painted that when he was in school." Dick said, so I started to ask Dick some more questions and he had then told me that my real dad was Jim's art teacher.

I turned on the computer and typed all the things I could remember of my father into Google. By the end of the day, I had found a Michael Wilkey taught at the Prince of Wales school in Kenya, but now lived in Vancouver, Canada. I even had an email address for him. Isn't Google just the greatest thing?

I sat back in my chair and exhaled for what seemed the first time in hours and stared at the email address. I had reached a point, a junction in the road. Making contact with this man after thirty-eight years was going to throw up all kinds of emotions on both sides. He may not want anything to do with me, he may have his own family now and they may not even know I exist. The thought that he might in fact be the cruel man my mother had portrayed him as flashed through my mind. I thought about all this and more. I decided to send an email.

It was hard to decide how to phrase the email. Firstly I may even have the wrong man. I just simply said who I was and that I was looking for Michael Wilkey, I then said if I had the right person could he reply. I pressed the send key and the email was gone.

Within days I had a reply - this Michael Wilkey was my father!

We emailed each other over the coming weeks, each gathering more details of the others life over the past thirty-eight years. It was very emotional and I think tears were shed on both sides when replies were read.

After some weeks I received an email from my father, it contained an image file attachment, "So you can see what I look like" the subject said. My mouse hovered over the open button on the screen for several minutes. This was my father, the man that I had no memory of, and I had never seen a photo of him in my entire life. Finally I gathered the courage to click the icon and the photo opened.

There was my father, sitting in the doorway of a helicopter, aviator sunglasses on, holding a 35mm SLR camera, dressed in khaki; on his feet he wore safari boots. I looked down at my feet; I was wearing the same safari boots! He's my father I spoke allowed and cried.

I won't bore you listing the similarities that we share, but the list does contain a love of Africa, Land Rovers, photography, art, and he has a Private Pilot's Licence. He also writes, having published several books. He was also born in the same hospital in Sheffield as I was, Netheredge Hospital.

We have now met several times both in the UK and in Spain. Last year I went over to Canada to spend some time with him. We get on better than I could have hoped for, due in no small part to my father. He and I have both lost many years and we will never catch up on them all but he has given me an identity, an idea of who I am. We are extremely similar in many ways; I can see my traits in him and I guess he can see himself at times when he looks at me. Following the contact with my father I have been in touch with many people from the "old Kenya" days who were in Kenya at the time of my parents' separation and final divorce; and they all confirm my father's account of what happened. People like Dick Wissolik, a man who remains my fathers' friend after nearly forty years. Geoff and John "Angus" Welford, who were at the Prince of Wales along with Jim, in fact John "Angus" and Jim were best friends at the time. No one has ever had a bad word to say of my father, quite the contrary. I just feel sad that so many years were painfully wasted through deceit, lies and cover-ups, which could so easily have been avoided if there had been a little more thought for me.

As I have said, I cut off all contact with my mother and Jim, and my half-sisters Amy and Isabel, and their respective partners. "They're your family!" I hear you cry. Yeap, I guess they are but I wouldn't accept what they have done from anyone else so why should I have to accept it from them just because they are "family"? I'm sorry; I can't see grey on this one, they were wrong and that is that. After all it was them who said "you're not family", not me.

I am not sure if they know that I am in contact with my father and I don't much care. Divorce happens and when children are involved it's even harder; but to fill a child's head with lies about his real father for no more reason than to hide their own guilt, well that's just wrong. I assume that the lies were started in the weeks after the separation and once they had begun, they couldn't find a way out of them. To stand up after all these years and say, "you know what, we lied, your father is not such a bad guy after all, and we're sorry" takes some guts.

I'm happy with my life now. I have my Dad, my half brothers and a huge extended family. Christmas is a better time, with cards, phone calls and emails of festive wishes.

I feel at peace with the world.

In 2019 I made my first trip to Canada to visit my dad as he approached his 85th birthday. It was the third time we had seen each other since being reconnected in 2005, although we communicate via email almost daily. It was a very emotional visit as I also met by half-brother Mitch for the first time.

The photo that my dad sent me by email. The first time I'd seen what he looked like.

Anyway at the end of the visit, my dad went to his bedroom and brought out a folded cloth.

"I want you to have this son" he said and handed it to me.

I instantly recognised the cloth. It was the kikoy I had been wearing in the photo that my dad had taken in the garden in Nairobi.

"I've carried it with me for over fifty years and now I want it to go home with you. It was in the washing when your mother left the house with John. It was the only item of yours she didn't take with her. I guess she didn't see it in the laundry room."

I was in tears and so was my dad. He had carried this cloth around the world with him for almost fifty five years.

We cried and hugged each other.

The Kikoy cloth that my father had carried with him for half a century.

CHAPTER 92

THINGS WE STILL DO

I just wanted to include this section, part as humour but really because these are things that I find myself doing and friends think I'm either eccentric, simple or just plain losing the plot.

Anyway, enjoy and I hope a smile comes to your face as you read through these things, because you will think to yourself "yes I DO that too".

You know that you grew up in Africa when:
You find it hard to go to sleep without someone yelling "Lights Out" first.
You know how to tell when an avocado is ripe.
You always shake out your shoes before you put them on just in case of snakes, scorpions and spiders.
You expect the water in your taps to turn brown after a rain.
You think 'direct dial' is a new invention.
You miss the handle in the side of the phone for calling the operator.
Your parents dropped you off at school in a Land Rover.

The night seems empty without the sound of Tree Hyrax screaming.

You cannot go shopping without at least 40 other people going along.

You cannot go to the doctor without at least 40 other people going along.

You keep expecting the water to turn hot in the shower.

You keep expecting the hot water to run out while you are in the shower.

You keep looking for a guy roasting maize while shopping.

You know what a Cholera shot feels like.

You have a clock made from copper in the shape of Africa on your wall.

You have been to most of the places used for scenery in Africa movies and documentaries.

You think of termites (flying ants) and grasshoppers as a food group.

You automatically break when you see a pile of leaves in the middle of the road.

You find yourself addressing people as 'Bwana'.

You know all the words to *"Ak pleaze Daddy won't you take us to the Drive-in"*.

You've been to a Drive-in.

You call it a Bria when you cook meat on a charcoal grill.

You planted a Jacaranda tree in your garden.

You don't see a problem with transporting a single bed on the back of a bicycle.

You know what a District Commissioner is.

You know how to open coke and beer bottles by using another bottle.

You still open a coke bottle with your teeth.

You had a driver named Salomon, Babu, Kiplangat or Boneyface.

You own a laundry bag, and wash clothes only once a week.

You know that when a car puts its hazard lights on at a X-roads it means it's going straight ahead.

You can estimate the weight of a suitcase within two pounds.

You prefer your sugar in 7 foot stalks, rather than by the spoon.

You sift your flour before baking anything.

You check for 'safari' ants before sitting down.

You can't dig with a spade and use a hoe instead.

You cut your lawn with a "slasher"

You play football better in bare feet.

You are not bothered by sell-by-dates, they are more of a guide.

You use whitewash to paint your lounge instead of emulsion.

You never assume that a petrol station will have petrol for sale.

You still check your dog for ticks, then your children.

You own a shortwave radio.

You think camping means you sleep in a tent.

You prefer countries with only two seasons: wet and dry.

You know the lines on a map don't necessarily represent a road.

You feel free to drop in on people that you have not seen for years.

People who speak less than five languages aren't impressive.

You know all the answers to the National Geographic quizzes.

You have dogs named Jomo, Kaunda, Banda, Kamuzu or Moi

You drive on dirt roads just for the fun of it.

You think money is fake because it doesn't have the President's picture on it.

You have read every Wilbur Smith book.

You think the only way to make coffee is by grinding your own beans.

You miss the smell of fresh diesel in the morning.

You miss goats running across the road when you are doing 60 mph.

You drove for years without a licence.

You had your first car accident at age 12.

You stay out of lakes because they may have bilharzia.

Any car less than 10 years old seems new to you.
You purchase maps of Africa just to find the mistakes.
Your mouth waters when anyone says 'samoosa'.
You start a lot of sentences with, "In Africa, we ..."
You did not meet your grandmother until you were four.
You drive by large fields and still look for zebra.
You once had a wild animal as a pet.
You look out for leopards when walking at night.
You own a pair of Bata Safari Boots.
You don't wear socks when wearing your Bata Safari Boots.
Bundu-bashing was once your favourite pastime.
You still wear a Kikoy in the house and garden, even though
your neighbours think it is a dress.
You still refer to trainers as "tackies".
You own a pair of tyre shoes.
You know what a Yarpi is and where he's from.
You're happy to watch lizards running around the walls of your
living room
You think a Peugeot 404 is the best car in the world
You still own a panga.
As a child you could imitate the calls of a lion, a hippo and a
hyena before you said your first word.
You search car websites to see if someone is selling a Peugeot
504 saloon.
You have the nickname 'Njeroge' for your automatic dishwasher
after your old houseboy.
The names in 'The Lion King' don't strike you as exotic.
You know what a rabies jab feels like.
Baboon Spiders become almost part of the family.
You water ski over a family of hippos and don't get scared.
Your first pet was a chameleon and you call it Bwana.
You keep your flour in the freezer to prevent weevils.
You know what Chiperoni is.
The smell of dried fish doesn't offend you.

456

You know the difference between an Impala, Kudu, Sable and Waterbuck and you don't call them Deer!
The first doll's house you ever had was a mud hut you made yourself at the bottom of the garden.
You keep going on property websites and look at the prices of houses in Africa and dream of buying one.
Most of your memories are of Africa.
…….. and finally, people, Land Rovers are not SUV's!

ALSO BY RUPERT WILKEY

HERPETOLOGY

A Checklist for African Snakes Vol. I

A Checklist for African Snakes Vol. II

Chameleons of Malawi

Venomous Snakes of Malawi

Snakes of Malawi

Snakes of Bulgaria

Snakes of Spain

Reptiles of Malawi (with Gary Brown)

A Few Moments

BUSINESS

Starting your own business

Transforming your business

BIOGRAPHY/AUTOBIOGRAHY

In the Shadow of the Baobab Tree

The Claws of Africa - Biography of Dick Prickett

HISTORY

The Masters of Magdalene College

ABOUT THE AUTHOR

Rupert Wilkey grew up in Kenya, but it was when his "family" moved to Malawi in 1975 that his passion for reptiles and amphibians started. He caught his first snake at twelve years old and has been studying them ever since. Over the past forty years, Rupert has collected, catalogued and released over 5,000 snakes as part of his research.

Rupert has gone on to write numerous books, including *Snakes of Malawi*; which is the most comprehensive work on Malawi's snake species since 1962. Other works include *Snakes of Spain* and *Snakes of Bulgaria*. He contributed the snake section *Reptiles of Malawi* written by Gary Brown in 2019. *Venomous Snakes of Malawi* was his most recent publication. *A Fish Eagle Calls* is his nineteenth book.

He now lives in Spain with his dog.

Printed in Great Britain
by Amazon